BROODING UPON THE WATERS

BROODING UPON THE WATERS

A Memoir of Farming, Fishing, and Failure in America's Lost Landscape

HOWARD SCHAAP

SL/.NT
BOOKS

BROODING UPON THE WATERS
A Memoir of Farming, Fishing, and Failure in America's Lost Landscape

Copyright © 2025 Howard Schaap. All rights reserved. Except for brief quotations in critical publications or reviews, no part of this book may be reproduced in any manner without prior written permission from the publisher. Write: Permissions, Slant Books, P.O. Box 60295, Seattle, WA 98160.

Slant Books
P.O. Box 60295
Seattle, WA 98160

www.slantbooks.org

Cataloguing-in-Publication data:

Names: Schaap, Howard.

Title: Brooding upon the waters: a memoir of farming, fishing, and failure in America's lost landscape / Howard Schaap.

Description: Seattle, WA: Slant Books, 2025

Identifiers: ISBN 978-1-63982-209-6 (hardcover) | ISBN 978-1-63982-208-9 (paperback) | ISBN 978-1-63982-210-2 (ebook)

Subjects: LCSH: Farms--Minnesota | Lakes--Minnesota | Natural history--Minnesota | Fishing stories, American

Contents

1. This Place Makes Me Sick | 1
2. The Miraculous Catch of Fish | 16
3. Ebenezer | 28
4. Acquiescence | 41
5. The Interdict | 55
6. Walking in Water | 68
7. Cross Lake | 81
8. The Long Winter | 94
9. Pond Fishing | 108
10. Prayer Bouquet | 121
11. The Dead Sea | 134
12. Charon | 146
13. Pal | 160
14. Reprieve | 172
15. Lake Independence | 183
16. Shit Buckets | 193
17. Minnesota Wild | 204
18. Lake Wilson | 217

Acknowledgments | 227

I

This Place Makes Me Sick

I LIKE TO THINK of it as something Pa Ingalls might've done. When my sister Heidi called from Mom and Dad's house in the Big Woods and said that Dad's sharp decline over the past six months had bottomed out in not one but two 911 calls in the same night and that now he was on the way to Mayo Clinic, I like to think my response was worthy of Pa. I shrugged my shoulders, kissed the wife and kids, and got in the car.

I've picked Pa Ingalls—not the perfectly tan, perfectly noble Michael Landon version from TV's *Little House*, set in a country of too many hills and trees, but the real one—because I've come to think of him as the ultimate shoulder-shrugger. Here comes a prairie fire, a plague of locusts, a blizzard to bury us. Shoulder shrug, let's plow a fire circle, block up the windows, dig a tunnel to the barn.

This is the way of things in the Midwest. You live with weather and fate, you shrug your shoulders, you go on. The dailiness gets punctuated by having a beer with a neighbor, digging some fool out of a snow drift, buying a T-shirt for someone fighting cancer, and so you send slow roots down through the soil. But you don't think of it that way. Just one thing followed by another and then another. This is heroism, meaning it's nothing.

Our particular fire / plague / blizzard happens to be Dad's bipolar disorder—bipolar II to be precise, the one with less ups and more downs, kind of like the landscape itself, like it's the boredom that'll kill you. This time, Dad had fallen twice while Heidi was there to witness, once in the shower, once behind their bed, and they had needed to call the ambulance both times just to pick Dad up, he was that awkward and unmanageable. On the second call, they took him to Crosby hospital, where they dropped his lithium and replaced it with Ativan, which Mom recognized by name as the drug that made him psychotic. Too late. By the time Heidi called me, Dad was a time bomb of raw nerve endings and explosive chemicals—as he had always been—but now he was bouncing in the back of an ambulance somewhere in greater Minnesota.

Shoulder shrug. Hop in the car and jump on I-90. See you in three, three-and-a-half hours.

I wasn't looking forward to the drive to Rochester, to the Mayo Clinic, a great boring plains drive. I love the prairie, but I've got standards. Like, the slightest roll to my landscape. Like, not so Fargo flat, where even the mounds clawed together to create interstate overpasses seem like alien architecture. There's a lovely undulation where I live, in southwest Minnesota, on the downslope of something called the Buffalo Ridge, but already down past Worthington on I-90, just forty-five minutes into the trip, it gets to be that North Dakota kind of flat. Then, over by the I-35 junction at Albert Lea, you get the first scrub of oak savannah, meaning haphazard trees that muck up the prairie's greatest feature, horizon, and make everything just look messy.

Of course, maybe that's just the grid talking, the Thomas Jefferson mindfuck. It was Jefferson, that Age of Reason geometry-lover, who determined the American West would be laid out in 5,280-foot squares, making that almost unimaginable space both manageable and salable. The grid seems especially fitted to the nowhereness of the Midwest, where we give directions by saying "the second mile road east and then one and a half north." The grid also teaches you to look for order, straight lines within straight lines. But if you stop to think about it, all that straight-line geometry over dead flat places is as unnerving as mind control. Laid over a landscape that bends and turns and rises and dips, it becomes a straitjacket, prepping the land to be leveled and raised and straightened and drained for the largest equipment to farm—in straight lines. That's what they've done all over the prairie, like at Great Oasis, the system of lakes just northeast of where I live that was once a fur trading outpost but is now drained to farmland. But they can't flatten it all. On the Buffalo Ridge there's still some nuance, in the last curves of creeks they haven't yet straightened.

"THIS PLACE MAKES me sick," Dad always said about the place we lived, on the former tallgrass prairie now converted almost completely to corn and soybean agriculture. Actually, what he said was, "This place makes me . . . just . . . tight," since mental illness was not a sickness to him, being by definition "all in your head."

"This place" centers on a farm in Moulton Township, Murray County, Minnesota, just above Champepadan Creek, three miles as the crow flies from Leota, Minnesota. There Milton Schaap and his wife, Hattie Jean (Schelhaas) Schaap, raised four children across four decades: Carmen (b. 1961), Lisa (b. 1964), Heidi (b. 1970), and me, Howard (b. 1975).

"This place." The detachment afforded by I-90 leaves me to contemplate again what was, what is. The Upper Midwest is certainly the landscape of melancholy, especially on the machine of the interstate. You might as well be in an airplane in terms of how far you are removed from what's left of the tallgrass prairie, the crannies where big bluestem still waves its princely head or sideoats grama flies its delicate line of flags. The tallgrass is more than ninety-nine percent gone in Minnesota. There's no there there in tallgrass country anymore, prairie connoisseurs like to say. The treeless flat leaves no place to hide on the one hand, and the rows and rows of corn and soybeans leave no room to imagine on the other.

But it's not like the place was ever exactly welcoming. The tallgrass prairie was the landscape of melancholy even prior to the decimation of the tallgrass, at least as long as white-settler history. In *Giants in the Earth*, that long, dry prairie epic I had to read in high school, the place—especially the wind of the place—drives pioneer wife Beret Hansa batshit crazy. As late as 1908, "prairie madness" got presidential attention from Teddy Roosevelt, the landscape president.

Today, beyond simple melancholy, the prairie produces plenty of suicides, attempted and actual: the man who tried to run his tractor over his own head; a father of four who shot himself in his car; a football player who killed himself the morning of prom; the valedictorian who went AWOL from the army and shot himself as authorities pounded on the door, a third-generation suicide. Closest to home, a cousin of mine who grew up a mile north of our farm, at the head of Champepadan Creek, who hung himself in his hog barn. He was a sweet kid, twenty-seven and newly married.

It's a haunted landscape, classically indifferent still. Or worse.

Of course, there's another story, one of deep-rooted alignment with the land: the intense tallgrass communities of flowers and forbs that take root in the black black soil; the Dakota, who knew the native plants intimately and moved with the seasons; the trivial towns that the machine of the interstate keeps you from entering, the Walnut Groves and Montevideos, the Ceylons and Guckeens, the Alphas and Granadas and Leotas.

Leota, Minnesota, dream name of the Jesse Ventura accent—Le*oo*ta, Minnes*oo*ta—our particular Walnut Grove version of small-town blessing and curse.

But mainly curse.

Here's Leota for Dad in one story.

We're sitting in Grampa and Gramma's living room, the front room of a hip-roofed house on a back street of Leota, population 250. This is where we come every Sunday after church at Leota Ebenezer Christian Reformed Church, and for Dad, it's torture. All five-foot-nothing of Grampa Hank is posed idol-like in his green rocking chair, hands on armrests, turned slightly away from the giant picture window. Uncle Klaas, an in-law, sits in the chair opposite Grampa. Dad looks in on their conversation from behind Uncle Klaas, deferential to the older man or shouldered out—or perhaps the heckler in the wings. Uncle Klaas has a cue ball head ("Can't grow hair on a cement block," Dad will quip) and transition glasses still adjusting to being inside. Uncle Klaas's two long-legged boys are there, one blond-bald and one dark-bald. Heidi and I are there, Heidi who reads bullshit and the tea leaves of adult conversation like Charles Ingalls reads the seasons. It's Heidi who saves me from the floaties in the stale Pepsi from when Gramma sips from the bottle during the week. Now we're tired of Gramma's five toys, having spun the metal top two or three times before plopping down on the couch, wanting above all to turn on the TV at one end of the room, which is forbidden. The smell is dust plus something sour, something turning.

Conversation is formulaic and slow. Did you get rain. Did you see who was in church. That minister does a good job.

The women, finished serving the coffee in white cups and saucers and nut cookies and nut breads ("Always nuts and never chocolate!" Heidi will comment) on little white plates, trickle into the living room and find seats. Conversation turns, takes a focus in the room.

"Gonna cut alfalfa this week, Milt?" asks Uncle Klaas.

"Oh, we'll see once," says Dad.

Grampa bought the original 200 acres that was now our home place, sowed it all in the light blue flowers of flax when he was forty-eight, hit the market just right—one might say providentially—and paid for it in one year. Dad has bought the 200 from Grampa at prime market value, financing his hip-roofed house in Leota, then another quarter to the west, the Vis quarter, as well as adding new silos and sheds and modern equipment. Ours is a postage stamp-sized farm compared to Uncle Klaas's, who has been steadily buying and renting land that he and the boys farm with the biggest equipment, but Dad's still up to his eyes in debt.

"South of Leota it's in bloom already—you know it loses all its nutrients if that happens," says Uncle Klaas the cattleman to Dad the dairyman, whose livelihood depends upon maximizing the nutrients of alfalfa.

"Well, you don't say, Klaas!" says Dad. "Boy, I'm sure glad you told me! I'd a never thought of it!"

"The boys cut theirs?" asks Grampa.

"Cut it yesterday," says the dark-bald one.

"Milt, you better have the boys cut yours. On Monday," instructs Grampa.

"Klaas Wierenga tells Henry Schaap when to shit," Dad will say later. Now he shifts his elbows to his knees, says, "Mine won't be ready till Friday."

"Well, don't say I didn't warn ya," says Uncle Klaas.

That done, the conversation turns again to the review of who was in church, settling on someone who'd left Leota and had returned that morning for a visit, a prodigal.

"He was never any good," Grampa says.

"Daughter had a child out of wedlock, I believe," says Uncle Klaas.

"That right?" asks Grampa, and then something in Dutch that sounds like an oath.

"I knew him when he was here," says Uncle Klaas. "Never could finish anything."

Silence.

"His farm—always a *throop*," says Grampa Hank, a Dutch term that even I know means a broken-down, ill-run mess.

"He was always in town," says Uncle Klaas. "That's no way to make a farm go."

"But he was handy—could fix anything, that guy," says Dad, the minority report.

Silence.

"Bounced around a lot," says Uncle Klaas.

"I heard people liked him when he worked in the stockyard," Dad says. "I heard he made a good bit of money there." Dad sits back, locks his hands atop his crew cut, smiling with his eyes. He's baiting Gramps.

"He did?"

"Worked at the lumberyard. The bank. Then the stockyards in Slayton, I believe," says Uncle Klaas. "You don't make money when you move around that much."

"That's right!" says Grampa. "Jack of all trades and master of none!"

Afterward, on the drive home, Dad is usually on jailbreak, rubbing his hands, calling himself "Milt Andretti" as he careens the car over the empty road, singing a few bars of some nonsense song. Today, all the way home to Grampa's farm that has yet to become his own, driving the Caprice Classic straight and just a little too fast, Dad rubs his crew cut, repeats, "Jack of all trades and master of none!"

Leota, and all it entailed—Dad would say *that* was the place that made him sick.

Leota—and the farm itself.

Even from the distance of interstate you can read the history of the land, in the farm places. Always, driving through the countryside like this, Dad would muse on all the farmsteads dissolved out of the landscape, houses and barns and outbuildings burned and bulldozed, or replaced by one long, low, unremarkable tin hog confinement, or sagging in on themselves, hollow-eyed and empty, or preserved as artifacts and painted quaint red.

Dad's farm will always be a little jewel of a farm to me.

From the road and across an open lawn, the white farmhouse greets you with wide-eyed windows accented by the simple mascara of brown shutters. The straight gravel drive leads back to a cul-de-sac gravel yard, around which huddle various barns and sheds painted in a brown and white theme with wood shingle roofs: the calf barn / chicken coop, the granary / tool shed, the hog house, the barn / milkhouse / parlor. Behind the barn, the tin freestall barn hunkers and three stave silos stand guard. Up the hill from the cul-de-sac, more modern structures await: the cement bunker for piling silage, a modern pole barn, another silo, and a big tin machine shed.

That farm was happiness to us kids.

In winter, unlatching the big wooden door to get into the calf barn's warmth, the various pitches of the calves all bawling for milk. The big plastic bottles, hot water and soapy-dusty milk replacer, the comically large rubber nipples. Teaching the newborns to take the bottle; teaching the older ones to drink from a pail by getting them to suck your finger and drawing them down into the milk; scooping the molasses-y feed into the wood trough—a real-life Bethlehem manger—for the oldest. Cats, tame and wild, surging forth from various holes for excess milk. My sisters, seeking out the absent ones in the haymow or in the loose hay under the trough, finding new litters of kittens, blind and huddled tightly to their mother, naming them as they grew playful or wild or sickened with matted eyes.

Or the milking!

The hum of the bulk tank and compressor kicking in and out. The rhythmic clicks of the milk machines, like some Lawrence Welk beat you couldn't help tapping your foot to. The suction of a milker coming off and the sluff of Dad's rubber boots on concrete as pleasant variation. It was a pageant, morning and night: the procession of large beasts, the cutting smell of manure and urine, the wet of cement and acidic sanitizer on stainless steel.

Calves in straw, cats in haymows, pigeons in the crowns of silos, and raccoons in their pits. Empty silos meant it was time for another pageant: chopping alfalfa. Until Dad got the new John Deere 4440 and I got to ride along, I'd watch from the apple trees across the driveway beyond our large garden, gazing across the cattle yard where the cows rode each other in sexual frustration to the field beyond where one of Uncle Klaas's long-legged boys, the dark-bald one, swathed the silage in cool wrap-around sunglasses. We were drenched in the sweet smell all morning. Then, a few days later, Dad drove the tractor that pulled the chopper with yellow head and banana spout that blew the silage into a trailing wagon, a procession of three.

Chopping silage was all I wanted to do with my life.

The powerful engine and warm heart behind all of this was Dad, always with something left for us. Summer evenings, even after hard work among large beasts, he'd grab an old glove and we'd play catch. The first ball might rocket past me at my feet. "Gotta warm up," he'd say. "This old arm ain't used to it anymore." But he had a fluid motion, an easy leg kick, a throw that came not just from his shoulder but out of his whole body. Where Heidi and I worked on pop-ups and grounders under the apple trees for hours, Dad and I just threw straight catch for ten minutes near the house. He'd maybe make sound effects with his mouth, "Pfeeewww!" as it popped in the leather and burned your palm. With anyone else, it would have gotten boring, but this was catch with Dad, and as such it was pure.

This was the kind of space I figured I could live in forever—figured I would, repeating the rhythms of hard work and then comic play. Dad doing voices and crow calls. Dad at meals pointing out the window and stealing your pancake or wiping butter on your arm or starting a spaghetti fight. Dad singing, "Well I woke up Sunday morning / With no way to hold my head, that didn't hurt / And the beer I had for breakfast wasn't bad / So I had one more for dessert" before you all went off to church.

But there was something else about the farm, the part that ground Dad down.

The number of buildings seems extravagant when I list them now, but you have to understand how pointless and outdated they were. The barn was a hundred years old and sagging in on itself. The calf barn, hog house, and granary were too small for conventional farming. They were leftovers, nothing like the squat, steel hog confinements and cattle sheds and turkey barns that now litter the countryside and house thousands or tens of thousands or hundreds of thousands of animals.

One of my earliest memories is sitting in the gravel in front of the dark hole of the lean-to toolshed, while Dad lay under the chopper. We were "broke down," and the alfalfa crop, cut down just before it bloomed, was lying ready in the field but would quickly rot with tonight's forecast rain.

"You're not gonna farm," Dad said. "You are going to college."

There were plenty of these moments that piled up over the years: Dad jacking up a section of the barn to support it with a post; Dad climbing the ninety-foot silo to fix the silo unloader; Dad "doing bookwork" by the fluorescent light at a particle board desk; Dad talking with milk testers who monitored how sanitary his milk was; Dad looking at blueprints for his new parlor but shackled by finances; Dad pulling his prize John Deere corn planter around the slight hills of the 200, creating elegant contour rows to prevent erosion.

He was indeed a jack of all trades. Mechanic. Carpenter. Herdsman. Financier. Manager. Prophet. Scientist. Artist.

But when Grampa put it into words, it was an unmistakable insult—too half-assed at everything to be good at anything, to be *successful*. It felt like a prophecy of doom in a landscape of necessity.

And over time, that prophecy worked its woe.

First the calves went, the music of the milking parlor, the stainless steel bulk tank cut off at its metal feet in the milk house. He hadn't mastered the dairy. We briefly transitioned to hogs. Then they went, too, a failed pig farmer. Then the implements, the chopper, the wagons, our prize tractor, the John Deere 4440.

After most everything was gone, we kept one or two pigs around as projects, but these inevitably developed into asthmatics and neurotics with limps and goiters. The doors of the empty buildings banged in the wind, the silos howled.

"Jack of all trades and master of none," he'd mutter.

COMING INTO FAIRMONT, just an hour forty-five into the trip, the trees psych me out. I think it's the start of oak savannah, the beginning of the end. But it's not. These trees signify something much more important to the prairie: lakes.

When Grampa's badgering got to Dad, there was one antidote. Our corner of the state is not blessed with clear blue lakes, festooned with pines and the occasional birch right down to the sandy shoreline, like the Bob Ross painting people think of when they hear "Minnesota." The shallow lakes that dot the tallgrass on and around the Buffalo Ridge are called "prairie potholes," gouged by the Wisconsin glacier in retreat. They tend to be shallow and muddy, sometimes treeless, breast bared directly to the unyielding sky. For all that, they are lifelines. Lakes on the prairie mean oasis, life, hope.

But for us, especially hope.

Though the counties just to the west of our farm, Pipestone and Rock, are two of the lakeless counties in Minnesota, "land of 10,000 lakes," Murray County, where we lived, had the premier lake of southwest Minnesota, Lake Shetek—a muddy and in fact tree-festooned oasis (hardwoods, primarily ash and oak)—located in Dakota country but bearing an Ojibwe name. The more the pressure of necessity built within Dad, the more Lake Shetek—The Lake—became a release valve.

The Lake was synonymous with peace, freedom, even bounty. On certain Saturday afternoons of early summer—never Sundays, no matter workload or seasonal demands—Dad and Mom loaded the family into the car with fishing poles and cane poles and tackle boxes and picnic baskets and off to The Lake we went, to the dikes of Lake Shetek. There, Dad spent the afternoon baiting hooks and removing them from the bellies of stubborn bullheads, then dipping down for a slippery minnow to rebait those same hooks until the crappies started biting—plate-sized, silver-white angels that came flapping into shore and flopped off our hooks and between the rocks of the shoreline where Dad searched them out with fingers thick from milking, then slid them on the stringer. Any fish we caught were received like grace itself—a free gift, given to Dad without requiring the sweat of his brow.

As the prophecy took shape over the years—lopping off first one limb of the farm, then another, Dad cobbling together odd jobs to keep us afloat another season—more and more he and I would get into our Scottsdale pickup and go fishing. The more we went, the worse things were. The older I got, the more Dad would recite the litany of what went wrong.

Incompetence: his dairy herd had been ravaged by "red nose," a disease the local vets should have caught but didn't. This was the first domino.

Obsolescence: Grampa's quaint old buildings were not the stuff of modern farming. Government officials declared them so, downgrading Dad to grade B milk and gouging his income.

Economics: land prices dropped and banks began measuring Dad's worth in cash flow instead of net worth.

To that list I've since added at least two items.

Politics: Jimmy Carter decided to use food as a weapon, declaring a grain embargo on the USSR for invading Afghanistan and sending corn prices plummeting. Then Ronald Reagan determined to teach farmers a lesson and tightened lending practices as a way to eliminate the "bad operators."

Theology: the hallmark of Leota theology is the sovereignty of God. This God—the God of Grampa's living room—is known for being a contractual God, a law-giver and covenant maker. If it's written down, there's nothing you can do. About the same time as he was "losing the farm," Dad also lost a run-in with Leota Ebenezer over my sister's teen pregnancy. After that loss, Dad pulled back from the people of the church, even his friends and relatives, leaving him isolated in an isolated place, without the resources to improvise or resist politics or the invisible hand. It was hard for him not to think of both losses as written in The Book.

All these years later, it's the theology that still pricks, like the sharp steeples of prairie churches scattered along the interstate. As Dad worsened last fall, Mom lamented to Heidi on one of their phone calls, "God is punishing us!"

Punishing for what?

Who knows?

Always, the God of the Leota living room lurks, ready to apply his mysterious standards to your miserable strivings, blessings or punishments, without an object or even a preposition.

Driving east on I-90, a crosswind buffets the car. The scrub ash invaders in the ditches, sorry-ass excuses for trees, wave a mocking goodbye.

HEIDI WOULD CALL bullshit on this, on living into the story this way, the-world-set-against-Milt-Schaap. She fears for my sanity, living so near to Leota as I do, beneath the same cultural umbrella as he did. It's Leota theology, she would say, that has prevented us from naming Dad's problem, from actually doing something about it.

She's not wrong.

I know what the solution would be these days, drugs and talk therapy, balancing him chemically.

Yet I can't quite buy it. That if we had just gotten his brain measured and calculated, all his salts and elements balanced and managed by some sane and logical therapist, a fixed point, then all would be well. And if we could just jettison that immigrant culture and its backwater religion, too, with its sin and guilt and servile work ethic (but also grace and wonderment), then we could all move on with our progressive lives. There's something grid-like about that solution too.

I've witnessed the effects of the chemical imbalance hypothesis. Years on lithium that made life manageable but during which Dad was only occasionally his sparky, jocular self and was instead quiet, often sleepy, though still with too many nights when he would tighten his jaw and clench his fist like he could kill someone, muttering who knows what under his breath.

So there was always an explosive quality to Dad, though back in the 1980s in rural Minnesota that's just what I thought masculinity was. In 1985, you couldn't just google the DSM-IV definition of bipolar disorder that would declare it a "severe mental disorder characterized by extreme mood swings and episodes of depression and mania" or explain that bipolar II "patients... will primarily suffer with major depressive episodes," with symptoms including "insomnia or hypersomnia nearly every day" (which would have explained all the afternoons Dad snored away on the couch) and "feelings of worthlessness" (which would have explained his mantra, "I'm a failure") or "excessive or inappropriate guilt... nearly every day" (which I just thought was good theology). There was no explanation so you just looked on as he sobbed into his Cheerios.

No, I wouldn't go back to that.

But I also don't want to discount how we *did* deal with it, the story of it.

When we turned to lakes with names like Shetek and Talcot, Sarah and Shaokotan. When we tried to leave Leota. When he went commercial ice fishing. When we turned the land back over to grass. When Mom asked me to put the guns upstairs. When he went to the promised land of California. When we changed churches and he clung to sermons with titles like "The Refiner's Fire." When he told me how he would kill himself. When we thought Up North would save us.

"This place makes me sick." From the vantage point of I-90, looking again out over the landscape of melancholy, ninety-nine percent of it plowed under and under, with its residual doctrines of sin and grace, of Manifest Destiny and the Promised Land—if you knew Dad, knew where we lived—hell, if you looked out across the landscape and knew anything about its history—you wouldn't reduce it to a chemical hypothesis.

So I'm ready to reconsider the role of place, a place hypothesis.

And then there's Charles Ingalls. I have Caroline Fraser to thank for that. When I read her book *Prairie Fires: The American Dreams of Laura Ingalls Wilder*, it explained my whole life up to the present moment.

It's maybe too harsh to think of Charles Ingalls as the original manic-depressive on the prairie. His granddaughter Rose had it in spades, and these things tend to run in families. But even if he wasn't, it's right there in his choices, in the kind of behaviors I've come to associate with the place. In Pa's "itching foot." In bizarre moves in the middle of the night. In building a house then abandoning it. In awkwardness with "foreign" neighbors. In claim-shack living in the face of killing winters. In the woman who holds it all together. In his move, not just farther right, but from someone broad-minded and warm-hearted to someone narrow and bitter.

Near the end, Dad sat in the corner of his mobile home in Crow Wing County, Minnesota, and nodded along to the talking points of his favorite news channel. That there were too many foreigners, too many handouts. That it was everyone's own fault if they didn't make it.

As Charles hadn't. As he hadn't.

It's really after Austin, Minnesota—Spamtown, USA—that the landscape changes, that the oak savannah begins. I'm resigned to leaving the prairie, resigned to what I'll find at Mayo.

But I have to go.

I have to go because I am my father's son. Dad was 38 when I was born in 1975, twelve years past his Minnesota Young Farmer of the Year award, but still in some of the prime years of farming. By the time the farm crisis hit and Dad's manic depression flowered forth in blue flowers, it was 1986 and he was 49.

I'm 38 as I drive to Rochester. I rub my hands together uncontrollably when I'm excited, like he does. I've had one bout with anxiety that left me unable to sleep, unable to get it up. At 38, all of his overreactions, his fascinations and obsessions don't seem so extreme. I'd be naïve to think my path is so self-selected that I can simply choose to avoid that darkness.

Or avoid passing it on to my own kids—these things tend to run in families.

I have to go because he's got his place hypothesis, and I've got mine. "This place makes me sick," he said. "Leota—that's a cult," he said. "Move away from here as soon as you can," he said. "Get a college education and you can do whatever you want—never look back."

But I did come back. I attend church in the same tradition. I fish the same lakes we fished, hunt the same draws we hunted. It was the landscape that called me back. And when I returned I found clumps of original tallgrass in the ditches—prairie cord grass and Indian grass and sideoats gramma and switch grass and of course big bluestem.

If Dad's theory is right, I've committed myself to the landscape of melancholy. If mine is right, it's the place that can make us well.

In going to Rochester, I'm still hoping for his healing and mine.

And then there's this: I have to go because I love my dad; my love for him is not a resignation. There were times over the last twenty-five years—one more time declaring himself a failure, once more down the rabbit hole of theological speculation, one more murderous clenching of the teeth—when I had to turn away. This is not one of those times. The man who was the joy of all of our childhoods is crumbling from the inside, and the one thing I want to do is hold his thick, calloused hands.

In Rochester, I will find Dad in storm. That's the better metaphor, truer to the place. Dad as collision of high and low pressure systems with a psychotropic updraft. That's what so many plains men are, Charles Ingalls included—men who embody the frontal conflict of highs and lows, who believe themselves to be the boundary between the semblance of order in our lives and the chaos that would stretch forth to wreck us did they not throw themselves bodily in front of it.

"No. Bullshit," says Heidi's voice again. In my memory, Heidi and I are two beers in at my kitchen table, meaning shit's about to get real. "It's Dad's martyr-saint complex that's so dangerous," she tells me. "It's held us hostage with its call to silence, to not making waves." Tiptoeing around Dad for so many years has made us into adults who stay silent in marriages until they erupt in divorce, she says, who become paralyzed by indecision before bosses and careers and "necessity," which result in our own mania or despair. We all continue to live with Dad's moods well into adulthood. It's time we stop bowing before Dad in storm.

Maybe she's right, too.

When I finally exit I-90 for US Highway 63 and then 52, I've left the oak savannah. The road descends between crumbling rock cuts, snakes along the rivers and contours of a different sort of landscape. Rochester sits upon some of the oldest land in Minnesota, "the driftless region," the Paleozoic Plateau. It feels ancient. It feels like a betweenness.

I turn right on Second Street SE, and in a few blocks find Mayo Clinic's St. Mary's Hospital, a modern marvel of the Midwest.

Dear God, may this be the answer.

I pull into a lot across the street that says, "Hotel Parking Only." The façade of St. Mary's from this view is old timey, with aged brick and many windows, though the entrance is made of lighter, modern slab. It's a different kind of place, a different kind of vision of place.

I call my sister Carmen. She's somewhere inside, in Dad's room.

"Hello?" she says.

Shoulder shrug. Let's go.

"I'm here," I say. "Where should I park?"

2

The Miraculous Catch of Fish

"I FELL FOKE."

In Schaap family lore, my sister Heidi spoke these words at four years old into the void of a Black Hills campground late one night to give notice that she was here and she was paying attention. That story, and the one about how she quietly stuck peas up her nose one family mealtime until Mom noticed and squeezed them out, 1-2-3-4, are probably her least favorite stories about herself, like jokes told too often. But smelling smoke means, all these years later, that Heidi picked up on Mom's hints about Dad's decline. The rest of us had shrugged, chalked it up to old age—Dad was going, sooner than we'd like at 77, but he'd had an almost impossibly hard life, and who knew what that had done to his body? But Heidi felled foke, damn it, and she went in and saved them.

It's Heidi I see first coming into Dad's room.

"Howie," she says, and it's all she can say. It's clear that Heidi has been through the fire. Her black eyes are both tired and relieved, showing her age, 43, for really the first time. Her auburn hair, a mysterious gift of ancestry, usually worn straight and neat and just above shoulder length, is slightly rumpled. She's borne Mom and Dad back from the brink, and she's been shaken by the journey.

Mom and Carmen tend to Dad in his hospital bed. I hug each of them in turn.

Heidi got them here and Carmen came in as reinforcement. A lifelong nurse whose Myers-Briggs suggested talk show host, Carmen is high doses of energy and action and logic and clear communication. She fills me in. "So, they think Dad is lithium toxic and that's what's causing his body to shut down, as well as his confusion and delirium," she begins. "Heidi and Mom did a great job of getting him to a hospital. At Crosby, they dropped him off lithium and started him on Ativan without asking Mom. Ativan—Dad's had bad reactions to that both in the state hospital and then one other time when Mom took him to Brainerd. As soon as Mom and Heidi found out about the Ativan, they stopped it, but he already had a bunch of it in his system, so we'll see. Anyway, they did a CT scan at Crosby and after seeing the results of that and talking to Mom and Heidi, Crosby suggested sending him here, which Mom has also wanted to do for a while, haven't you, Mom? Now the doctors here are waiting to put him on other mood stabilizers until the lithium and Ativan clear out a little bit. They're also concerned about his kidney function—his blood test had high levels of calcium which is probably from the lithium toxicity. And, I almost forgot, they're testing for a UTI, too, which could explain some of his confusion. Now, what questions do you have?"

Carmen is the pioneer of the family: first one to graduate college, to marry outside the tribe, to leave our Reformed churches for something approaching evangelical megachurch—the first to leave Leota. She's 52 with large brown eyes, sharp cheekbones and pointed nose, and a clear manner that carries authority with it. We look to Carmen to get things done.

Lisa, sister number two, between Carmen and Heidi, is en route.

I look around the room, from Carmen the rock-solid family-values Republican evangelical to Heidi the agnostic liberal feminist. Lisa is currently married to a stand-your-ground Texan; I'm married to a Laotian refugee. Between us kids we tally two-going-on-three divorces and six-going-on-seven marriages and political views so divergent it's a wonder we can be in the same room. Then I look at Mom, her body beginning to shrink and warp, reduced to TV preacher Christianity, and Dad, lying delusional in a hospital bed below the TV news. My question is: what went wrong?

"I'm sorry," Carmen interrupts. "That's a lot to take in, isn't it? How are you? Been doing any fishing?"

It's a different first question: what went right?

THE FIRST TIME Dad went fishing was at the invitation of friends. He had absolutely zero equipment, so he had to make his own pole, which he did, out of an old broomstick. They went to Lake Wilson and caught bullheads. That's the story.

But because it's the origin story, I need to imagine my way into it a little bit.

Saturday night after milking, Dad's friends show up in a '49 Ford pickup, with their equipment in the back. They have cane poles and a couple legit fishing poles with open-faced, spiral-wind reels that look like small engines, and even one closed-faced reel, with just a hole for the string to come out, like something space-aged, made by Zebco, short for the Zero Hour Bomb Company.

"Where's your pole, Milt?" somebody asks.

"I haven't got one," he says. "But wait a minute once." He disappears into the lean-to tool shed, grabs a broken-down broom, and knocks the end off with a handsaw before notching a groove in the end. "There. Now, I've got my own cane pole," he announces, triumphant.

At Lake Wilson, the boys sit along the stones that line Highway 30 which runs right through the middle of the lake. The bullheads are biting regular but Dad first has to rig up his pole. As the fish come in, the boys hoot and holler, tease each other.

"Ho, that's the biggest one yet!"

"And the ugliest!"

"Looks just like that girl you like from Lismore."

Once ready, Dad joins in. "Alright boys, now I am going to out-fish you all with my broomstick pole. Get ready!"

And sure enough, down goes his bobber and Milt hauls in a yellow belly, fat through the stomach with eggs, flopping onto the rocks of shore.

"I told you, fellas!" he says.

As Dad laughs and jokes and catches bullhead after bullhead along the fieldstone of Lake Wilson, the evening unspools before him.

Though Grampa's farm and its unyielding schedule lies just eight miles south down highway 91, it feels a whole dimension away.

By the time us kids rolled around, Dad had upgraded from muddy Lake Wilson to the larger Lake Shetek. We sat on the rocks that lined the road that ran to Valhalla Island and then Keeley Island, creating three dikes that were perfect for fishing bullheads, crappies, and walleyes. Likewise, Dad had upgraded from his broomstick pole to cane poles and even a Zebco 33.

See them sit there on a Saturday afternoon, the Milt and Jean Schaap family part one: Carmen, the oldest and type-A all the way, holding the pole correctly but so busy instructing Lisa on proper etiquette that she misses her own bobber going down. Lisa, the wild one, jumping from one thing to the next and up and down the rocks, grabbing a minnow from the bait bucket just to feel it wriggle in her hands before dropping it in the lake so she has to grab another one.

They fished primarily with cane poles in those days, wooden poles assembled in sections to something eight or more feet long. You hung one long line from the end and swung it out into the water; catching meant you just lifted up and pulled the fish right out of the water. Legend has it that one time Lisa jerked the pole so hard and high she flung the flapping crappie up onto the road behind her. Carmen still tells that story.

The other story is about ice cream. Fishing trips to Lake Shetek always ended with ice cream at The Hub, a summer-only café in nearby Slayton that hired high school girls as carhops. Carmen and Lisa would whisper in the back seat of various old cars on the return trip, wondering if Dad was going to stop, not daring to ask. Dad, knowing this full well, would drive right past The Hub on purpose, no doubt listening for the girls' whispering to crescendo and fizzle before he would turn around.

"Oh, I forgot something! We gotta go back to Slayton a minute!" And the girls knew they were getting their ice cream.

Heidi and I, part two of Milt and Jean's family, had the Lake Shetek-followed-by-The-Hub experience, too, though things had changed somewhat by the time we came around.

Heidi was early labeled quiet, introspective, and she probably took in Lake Shetek in ways the rest of us didn't, studying the cloud formations and rock striations and the way the threads from Dad's cut-off sleeves flicked in the wind and how many damn mosquitoes there were and the way her sisters fought and the way Mom had to watch over me, the prized son and whiny brat, and how she would have preferred to skip the whole fishing part to just walk around and explore but played along on account that it was so important to Dad.

Heidi could stand apart and see the whole situation. And she had the ability that Dad long praised to call a spade a spade.

And then there was me, a pukey baby who grew into a snot-nosed little kid, who got a special kid-fishing pole before I had even proved myself as a fisherman.

As the youngest and the only boy, I would have had to work a little to screw up my golden child status, but it also wasn't a slam dunk. Word is Dad was so ambivalent about having a son that he just sort of looked away at the announcement that it was a boy. Mom says he didn't want to make the same mistakes Grampa Hank made with him but that as a good Calvinist he was afraid of predestiny or total depravity or the law of eternal return or whatever.

Then it turned out I had the demeanor of Grampa Hank.

In short, I was a little shit.

MOM IS STANDING at the white double sink with drain board in a *Leave it to Beaver* kitchen. I want a drink, and I'm looking up at her, unable to see the bloody meat she's working with, cracking it apart so it will thaw faster and she'll be able to get supper on the table at a reasonable hour.

"Be patient, Grampa Hank!" she hollers down at me. "You're just like old Gramps—you've gotta have it right now, dontcha!"

I stomp my foot. I *do* want a drink, I'm thirsty, but she's just turned this moment—the simple need of a child dying of thirst—into a double bind: choose death or align myself with my wicked hypocritical grandfather.

Grampa Hank, I know at the earliest of ages, is the name of the man whose dry, still house we go to Sunday after church, where the conversation is oppressed by long silences and Dad looks like he's being interrogated for crimes he didn't commit and Grampa hollers from his chair at Grandma for this and that.

"Mary! Get me a cookie!"

"Mary! Bring me that bulletin once!"

"Mary! Open the curtains!"

Not done quickly or to his satisfaction, he begins to raise himself against his immobility, cursing in Dutch under his breath.

Now, this man, Mom is saying, is me.

Even as I weigh the dilemma, being like Grampa or dying of thirst, my heart beating in my chest at the prospect, she's washed her hands and gotten the water. "Here—here's your water. Impatient, just like Old Gramps! That's what I'm going to call you—Gramps!"

After that moment, whenever I got impatient with her, Mom indeed called me Gramps and that insult began its drip-dripping on the rock that was my nature.

Dad's strategy was different. He turned to fishing.

Those were the Jimmy Carter seventies. With prices down and interest up, the banks said to borrow-borrow-borrow because everything would come back. So Dad did. He put up a freestall barn, future site of his state-of-the-art milking parlor. Then he bought a new, modern tractor, a closed-cab John Deere 4440. He and I took pictures on it one Sunday in church clothes, me standing high on its hood, he holding me so that the roaring south wind wouldn't blow me off, one picture with formal smiles, one with Dad cringing, as if he were thinking, "Dear God, what am I doing?" The dairy was brimming and the farm buildings were flush with life and we were tractor-tire-deep in debt.

And I was king of all I surveyed. Mornings, I'd wake up and farm the green shag carpet of the living room with a full array of toy John Deere implements, make a hundred bank shots on the basketball hoop nailed to the garage, hit whiffle balls into the lawn and maybe pet the cats. Half an hour later, I'd nag mom, "I'm bored—what can I do?" Rinse, repeat. It drove her batty.

And so, I got a special invitation to the fishing party. For Christmas one year, I unwrapped an orange and white Snoopy fishing pole complete with plastic plug to practice casting. Casting that plug into the lawn and fantasizing about reeling in crappies and walleyes got added to the morning repertoire.

A half hour later, back to nagging.

As the nagging increased and Carter stretched into Reagan, Dad hatched a plan to take me fishing, just him and me.

"He'll never have the patience for it—he's got too much Hank in him," Mom told Dad in confidence, so that I could hear perfectly. The idea that I might somehow have Grampa Hank inside me got my attention. It terrified me.

When we left the yard for the first time in our always-dirty Scottsdale pickup, ten-year-old Heidi forgotten somewhere in the house, I could feel Mom's doubt: "Good luck! We'll see how long he lasts!" I steeled myself against it.

Dad insured his wager with a safety net: he promised we'd always catch something; he bought snacks to eat while we waited; he promised (an unspoken promise) that if I would be a good fisherman (patient and not a complainer) I could spend hours away from home with him, just him and me.

Lake Shetek itself added to the magic. The rock-lined road with water on both sides was like the path of the Israelites through the Red Sea. We parked on the islands and walked back out to sit on the rocks and bobber-fished away the afternoon.

I memorialized that first trip in my earliest elementary school writing: we went to Lake Shetek; while it rained, we had our lunch of chocolate milk and powdered donuts; we caught a perch and a crappie.

BOBBER FISHING—Dad always called it a dobber—is good discipline, biceps curls for your patience. Dad set up my Snoopy pole with a dobber, split-shot weight, and a gold hook. We always used a fixed pencil bobber with a fire-red tip, yellow shoulders, and white underbelly, swelled out in the middle like a pencil had swallowed a marshmallow.

My job was to watch this thing. So on the puzzle-pieced rocks on the south side of the second dike on Lake Shetek, in the dry, still afternoons, I watched it.

As it slid almost imperceptibly up and down the bank. As it bob-bob-bobbed on the waves of a southeast wind. As it sent out almost imperceptible blips on the water.

"Dad, I've got a bite."

"That might just be your minnow. You've got a lively one on."

As I waited, hands braided to my Snoopy pole, I was the paragon of patience. Or obsession-compulsion. I didn't throw rocks or wander up the bank or ask to go home. For hours and hours I sat, baited by the promise.

And prophecy. "It's only four o'clock sun time," Dad would say. "In another couple hours the walleyes will start coming in to shore."

That prospect redoubled my determination to watch. And pray.

"Please, please, *please* let me catch a fish, *please*," was easily my earliest and most earnest prayer. Still is.

Then I made up rhymes. "Wall-eyes, wall-eyes come to shore, so my life won't be a bore."

I watched and prayed, chanted and incanted through the long afternoon. Mostly, my dobber prayers met silence. But I just kept asking. When it bobbed in with the waves, I casted again. And again and again and again.

I got false positives: when what looked like a bite was actually a snag. I endured suffering: when my reel wouldn't cast and Dad undid the front cover only to find a rat's nest of tangles inside, and it seemed like I'd never cast again. I met despair: when the thought arose that we were fishing in an empty puddle and the cars going by on the road were all laughing at us, that there were no fish and there was no God.

No, against this, I simply had to believe.

And endure. I endured through the long afternoons—because He wants this. So I determined to be the longest endurer.

Because with endurance did come answers. The down periscope bite, a submarine slowly submerging. The bob and weave bite, slight bounces this way, then that. The staccato bite of sharper ups and downs. And most unnerving of all, the dead man's float, when a bobber comes *up* instead of going down, a prayer sent back to you so you might reconsider.

"That's a crappie bite," Dad would prophesy, "get ready—tighten your line."

And just like that it would dive, as if to the abyss itself, as if God had just been teasing you, God, the creator of the teeming fishes of the deep.

"OK now, set the hook!"

And I'd reel in a madly flapping crappie with a plastic, dainty mouth. Dad would poke the stringer up through the slot of its gill, toss it in the water, and there it was, my own fish that I could always check on—check on as proof. There was a God.

MAYBE HALF A dozen trips into Dad's wager, we got skunked for the first time, and that meant everything was being tested.

Like Dad's benevolence. "Sorry, Pal," Dad said. "We've never got skunked before, have we? I usually get you to catch a fish, don't I?"

"It's not your fault, Dad," I said but didn't mean. I was trying my best not to pout, which is to say I was ready to go all blubbery-fist-pounding tantrum. I could almost accept his offering, that he was somehow to blame.

"Not even a bullhead!" Dad said, and it was the most frightening line of all. I felt the lack of even that universal devil-fish as great injustice, as if something was working actively against us. Or someone.

As if it were predestined.

Skunked.

That word and how I felt about it dredges up the whole apparatus of how I thought the world worked then.

On the one hand, there was Grampa's God.

Every Sunday at Leota Ebenezer and afterward in my grandparents' living room, even if the conversation was about the weather or commodity prices or who got a new car, the air was dense with theological principles: providence, depravity, election. It was a confined and confining world, where everything happened by the hand of God and the only real option was nose-to-the-grindstone diligence.

The God of Grampa's living room was dour—though, to be fair, the light that poured in through the picture window—that illuminated the whole scene—had a name, "grace." You just didn't know exactly what to do with that grace. It never quite translated into unrestrained joy for Grampa, and certainly never into any kind of bacchanal: at Grampa's birthday, when we gave him a bottle of Mogen David or King Solomon wine, he closed the curtains before he partook. Then, in a surprising move, he poured everyone a small glass, even us kids.

When confronted with this God on Lake Shetek, earnest prayer became a way to somehow move him to action, convince him you were worthy. He was out there, this otherwise-preoccupied Father was—hadn't he done enough already?—and you were asking him, impossibly, to just take a little more time and tie a fish on your line. So you endured to prove yourself and to move God out of torpor and indifference and convince him to bless you with his hesitant hand.

But there was another God, too. This was the God of the brimful farm, of a spooked herd of bovine trampling through a fence. The one who sometimes overdid things, who multiplied flicker tails in the pasture till they became a plague that dug out rows of newly planted corn, a hole for every regular seed dropped from Dad's John Deere corn planter. This was the fun God, the wild or even OCD God, the one who was busy tracking every loop de loop of all the iridescent barn swallows, who noted when even one of them was nabbed out of the sky by a tabby.

This was the crazy uncle God, who stashed away coins in the mouths of fish for a rainy-day fund. The God who would let you fish all night without catching and then show up on shore wild-haired and whimsical in the morning and say, "Oh, not catching anything?—here, hold my beer—OK, cast your nets on the *other* side of the boat—" and the waters would literally swarm with fish, to the point of creeping you out, to the point of terror.

This was Dad's God. Rollicking and chaotic, joyful and unpredictable, profligate and dangerous.

He was manic.

That manic God was why you endured.

BUT NOW WE were skunked; Grampa's God was in charge.

And then, miracle.

As we came out of the trees along Valhalla Road to the open water of the first dike, the last piece of hope before the never-ending prairie, we saw three clumps of fishermen standing around the culverts that ran underneath the dike.

"What's going on here? They must be catching something," Dad said. We drove slowly past the first two crowds, looking along the water's edge for stringers in the water, of which there were several, with long clutches of white-bellied fish on each.

"Do you want to try it here, Pal?"

Naturally.

The farthest culvert only had one or two fishermen by it. Dad parked at the end of the road and walked back up to the culvert to ask if we might fish there. When he came back, he was excited.

"He'll let us fish by him—he's a real nice guy."

I got placed right on the corrugated metal of the culvert, the prime spot. The water boiled out slowly beneath me, eddying and roiling in a way that was magic in itself. They were biting on black Mister Twisters, of which we had exactly none, but the guy—really a nice guy—gave us a couple.

They were like black licorice with yellow eyes. The lead head gave way to a body that was squishy, vinyly to the feel, tapering down to a fragile tail that flopped in the air and fluttered in the water. Genius. Gorgeous. Dad tied one on the Zebco 33, his rod and reel, and gave it to me.

"Here, I want you to catch one. You can't use your pole for this. Go ahead, you can do it."

And I knew I could because of practice on the lawn. I casted and reeled, pulling the Mister Twister through the water, watching its yellow eye and spinning tail the last few feet as it climbed out of the push of the current.

On one of the casts, true to the man's promise, something grabbed it.

"Dad, I got one!"

Dad, incredulous: "Really?"

"Here, use my dip net," said the man as the fish fought me across the current.

"Yeah, I forgot to bring ours along," Dad lied.

Its side came up golden in the late evening water, its large eyes dark and blue.

"Yep, that's a walleye." Dad's voice trembled slightly. I can't see the second fish in my memory as it came in. It was smaller but still a keeper. Dad, feeling like we had intruded on the man's territory—that we'd probably already taken advantage of the grace allotted to us—that his prayer had already been answered beyond what he could have asked or imagined—said we should go. When we left, the man and most of the crowd were still fishing. The sun had set.

"How was that? How's that for getting skunked?!" he said in the pickup as we drove away, playfully slapping me with the back of his hand. "I told you we'd catch something."

I couldn't stop smiling.

We stopped at the bait shop, Pete's Corner, where they weighed the fish, then snapped a Polaroid with us holding them, the weights of each fish written on a chalkboard behind us, something official, like 1 lb. 8 oz. and 3 lbs. 2 oz.

Considering the drought that came after, we should have framed that picture. To help us hold on.

"WHAT WENT WRONG?" is also a way of asking, "What went right?" The dikes of Lake Shetek went right. Ice cream at The Hub went right. We return to these things as common ground to remind ourselves of who Dad is, of what he's done, and of who he and Mom have made us, come what may in the next season, the next election cycle, the next instant.

Dad long needed reminding of what went right. Because he could only seem to remember what went wrong.

And now he needs a different kind of reminding. Of anything at all.

A nurse has come in and wakes Dad up to give him pills. When she puts a cup of apple juice to his lips, he trembles as he drinks, splutters, then gathers all his strength to cough.

"You OK, Dad?" Carmen asks.

He's spiraling down, the rest of us with him.

No, that's not true.

"I think you've got a hole in your chin," Heidi says, using one of his own one-liners from a whole menu of options.

Between us, we've got all the versions of all Dad's stories, each from our different vantage points, which just makes for better storytelling. We're here to pick Dad up, and with all the one-liners and all the stories, to put him back together again.

3

Ebenezer

IN HIS ROOM in the Domatilla Building of St. Mary's hospital, Dad is somewhere between resting and worrying his lips with his eyes closed. When he opens them momentarily, it's not clear he recognizes anyone. Mom straightens his hospital gown, which he seems to be crawling out of. She's her typical, positive self, if tired. Her body, always angular, is starting to go out of alignment, as if walking alongside Dad all these years is finally having an effect. She accepts these changes without comment, as long as we kids are there to help her. With Lisa on the way, all her children will soon be together to stand alongside her.

I check the view from Dad's window. A line of diners and coffee shops across the way with blocky, important-looking buildings in the distance. Dad's room is in the old part of the hospital, classic brick. The entrance I came in is newer, lighter slab that brings to mind the term limestone.

Brick and limestone.

Two materials as good as any to explain how we got here.

LICK YOUR TEETH rock picking and you can feel how fine the Wisconsin glacier could grind dirt.

Rock picking was the family job on the farm every June. Hitch up the cabless 3010 John Deere to a wagon of some sort and pull it up and down the fields of newly sprouted corn, grassy and weak and leaning over from the wind, a lazy green spider that would surely get squashed before it could suck its stalky strength out of the soil and the sky. Our job was to look for rocks, the new crop of assorted nameless varieties that were uncovered by the belching frost below and the scraping implements above. Up and down the fields, maybe twenty rows at a time, walking and spying rocks, fetching and humping them to the wagon. From softball size to skull size to the kind of slab it'd take two adults to trundle over, to occasionally one so big Dad would take the Bobcat out and dig it out of the field. Hit that kind of rock with a cultivator or send it through the combine and you'd land yourself in the shop at the worst time and there would go your number one commodity on the farm: time.

I came to consciousness rock-picking. Opened my eyes and there I was, slight sweat around the hairline already catching the fine dirt, plodding across the still loose loess, like an uglier kind of sand and just about as hard to walk across. Finding white, gray, and cheese-textured rocks to retrieve. Hucking them from distance. Grabbing ones more the size of baseballs because you could throw them and make a game of it. Skipping one accidentally off the wagon and onto the other side, where Mom was bent over with both hands to pull out a piece of basalt still mostly buried, rock glancing off her head.

Oh shit.

Mom was mostly humble diligence, tender compassion, but she had Grandma Cornelia's sharp tongue, too, which she unleashed upon me then. After, Heidi says, she just walked off the job, walked home.

REFORMED CHURCHES mean, to many people, Dutch Reformed Churches, but to us specifically they mean Christian Reformed Churches, a small subset of churches originating in the northern Netherlands, circa 1830. Reformed churches in this old country tradition—especially in the tiny towns of Leens and Ulrum from which the Schaaps hail—are typically stalwart, red brick structures with lovely if streamlined woodwork inside, support beams for the A-frame architecture and solid wooden pews, and simple, beautiful stained-glass windows. These reformed churches are as somber—some would say stuffy—as any church you've been in, toned down from the pagan ornateness of high church tradition but not as anorexic as clapboard meetinghouses. And some of us will be just that frank about how right we have got the balance of both style and theology. An ethnic joke about us goes like this:

What's a Dutch tip?

Not so much makeup and a little quicker with the coffee.

I'm not sure what the Dutch thought they were getting when they bought into southwest Minnesota in the 1890s. No doubt clan reports made their way back across the pond to announce that the Dutch had stumbled upon some of the purest black dirt in the world in Sioux Center, Iowa, and that new settlers were now moving up to Leota, Minnesota, only sixty miles north, with soil surely similar to that of Sioux County.

Except it wasn't. It was rockier. As it melted, the Wisconsin glacier dumped its cargo of rock all over southwest Minnesota. First-wave immigrants found this out in a hurry. Not only did they have to break the original prairie, but below all that grass, heavy as concrete, they found a hodgepodge of rocks to stop their plows cold or even break the moldboards.

Third-wave immigrants often bought farms that others were thinking better of. That's what happened to Jan and Frederika Schaap, my great grandparents, who bought a partially broke quarter in Moulton Township, Murray County, Minnesota, perched above Champepadan Creek. Maybe the view suckered Jan (who Anglicized his name to John). Compared to the dead flat land around Leens, in the province of Groningen, the Netherlands, from which he hailed, the Moulton County farm must've felt like a precipice, the romantic sublime. Or pastoral, a gentle stream winding through green hills a million miles from the angry North Sea—or any sea, for that matter. And then all that black soil!

By the time Great Grampa John realized what kind of farm he'd *really* bought, a rocky knoll perched above a trickle of water, the pasture only green—or green-*ish*—about April through June, he must have decided it was a great joke or maybe was still just thrilled to have rocks to call his own, because he settled down to have ten children on that rocky Moulton Township farm.

In general, the third-wavers around Leota Township got the joke. The pure black gold the Dutch settlers had found around Sioux County had indeed been too good to be true. The Leota land was riddled with rocks that they would be picking for generations. So when they set up a church in town, they named it Ebenezer.

"Ebenezer" is an Old Testament word, originating with the prophet Samuel, back when he was just getting going. Just as the Israelites are putting away their idols and Samuel is sacrificing for them out in the open, here comes the Philistine army—the Israelites are sitting ducks. But Samuel goes ahead with the sacrifice, a suckling lamb. God goes in for that kind of trust, and "thunders with a loud thunder against the Philistines" and saves them all. To commemorate that saving, Samuel sets up a rock and calls it Ebenezer, meaning "stone of help."

Naming a Reformed church Ebenezer in southwest Minnesota shows keen, almost comedic, insight. The God of Leota Ebenezer is a sovereign God; he had surely dropped all the rocks right where they landed. If Leota settlers were going to make a go of it, they would just enlist his help to pick them back up. "Thus far has God helped us," Samuel had said in the Bible at the first Ebenezer, the perfect name for a church out on the glacial till where families would be forced to pick rock for generations.

If Great Grampa John got the joke, his sons, who actually had to finish breaking the Schaap quarter, didn't find it all that funny. One by one the boys moved off that farm seeking better ones: first John, then Henry, then Frank and Fred and Lew and even the youngest, Bill, whose farm it was for the taking. When he gave it up, it was bought by Walt Buys, who with his wife Florence set to picking rock.

In the end, Henry—Grampa Hank—ended up the closest, on a farm right across the road.

THE STONE OF help that was Ebenezer Christian Reformed Church was where Grampa Hank expected to see us every Sunday. If we didn't show up in the unpadded wooden pews for even one service, we could expect a call. And if we didn't show for a few Sundays, we could expect a visit from the elders. Ebenezer was the focal point upon which Grampa Hank meditated from his rocking chair in his hip-roofed house on a backstreet of Leota.

I will always picture Grampa Hank in that swivel rocker. He is bald with a white-hair comb over. He wears horn-rimmed glasses, a white button-down shirt, and brown suspenders. There's a TV at the opposite end of the long room, but it's the picture window that is his world. Grampa can pivot in this chair and watch Leota, imagine his way through it. His neighbor the car dealer, with teenage children all in rut. Down the street to Main and the little repair shop where you can buy pop in cold bottles, drink them in air thick with the musk of oil, talk politics. Farther down Main to pop into the post office, then the café for gossip. Across the street, set back on a low hill in the very center of town, Leota Ebenezer perches, its A-frame architecture and light brick and square bell tower echoing the style of the Netherlands churches but in a fresh American form. Further down the street is the car dealership, the grocery store, the hardware store, another church, the bank where he checks his balance on Monday and Friday, and finally the brick town hall. And up the street in the opposite direction, on the outskirts of town to the east, the brick Christian school, founded by the brick church and built with all the old country distrust for government.

For Christians in our tradition, there's nothing that's not religious; everything is a belief in something, and every action is based on a belief; therefore, we believe we can bake the Kingdom of God into everything we do, that starting with Jesus as the central ingredient makes the recipe. That having Christ as the foundation is not just metaphor—it will actually mean you build better. The same goes for ditch-digging, corn-farming, movie-making, Amway-selling, or education-governing. It's high-minded and optimistic, with tendencies toward self-righteousness and triumphalism ("thus far God has helped us"). Like most things in Christianity, it hinges on who—and how made over in your own image—you think Jesus is.

It can be beautiful and intense. You bake you a cake, you build you a house, you do it before the face of God. This shit matters.

It can be ugly and self-righteous. You settle a town, get elected to school board or Ebenezer consistory, and you start musing on how everyone else should live. You *are* the face of God.

Two of our famous members illustrate the contrast.

Paul Schrader, screenwriter for *Taxi Driver* and writer/director of *First Reformed*.

Betsy DeVos, Secretary of Education during the first Trump administration.

One event would solidify Henry Schaap's work before the face of God: when he bought the 200 acres directly across the road from Great Grampa John and with one crop both made his fortune and convinced himself it was a better farm than the rocky knoll of his dad's place.

WHILE GRAMPA meditated in his Leota swivel-rocker, we picked rock.

Nothing symbolized the ball-and-chain labor of the farm quite like rock-picking. Up and back along the rows, picking all the rocks softball size and bigger. Then do it again the next year. And the next. Unthinking labor. So when we got to a particularly rocky knoll and Dad shut off the tractor and we humped rock after rock to the wagon, we kids would think up inventions so we wouldn't have to do it. Rock-sensing implements. Robots. Lasers you could blast them with. They could do that already in *Star Wars*. Yeah, but we would make blasters just for rocks.

Dad was not far behind us. He drew thick lines between us and Florence the neighbor woman who seemed to enjoy rock picking and who did it twice as long as us, both daily and seasonally, her head tied up in a red kerchief like some cliché painting of pioneers. We cut off at noon because according to Dad it was unethical to pick rocks under the afternoon sun. She did not.

"That's all that Florence knows is picking rock," Dad would joke. "She's got rocks in her head!"

GRAMPA HANK'S story about God's providence went something like this: in 1946, after building his dairy herd and working his way up in the area, Henry Schaap bought a 200-acre farm, directly across the road and upstream from his own father's two quarters. In 1947, thanks to the providence of God and his own insight, Henry sowed all 200 acres in flax. He hit the market just right and paid for it in one year. This is Dad's phrase, "And he paid for it in one year," like "He won the lottery on the first ticket he ever bought."

The truth is that Henry Schaap bounced around a bit, trying to catch on somewhere. First, he rented a place by Lismore where Gramma Mary brought two girls, Agnes and Lida, and a boy, Howard, into the world, all by 1929. Then they rented a place near Leota. The Depression put Henry into a holding pattern, because when Gramma Mary got pregnant with Milton in 1936, clearly an oops, the family was renting yet another place a mile northwest from Grampa John's place.

The other kids, now ages eight, nine, and thirteen, never knew their mother was pregnant. Typical of the time, Gramma Mary kept her pregnancy hid behind roomy dresses, and then one day in late March 1937 the kids were mysteriously sent to the neighbors. Dad was delivered in a snowstorm, the doctor traveling out to the farmhouse in an emergency snow machine that's like something from a comic book, complete with riveted metal sides and tracks in place of wheels.

After his birth, Gramma Mary, either in postpartum depression or just ground down from a demanding life and a demanding husband, did not manage the crying Milton well. Nine-year-old Lida rocked him when he cried, morning and night. It got so bad, the baby Milt not growing at all, that they took him to a specialist in Sioux Falls, a "woman doctor," who looked at the scrawny baby and declared him to be "starving." She directed Mary to get Carnation milk for Milt, who guzzled it down and slept all the way home.

All along, Hank must have been steadily building his dairy herd, for when Dad opens his eyes on a farm closer to Leota, he opens them to a 5:00 a.m. milking and to Hank's badgering: "Stop *nou eens met gapen!*" which Dad translated as "Quit yawning your head off!" This is part of a chorus of mixed Dutch-English lines from Hank that include "Aren't you done yet?" and the ubiquitous "Hurry up *een beetje*"— hurry up a little bit. Hank's dairy herd included twenty-six cows by that time, including ones named Frances, Bertha, and Audrey.

At the end of World War II, things finally started to break right for Hank, the second-born son of John and Frederika Schaap. First, the nice 200 across the road from his dad. Then, the flax jackpot.

The 200 must have been pretty that year, the blue flowers winking as they waved in the big south winds. It's a movie scene, a long pan, someone running through the flowers, excitement building in the family all summer, the threat of storm looming but breaking at the last moment. When it came time to harvest, Henry Schaap, with the help of his sons Howard and Milton, and daughters Agnes and Lida, pulled in the equivalent of a million-dollar crop, and his legend was made. He was forty-eight and feeling fine, feeling blessed.

Thus far had God helped him.

Then, rocks.

In 1951, Hank's son Howard was drafted to fight in the Korean conflict. While Grampa's fortune may have been made, the situation inside the Schaap household crystallizes in one image for the thirteen-year-old Milt: Howard reduced to tears at the kitchen table, begging for a new suitcase with which to go to the army.

And this personal regret: Milt shook Howard's hand when he left instead of giving him a hug.

Private Howard Calvin Schaap would be killed by mortar fire on October 7, 1951, in his second stint on the front lines as litter bearer, near Mundung-Ni, as part of the battle for Heartbreak Ridge. Almost a year from when he cried at that table, Howard's body would come back home by train in a box. Henry and Mary would ask two family friends to open the casket to make sure that it was their Howard. Milt wishes he would have looked, despite the men's testimony that they could just barely tell it was Howard, that they had nightmares for weeks afterward.

What happened next is curious. Daughter Lida hatched a plan for Hank and Mary to come to Chicago where she lived, to get away from everything for a couple of weeks. Thirteen-year-old Milt was left behind to do chores with a neighbor boy who had been enlisted to help. When that boy snuck away to the Twin Cities to himself secretly enlist in the military, thirteen-year-old Milt did all the chores, as well as grieving for his brother, entirely alone.

One would think that losing a son would soften Hank's character, would focus his attention on the other children a little bit more, but the opposite happened. To Grampa Hank, Dad seemed made for work. Out of the body of his wife and out of her line—Bolluyts, with French and Irish strains—plus an added generation of robust garden-grown diets, he'd gotten a six-foot-tall boy thick through the chest and arms, a fullback who could get one tough yard, who could stack hay bales all day and then earn extra cash at the neighbors' at night. A boy not quick in school. A body to harness. So Grampa, a little man, harnessed him.

"Aren't you done yet?"

"Hurry up *een beetje!*"

And Dad leaned into the harness, trying to fill Howard's shoes, to earn the blessing. Dad was the primary milker on the place well before age thirteen. In high school he'd do chores for Henry and then do chores for Uncle Bill across the road and still catch the bus that stopped along the highway to pick him up for a basketball game. During the summers he worked out for other farmers, stacking ten thousand bales in one summer, over a hundred racks' worth. The hardware man in town—a cousin, Conley, Uncle Bill's youngest—tells me a story from this era.

"I rode over his legs once."

What?

"Well, Milt always had to stack the rack so doggone high, you know right up to the front. And I was driving. And, yeah, we hit a bump—I couldn't help it—and Milt fell off the front and before I could stop, I had ridden over his legs."

So, was he laid up? Were they broken?

"Nope. Uh-huh. Rode right over them and he was fine—oh, maybe he was a little sore the next day. He was always such a brute."

AS OUR ALLY in rock picking and not just our boss, Dad actually tried his best to enact, if not our visions to make the job easier, then his own. Most people just pulled a flatbed through the field and piled up the rocks on it. That's what Florence, the kerchief-wearing neighbor, did on the original Schaap place. But pulling a flatbed meant that when it was time to unload, in some obscure corner, side hill, or soil bank that would never be farmed, you had to throw all those rocks off *a second time*, to in essence pick them again.

Dad would be damned. So first he bought a little crab-like mechanism with a hydraulic front scoop to pick up the biggest rocks and also dump the load after you had filled it. When that wasn't to his liking—too small, too impractical—he made his own implement, cutting down the sides on an old-style hydraulic dump wagon to eighteen inches so you could pick all day and then go dump the whole load by pulling one lever. He also mounted three metal tractor seats to each side, so when you drove through a rockless section of the field, you could ride in style, swinging your legs above the growing corn, now splaying out like a threatening green tarantula.

Saving graces for Milt the brute on the Moulton Township farm included fishing and music. And a girl, Hattie Jean Schelhaas, a brown-eyed, angular-faced looker from a marginal farm in the Chandler Hills.

Hattie Jean, who went with the more modern-sounding Jean, was the fourth child and second daughter of Peter and Cornelia. As second daughter on a hilly farm, Jean learned the magic of the public library and snuck away whenever she had the chance to read. Despite slim finances, Peter and Cornelia sent Jean to high school in Edgerton, to the newly opened Southwest Minnesota Christian High School, where she flourished. Dad would always say about their marriage, "The valedictorian married the dunce."

What to do with half a brain on the prairie? After graduation, Jean went away to Calvin College, all the way around the lake to Grand Rapids, Michigan, to a six-week teacher training program. Pictures from the era include one of Jean with the other girls out front of their boarding house and one of Jean in the back seat of a car riding the dunes of Lake Michigan. She looks like she's having fun but is noncommittal, maybe not homesick but counting down the days to return to Milt and the places she really knows.

Back home, Jean hit her stride in the classroom, teaching fourth and fifth grade in local schools. Jean's combination of work ethic, intelligence, and doe-eyed compassion—and her mother's sharp tongue, which she wasn't above using when the boys tried to run over her—meant the classroom became Jean's kingdom. To this day, grown men will come up to her and tell her she was their favorite teacher.

Jean gave Milt a lifeline, a connection to the wider world of ideas, a well of grace on the rocky prairie. Early on he determined that she was not to work alongside him, not to become slave labor. She would have her domain and he would have his and they would join together at meals and at nights in their kingdom above Champepadan Creek.

They married on the Schelhaas family lawn on June 7, 1955, a windy day, and moved into a small green house without indoor plumbing on the Schaap place, Moulton Township. When Grampa Hank managed an uneasy retirement, Milt took over the farm and the couple moved into the house with toilets. From then on, Grampa Hank contemplated his youngest son's mismanagement of his farm from his swivel chair in his hip-roofed house in Leota.

Dad kept telling the flax story like it was about the special blessing of God upon Hank, while he was shackled by debt. He picked rock every spring. He milked ever more cows, twice a day, seven days a week. Church at Leota Ebenezer twice on Sunday, where he felt the heavy hand of God and of Grampa Hank, week in and week out, for the first forty-five years of his life.

Stone of help, indeed. More like The Rock.

But there's more to Grampa Hank's story. In 1946, because of a trade dispute between the U.S. and Argentina over linseed oil, the Department of Agriculture instituted a price support of $6.00 per bushel to increase production of flax for the years 1947-1948. In a community that felt so strongly about government that they funded their own schools, Henry Schaap made his fortune by taking advantage of government handouts. The deck was stacked in his favor.

I'M TRYING to find sympathy for Grampa Hank, after a lifetime of feeling otherwise. One way is to think of him as the product of ancestry. Cobbled together from Uncle Bill and my own perusal of the archives in Groningen, the Netherlands, and cast into biblical form, the story goes something like this:

Jan Jans Schaap, *schipper* of a ship on the island of Schiermonnikoog, the Netherlands, begat

Jan Jans Schaap, infantryman, of Groningen, the Netherlands, who begat

Jan Schaap, farmhand, of Leens, the Netherlands, who begat

Jan Schaap, farmhand, of Leens, the Netherlands, who became John Schaap of Leota, Minnesota, USA, who in 1900 begat the first truly American

John Schaap.

The next son born to the immigrant John Schaap, in the very next year, 1901, the second-born son in the second-best year, would be named Henry.

Almost forty years later, Hank would buy the farm across the road from his father and sit on it, like the good thing it is in a rocky world. It was that landscape that would shape Grampa Hank's character.

THERE WAS ONE major flaw in the 200. Behind the house to the east, Grampa's plow hit a rock. And not just any rock. When they tried to dig it out, to find the edges with spades and pry it up, they couldn't get around it. It was as if all the rocks that the Schaap boys and then Florence had picked across the road on the original Schaap homestead had melded into one rock on Hank's farm, one giant rock to test him. It could have been his Ebenezer, but no, Henry would have it out. He called a munitions expert, home from WWII, Hank Buys, who brought sixty-six sticks of dynamite that they plugged all around that rock. "They blew it half out," Dad remembered, "a rock as big as a room, a rock that you could drive an M Farmall into."

From there, with tractors and manpower including two sons, both Howard and Milt, they loaded the broken half up to haul it away. Dad had a large scar on his arm, transverse to his bicep, from some of the shards of this rock. I always imagined it as rock shrapnel, a spontaneous arrowhead splintering off during the explosion and glancing off Dad's arm, a miraculous near miss. The truth was a lot more mundane. Hauling a piece of it out of the field in some wagon or truck, the rock shifted, and a shard of it, sharp from the explosion, caught Dad's arm and sliced it open, a three-inch gash. Dad was twelve years old.

AT MAYO, ANOTHER nurse comes in to get Dad's vitals. He stirs enough for her to get a blood pressure cuff on him, then immediately his

head falls back on the pillow. He's heading toward sleep again or at least turning back into himself, into whatever interior landscape he's sojourning in. It's fine by me. I wish we could just let him sleep until he's better. But I know what we're headed for, for all kinds of rocks turning up in the upheaval of his mind. And we will subject ourselves, bend down to pick them up again. The sleeves of his hospital gown are pushed up to his shoulders like the cut-off shirts he wore to pick rock. There's the scar on his right arm.

It's a story he doesn't mind telling. Even in good times, Dad's stories about growing up, about Grampa and his brother Howard and characters from Leota Ebenezer, are always a mixed bag. They laugh at Grampa's foolishness; they paint him as immovable tyrant. They recall bullying; they recount hilarity. They cycle through, seasonally. Dad's stories taught us that there will necessarily be rocks in good soil; that's just the curse, that's just life. So you pick them up. You ask God to help you. You keep going.

And sometimes, when you've done the work of picking them up, you set one up, as an Ebenezer.

Thus far has God helped us.

Then Mom gives me the gift I don't really want.

"Milt—hey Milt. Open your eyes. Look who's here."

Dad lifts his head a little. His eyes open, begin their search. He's surfacing from deep water.

"Who is that?" she quizzes again.

"Howard," he says.

4

Acquiescence

DAD HAS DEVELOPED a new habit at St. Mary's. Even when he's awake, Dad squints his eyes shut and lips something invisible, like he's got his usual toothpick in his mouth, except he doesn't. When we ask him pointed questions, you can see him trying to surface but his answers are grunted yeses or nos that tail off into mumbles. Then his eyes go vacant again and he slips into drowsiness, worrying those lips. It's the expression of people tied into wheelchairs in nursing homes. We're told the doctors will do their rounds sometime in the late afternoon to evaluate him. We can't wait. We need hope, direction.

Ordinarily, when doctors ask Dad questions, his one goal is to mess with them, to see if there's a human in there or just a medical machine. At the intake in Worthington, after he threatened Mom and we were committing him to a seventy-two-hour involuntary hold, Dad tried his usual routine, even if he wasn't at his rebel best.

"Can you tell me your name, sir?"

"Yeah, I can tell you my name—Clem Kadiddlehopper."

Then, when nobody laughed at the same old joke, the one that had lost its snap when his favorite comedian, Red Skelton, went out of style eons ago, "No, my kids want me to—Milt Schaap."

"It says here 'Milton.'" First sign that our intervention wasn't as good of an idea as we thought: a humorless doctor. "Do they call you Milt?"

No wonder Dad messed with them.

Dad has never been self-aware about his moods, but with "experts" he relished using subterfuge.

"Can you tell me what day it is today, Milton?"

"Yeah, the day after yesterday."

"OK, but do you know the date?"

An almost snort, then an intake of breath.

"September 25, 2006."

"What seems to be the matter today, Milton?"

"Oh, I seem to have—" he no doubt wanted to go off-color—"a hole in my pecker, all it does is leak!" but stuck with something safer "—a rogue tooth."

"Dad...."

"Well, my kids want me here because...."

We helped him with the story, Mom helped him. Eventually we got to something like what had transpired, that he had threatened Mom's life with that clenched-jaw look that scared us all. "Well, I guess I'm a little—oh, I guess you would say tight."

"You're depressed."

"Yeah, I'm just down. And I'm tired. I can't fight it anymore."

It's a present-tense moment for me still. This doesn't happen. Dad is suddenly playing it straight and it feels like a breakthrough.

"When would you say was the first time you were depressed?"

"Oh, when I was ten years old, when I thought about killing myself behind the axle of the car."

"Why was that, Milton?"

"Well...."

Grampa figured heavily in what Mom prompts him to recount. A story about Leota comes to the surface, too, one I haven't heard before: "And at parent-teacher conferences in Leota school, when those teachers put my Fs up on the wall with everyone's As. And then Hank Schaap still took it out of my hide when we got home."

Leota, still and always.

We had just driven through Leota to get Dad to Worthington. When we got out of our cars, Heidi said, "Wow, driving through Leota—it gave me the shivers."

AT MAYO, Lisa sweeps into Dad's room. "Hey everybody," she says.

You don't miss Lisa. Not that she's big or extraordinarily tall at 5'9", just a presence. She's what they call a dishwater blonde, with eyes dark brown to the point of black. She has long legs, Mom's high hips, and she's strong, even powerful—a wonder woman.

Carmen gives Lisa the update and ends the spiel as she did with me: "Now, do you have questions?"

We look at Dad. He looks like a crazy man, like he's wearing his subconscious on the outside. He picked at his sheets and his hospital gown so much that we took them off so he's naked from the waist up. His torso is still bale-stacker thick, though the skin of his arms is starting to sag.

"Hi, Dad," Lisa says, but it's all he can do to glance up and open his eyes once before he closes them again, working those lips.

Lisa directs our attention elsewhere. "We're getting Mom a room at the hotel across the way, right?" she asks. Mom is out using the bathroom. "Let's just get her a room, split the cost once it's all over—make it easy on her. She needs to get her rest on a good bed and not try to sleep in here."

Lisa, not thinking about what she can't control but only what she can: Mom's relative comfort, her physical, bodily rest. Lisa, who is probably most like Dad in her love of bodily things, in taking his rebel stories to heart. And who gave Dad the best run for his money.

Of any of us, it's Lisa who has the most right to get shivers when thinking about Leota.

LISA SITS at the foot of the family table in my memory. She's in her late teens and her life is an adventure. She eats what she wants, goes where she wants, tells the stories she wants. Story is, on trips to McDonald's she'd eat two Big Macs and finish her friends' besides. She's strong, even preternaturally so. She set the girls' basketball scoring record at the high school. She broke a girl's nose with a volleyball spike. She's a state hurdler. Now, she's talking about hickeys, about the constellation of hickeys a girl she knows has. It's summer and she's wearing a loose T-shirt. "She had one here," she narrates, pointing just below the neckline, then, pulling out her shirt and moving her finger down her chest, "and here and here and here and here and here."

The stories just keep coming. About picking up the principal's daughter and saying they would take her to school, then riding around just to make the girl tardy. About the red and blue cop-car lights dancing through the cornfield as everyone fled a party. About a farmer who paid a girl to paint his farm buildings red, then paid her again for other things.

I learned plenty about the world from Lisa. With Carmen off in college, all three of us remaining kids slept upstairs. I slept in the cold north room. Since I was afraid of the dark I slept with the door open and the hall light on, which fell in a patch across the candy-striped carpet of the hall. Across that hall was Lisa's room—Lisa, who kept late hours, who was comfortable with her body.

Once I came downstairs to go to the bathroom in the middle of the night and peeked into the living room, lit only by the white light of the TV, and glimpsed Lisa and her boyfriend wrestling on the green shag carpet. That boyfriend came around a lot, even to Sunday dinner.

The meet-cute of Lisa and that boyfriend is its own story.

It is the time of muscle cars. Lisa is maybe sixteen and on her first date with some other guy, perhaps on the sly. That guy takes her out into the country in his car. He tells her to put out or he'll leave her there. So she opens the door and gets out. It's freezing and dark, November, in the middle of nowhere. She starts walking. A guy in a *Smokey and the Bandit* Trans Am, complete with full-hood eagle decal, except in dark blue, stops to pick her up. He's the son of a local dairy farmer, and though Lisa's not exactly a damsel in distress, there is no turning back. He will become her steady boyfriend, then, when she gets pregnant her senior year of high school, her husband.

The stories at the foot of the table include the trauma of the premature birth, of bleeding in that Trans Am all the way to the hospital, of catching the doctor at just the right time, of the child who was born weighing four pounds, four ounces.

Lisa is eighteen or nineteen as she sits at the foot of the table in my memory. Whatever the story, the perfect wonder that is her daughter sleeps in her car seat in the living room.

While Lisa turned many stories into adventures, they weren't all happy ones.

One time, when I had fallen asleep and Lisa came home late, I awoke to Dad's voice. Dad never came upstairs. He was talking in his low bass whisper and Lisa was replying in her warm alto. Then, there was a swish and a gasp and half a muskmelon rind and spoon bounced into the spot of carpet I could see from my room.

I heard Lisa gasp, sob.

"Yeah, I guess I wasn't hard enough on Lisa," I heard Mom say on more than one occasion. "I shoulda broke her spirit, I suppose."

THERE'S ONE story that never gets told, that I have to piece together: Lisa's trouble with Leota Ebenezer.

In 1982, the baby-belly of an unmarried teenager was still a flag of public offense in Leota. Church practice regarding teen pregnancy at that time went like this: the two sinners would go before the consistory, the elected board of men that led the church, and admit that they had sinned. Then, on Sunday morning, they would do the same thing before the congregation. In Lisa's case, it would have only been her confessing, since Lisa's boyfriend didn't go to our church.

Talk about your Hester Prynne experience.

Dad knew a shit show when he smelled one, so he and Lisa hatched a plan. Since Lisa would be moving over to the church of her husband-to-be, a tiny church on the peak of the Buffalo Ridge where she would presumably live out the rest of her days, a church that had stopped being quite so uptight about church discipline, Lisa would just profess her faith and marry there, skipping the whole step of public humiliation. Dad broached the idea to someone in the consistory, and an agreement was struck. If Lisa confessed before the consistory, the move would be approved.

So there they are—this is how I imagine it anyway, since no one will actually recount the story—a dozen men around a long table, the minister and consistory president at the far end. The minister reads a Bible passage, opens with prayer. They ask Lisa what she has to say and she makes her confession—knowing Lisa, not breaking down, not giving them that. Then they make Dad make the request to transfer

Lisa's membership, and he does, and clenches his jaw afterwards. They come to an uneasy agreement. Someone closes with a prayer.

Our house was upset that night, meaning Heidi and I got sent upstairs so Mom and Dad could talk. We tried to listen through the register in the floor but didn't hear anything. After lights out, we could hear urgent whispers coming from their bedroom. Then silence. I'm sure Dad didn't sleep, replaying the scene and lines that were said and by whom over and over, mouthing words to himself in the dark.

In the bulletin on Sunday, Dad read this announcement: "The Consistory acquiesces to Lisa Schaap's request to transfer her membership to the American Reformed Church of Woodstock."

It was the Latin that did it.

After forty-five years, the fact that they reached for the Latin really pissed him off. "Acquiesce." In a country of dirt and rocks and cricks, on farms of corn and hay and milk and cow tits, they were going to pull out "acquiesce"?

He couldn't stop saying it.

"Acquiesces. Acquiesce, acquiesces. The consistory acquiesces. . . ."

To Dad, it was the same judgment he'd stood under all his life.

It was Leota.

DAD'S EARLIEST stories of Leota rend the historical fabric a little.

Like this: young Milt rides a horse to school. It's the early 1940s, and Grampa Hank sets him on in the morning and a mile down the road, the horse bucks him off and runs back home. Dad picks up his lunch and follows, in tears, but Grampa Hank sets him firmly on again, tells him not to let the horse get the better of him.

When Milt finally gets to school, late again, he gets off smelling like horse and the kids tease him.

At recess, the big boys rip the buttons off his pants so they won't stay up by themselves but keep slipping down for those boys to point out Dad's underwear to the girls, including Mom. It took years for me to understand that these were button fly pants. As in, someone took the time to rip multiple buttons off his jeans, a targeted attack on the crotch. On a kid in first or second grade.

When he gets home, Gramma asks, "What happened to your buttons again, Milt?" She's tired of cooking for Henry and gathering eggs and sewing on buttons and Grampa hears her and takes it out of Milt's hide.

When Milt starts to grow into a tall, athletic frame, the problems get bigger. Once, coming in from recess, for reasons forgotten to mankind, one kid jumps him from behind and puts him in headlock while a little kid, a Vander Meer from a powerful local family, kicks him in the balls until he falls to the ground. When he looks up from his knees, he sees the teacher watching out the window.

This boy, whose Fs are also tacked up in the classroom at parent-teacher conferences, contemplates how he might kill himself with the family car at ten years old. At thirteen, Howard dies in Korea. At fourteen, Milt graduates eighth grade from Leota Christian and escapes to Chandler public high school. First day hazing for freshmen is to wear their clothes backwards, but Milt loves the high school atmosphere, the hijinks, the friendships. It's four years of some freedom from Leota.

Fast-forward two more years, and Milt and Hattie Jean settle down on the Schaap farm in Moulton Township and orient their lives around Leota as their social hub.

Even before the acquiescence, Carmen and Lisa remember Dad as a fringe player in Leota, ruminating on sermons, finding excuses in the dairy—not hard to do—to stay away from church after a sermon bothered him in some way. Dad turned down consistory and school board service, citing his own inadequacy to sit on any formal board with the proud men of Leota, instead cobbling together his own common-man theology, "Christ and him crucified" and "my sins are always before me"—the language of the penitent David.

When a new minister came to town, Dad avoided him for months. This one, Reverend Henry Entingh, took notice and sought out Dad on his own turf, in his milking parlor, and asked Dad why he was avoiding him. "Well, I drink a little bit and I swear a little bit," Dad reports himself saying, "so I think I'm the kind of guy who should just stay away."

"There's nothing wrong with a beer a day," came the reply. "And call me Henry, not Reverend."

The Reverend Entingh earned his title that day and often came to get milk from Milt's parlor, where they had a Hamm's beer together as they discussed life and politics and theology.

But it was not to last. Leota, Dad says, drove out Henry Entingh, drives out all its ministers. To this day, Dad blames Corny Jelgerhuis for picking at everything Reverend Entingh did until he left.

After the Reverend Entingh's departure, just at the dawn of my memory, Dad started making Leota the butt of his jokes: "You better not lie," he'd tease us kids, "because you know where liars go, don't you?" Beat. "Leota." Or frontal assault: "Leota—that's a cult!"

LEOTA EBENEZER was not unique among Protestant denominations in its attempts to deal with sin. The forefathers of the men and one woman in that tableau, many of whose ancestors came from the tiny Dutch towns of Leens and Ulrum, had staked everything on the freedom to make decisions about all manner of sins among their congregation, from card playing to adultery.

While I had confirmed the family line in the Groningen archives, Uncle Bill—Grampa's youngest brother and a noted bullshitter—filled in the details. The story gets interesting with my third great-grandfather, Jan Jans Schaap, the son of a *schipper* who enlisted in the infantry, got in a bar fight, and put a guy in the infirmary. For that, Jan Jans got thrown in jail and the book thrown at him—assault and murder if the guy dies, or just plain assault if he lives. Either way this was a bad deal for Jan Jans because it was the 1830s.

But there was light in the darkness: a girl named Grietje, who worked in the jail serving Jan Jans "victuals." This is the term, victuals. Grietje was evangelical about her faith and dirt poor and through her testimony or something, Jan Jans converted. After he spent some time in prison and his crime was indeed declared self-defense, Jan Jans married Grietje, and they went back to her hometown of Leens and joined her people—the landless, rural poor.

But when Jan Jans Schaap and Grietje Adolfs Siekmann were married in Groningen, the Netherlands, on August 3, 1834, their timing couldn't have been worse (or better, depending on your theology). Within two months of their marriage, the minister Hendrik de

Cock has led his Ulrum church to secede from the Dutch Reformed Church and formed a new sect. So in a very short time Jan Jans went from the son of a *schipper* to a son of a bitch—a shipless, landless felon, a religious dissenter and enemy of the state.

It's a real resistance to empire story. But it's not at all progressive.

For the people in Ulrum and Leens, the problems started with the Church-State-University alliance. As this unholy trinity strived for progress in the modern world, the university at Groningen pumped out ministers preaching good citizenship: that we are all basically good people who, if we think logically and pay our taxes and obey state institutions, can go to heaven when we die. Or not—does it really matter as long as the machines of modernity hum along toward progress? Which is always a cover for someone getting rich, and it's not the landless poor around Ulrum and Leens.

Hendrick de Cock was one of these ministers, assigned to the church at Ulrum. One day, one of his parishioners called bullshit, gave de Cock a copy of the Canons of Dordt, often summarized as the five points of Calvinism in the acronym TULIP: Total depravity, Unconditional election, Limited atonement, Irresistible grace, and the Perseverance of the saints. Some would call it a dark document, especially for the way it outlines sin: without grace, humans would all be pretty much Görings and Hitlers right from birth. This reality makes salvation unachievable, nothing you can strive for: there's nothing we can do, no calisthenics or good works, to pull ourselves up by our bootstraps. Only by God's grace and choice is anyone saved.

Few would call it revolutionary or democratic today, but that's what it was for poor churchgoers around Ulrum and Leens: wealth and status be damned, they could understand God's saving hand reaching down into the dark waters of sin and misery to pull them up—pull up all people equally—kicking and screaming.

Though not really all people. Only the chosen, the elect. Why not everyone? Because God is sovereign. Which is just another way of saying that God is mysterious but in a way that no one likes—because no one likes woe and no one likes a know-it-all, especially if they act like they're the only ones on solid ground but y'all are going to hell, and especially if they're poor and uneducated. And of course that *is* looking down the wrong end of the sovereignty-scope, and not counting grace as the mystery it is.

Because of the Canons of Dort and Calvin's *Institutes* and, of course, the mysterious working of the Holy Spirit, sin and misery made their way back into de Cock's sermons. Word spread. Surrounding parishioners started bringing de Cock their babies to be baptized. Other ministers felt threatened by de Cock and blew the whistle. Eventually churches in Ulrum and nearby Leens seceded from the Dutch Reformed Church, and called themselves the *Christelijke Gereformeerde Kerk*, what would in America would become the Christian Reformed Church.

In this poor-farmers-on-Tatooine-resist-the-empire tale, Jan Jans and Grietje planted themselves among the rebels of Ulrum and Leens, a poor, primarily landless class of *boerenknechts* (farmhands) and *dienstmeids* (maids). That's what their son Jan and his wife Anna also were, my great-great grandparents. Of course, the state couldn't bring itself to shrug its shoulders and say, "Meh" to these poor Tatooine farmhands. The empire sent stormtroopers, who forced their way into homes and enforced martial law. They prevented assembly and leveled fines, and then, naturally, when the people couldn't pay, confiscated the property they did have and sent them to jail.

But Jan and Anna dug in their heels, scraped by. When Jan died at 36, leaving Anna the maid with several children including another Jan, the family hit rock bottom. They subsisted off Anna's fish-mongering until son Jan, at age 25 but still with no prospects, left for the promise of the New World where the government would leave you alone.

In America, in a town called Leota, Jan became John and had a hand in founding a church and then a Christian school where the new Dutch-American settlement would educate their own children beyond the reach of the state and bet on tighter ethnic and religious ties in order to weather the weather and the economic winds of America. That's the Leota wager.

Bringing us to Grampa Hank and his swivel chair meditations.

Bringing us to his granddaughter and that Leota tableau. The right to make the call about sin was deep-rooted in the men of that consistory room, down in their very stubborn, sober Dutch DNA. Their power had dwindled to rendering judgments about teenage sex, but they wouldn't give it up. "He's so stubborn they'll have to push him over when he's dead," Dad said about one of my Friese uncles, the tribe reputed to be the stubbornest of Dutchmen. Quite true. He died of a heart attack at his desk, sitting up.

Dad was just as stubborn, with maybe one difference: the leaven of his sense of humor.

Leota brought out the jester in Dad best of all.

In the days before Dad sold the cows, we had a telephone in the milk house. Dad was freer with his language there in the barn, more willing to improvise, to go off color. That was true throughout the Leota countryside. Solemn and formal language in churches gave way to a sharp earthiness and a coarse creativity in barnyards and backrooms.

The jester was on full display in the barn telephone conversations. "St. Kilian Cemetery, one plot left," Dad answered once. When the person hung up, then dialed right back, Dad repeated the line and heard one of the neighbor kids say in the background, "I keep gettin' the cemetery."

I didn't realize at the time that lines like, "Undertaker, you stab 'em, we'll slab 'em and send 'em to Hell-o!" weren't originals, that Dad had gleaned them from *Reader's Digest* and Red Skelton, who was behind a number of Dad's voices and gags. That's where his typical introduction, "Clem Kadiddlehopper," came from. It took me years to figure out that name's origin, but Dad kept using it right into the 1980s when Red Skelton was long forgotten. As a teen, I was embarrassed by it.

But back then, the only thing that mattered was that he would use these one-liners on real people. It made us die with laughter.

The best one got used on a preacher—"Schaap's mule barn, which ass do you want to talk to first?"—the very preacher who would preside over the acquiescence.

But after the acquiescence, we were done with Leota. We left Leota Ebenezer, which meant both church and school, which meant we didn't sponsor a float to go through the Fourth of July parade, which meant we didn't get together with our neighbors to build it. I know Dad has not talked to some of the men in that council room since the acquiescence, some of them at one time counted as friends.

No one from Leota was really welcome on our yard anymore after that; Dad would go it alone.

But it doesn't make sense. Dad had plenty of friends from Leota, often from the fringes. He was more of a man for the Leota café, a long, narrow, wild-west boom-town type building. In its plastic booths in midwinter, Dad played Rook, the faceless card game that was the Protestant answer to a regular deck and the dubious morals of those two-faced queens in threesomes with jacks and kings. He played with Marv Acterhof who never failed to start the bid high, at 125 or above, the Leota equivalent of a steely-eyed gambler. Other friends included Don DeBoer and Johnny Hofkamp, the car dealer and the junk dealer, Dad's hunting and fishing buddies. There were shirttail Schaap relatives who would always stop me to ask, "How's your dad doing? You know one time at a family reunion, I'll never forget. . . ." There were kids long grown into men whom Dad babysat or drove to Leota School in the "school car," who remembered him turning off that car at the top of the hill just east of Leota and coasting all the way in, to stop dead perfectly in front of school.

The darkness that the acquiescence brought out of Dad was profound. I had a dream during those days that Dad wasn't allowed into heaven because he couldn't forgive. I woke in tears.

"This place makes me sick," Dad always said, and chief in that equation were the people of Leota whom he assumed were gossiping about him, his family, and his farm. But as often as not, these people were his lifelong friends. Famously, desperate animals who are trapped will chew off a leg to get out, but Dad cut himself off from friend and foe alike. In isolating himself from Leota, it was as if Dad had chewed off both his legs.

Just as the storm of the 1980s bore down on him, bore down on us all.

OF COURSE, making Dad the center of this story, or making the Ebenezer consistory the center, or the Leota wager, ignores Lisa, seventeen, the focus of all these men's gazes. Including mine as I write this. The least I can do is imagine the defiance in her eyes throughout the meeting, remember how much she loves her dad beside her, despite his own missteps, how much she loves life, her indomitable self.

Another of Dad's jokes about Dutchmen is that you only have to be mad at one of them: the one who plugged the hole in the dike. I never liked that line, or the story. No systems are so airtight that water or people won't slip through.

The truth is, the Leota wager can't work because of this very scene, because of people who slip through the cracks.

WHEN THE intake finally happens at St. Mary's, the contrast with Worthington is stark. Dad is fully awake but searching not just for the right answers but for any answers, like a cartoon character feeling around blindly for his glasses.

"What's your name, sir? Can you tell me your name?"

"Oh . . . I'm. . . ." He's searching for one of his stock jokes, not finding. I'd give anything for a little of that old spirit, even the bitterness. It's all the rest of us can do not to fill in for him, until Lisa does.

"He's Clem Kadiddlehopper. That's the name you always gave, right, Dad?" she says, stroking his forearm. "But now can you tell him your name?"

"Milt," Mom says.

"Milton Schaap?"

"Thass right."

"What day is it, Milton?"

"What day is it? Oh . . . it's . . . ."

"What month is it, Milt," Mom can't help but interject, "can you tell him that?"

"I...don't...know."

"Who is the president?"

We wait. He looks around vacantly.

Mom again. "Who's that president—you don't like him very much. It's not Hilary but . . . who?"

We wait.

"Remember? Barack Osama?" Mom prompts, digging into Dad's DNA for that old anti-progressive government sentiment and beyond, to something darker. "Do you like Barack Obama?"

The interview is over.

"That's OK, Dad," Lisa says. "We love you."

Dad is drifting from us. I'd give anything now to see the devil come into Dad's eyes, to anticipate the smart-ass answer he will reach for.

I'd give anything now for Clem Kadiddlehopper.

5

The Interdict

WE SIBLINGS AND MOM make camp in the hotel across the road while we wait for more clarity on Dad. We're all there next morning when a sudden urgency brings him momentarily back to life. He starts to get antsy with his hands, tries to shift himself.

"What wrong, Dad?" Carmen asks. Then guesses, "Do you have to go to the bathroom?"

"Yes!" he grunts.

We fumble for the call button since the nurses are tracking his urine output and he's a fall risk, and when a nurse arrives she's maybe 110 pounds, and it's clear with the way Dad's acting that if she leaves to get a second nurse, it will be too late. She leaves. We fetch the little urine bottle and try to get ready what we can.

"Le's go!" he slurs. Carmen and I consider helping him ourselves. We weigh the awkwardness of it.

When the nurse comes back because she's been unable to find anybody, we help her shift and lift him carefully without balance or strength and get him aimed in the right place and God am I glad he's not quite in his right mind as we hold him to pee.

Back in bed, he's winded for a moment, then comes around and slurs, "Howard, hel' me get out of here."

"To do what?" It's the UTI talking. Any personality flareup is a welcome sign of life though I fear having to stop him from whatever mad thing he conceives of.

"Well, I gotta get the Bobcat and clean out the—"

Oh, I can play this game.

"Already done," I say, joining the fantasy. "Did it myself."

A Bobcat or skid steer was essential equipment on a small dairy farm like ours, and Dad was an artist on the Bobcat. His canvases were the various floors of barns and sheds and yards and his paint dirt or gravel or shit. Smaller than a small car, in the Bobcat you buckled into a tight cockpit, the arms that lifted the hydraulic bucket running along either side of you. Push or pull the steering levers at easy arm's reach to go forward or back. Pull one back and push one forward to execute tight, on-point spins. At your feet are the bucket controls to lift and tip the bucket. Crank up the throttle and then just go, fly.

Dad had taken the protective cab off our Bobcat and set it somewhere in the grove, which made it even more of a death trap. Bobcats are notorious for tipping and for appendages and bodies getting caught in the hydraulics of the bucket, which were strong enough to lift the front wheels off the ground or to lift round bales high in the air. But it was a necessary or at least calculated risk. Without the cab, he could basically go full blast around any of the tight corners in the hog house, the freestall barn, or the barn itself. In the Bobcat Dad could scrape the holding area perfectly clean; he could dig up a bucket of dirt, dump it, and scrape it to the exact angle he wanted in a moment. It was like those movies where people in a cockpit fight with robots much bigger than themselves.

With the Bobcat working at the warp speed of his improvisational mind, Dad was shaping the kind of farm he wanted. Compared to Grampa Hanks's bury-your-one-talent-and-sit-on-it vision of the 200, Dad wanted a cup brimful, spilling over, a little economy. Dad's priority was to hire local young men, relatives from the city, foreign exchange students.

There were Aunt Lida's boys from Chicago, Doug and Gary, who came to work in the summers and learned to milk cows, drive tractor, stack bales, shoot a .22, take shit, and give it back.

There was Keith, earnest and in a hurry, legendary for leaving gates open so that we'd wake with cows bellowing outside our bedroom windows in the middle of the night. And Kevin, the milk-tester's son, who got perms—'nuff said.

Then, foreign exchange students. Englishman John Thwaite, whose Midlands accent was so thick we just had to keep repeating, "What? What? What?" Frenchman Jean Luc Boucher, who came to us wounded and homesick after having taken a bale hook to the ear at his first farm, which had used him as free labor. When he arrived, Dad gave him space to settle in, then took us all fishing Saturday afternoon. Irishman Paul O'Dwyer, whose curls and ruddy face charmed the Leota girls and almost stole him away from his girlfriend Trina, even when she came all the way from Ireland to visit, till Dad cornered him in the parlor and told him to shape up. And finally Dutchman Avert Vandersluis, who came to us as Dad was losing the farm and losing patience, summarized in one exchange:

Avert: I bet you're glad I'm here.

Dad: . . .

Avert: What would you do if I broke my arm?

Dad (deadpan): I'd break the other one.

Central to operations on a farm fast becoming too small to support our family, let alone these other characters, was the little, maneuverable Bobcat that made the work on the farm—and escapes on Saturday afternoons to Lake Shetek—possible.

The best Bobcat story: we had this bull who was a son-of-a-bitch with the nickname King Solomon. Dad got trapped alone with him in a yard once and had to jump through barbed wire to escape, injuring his knee. When it came time to sell King Solomon, he wasn't going to leave his wives and his concubines. Enter Jeroboam. Dad took the muffler off the Bobcat and it went from a high-RPM machine to a demon of hell and chased King Solomon right on the truck and into family lore.

After Avert, we got no more exchange students, no more hired men. And because the Bobcat was so dangerous, Dad wouldn't let me near it.

When you're a bored little kid on the prairie, marooned in space and cut off from your neighbors because your dad is pissed at them, pissed at everybody, without even hired men to follow around or to tease you, with no prospects of running the Bobcat, you find other stuff to do. You play in the grove. You shoot your BB gun at blackbirds, at squirrels, at your dog. And, inevitably, you wander down to the creek. It's there you find that you don't need other people.

IN *On the Banks of Plum Creek*, Laura makes friends with Plum Creek, meaning she gets to know its personality: its laughing waterfall where Pa plants a "fish-trap," its angry flood, its gravelly clear parts, its silted horrors. Then she enlists it as an ally, against the snooty Nellie Oleson.

What happens is this. When Laura gets invited to a "Town Party" at Nellie's, she is stunned by the Oleson's house, that they have carpets and wooden tables, beds and dressers. Then Nellie brings out her new doll that even barfs out "Mama" when Nellie punches it in the gut. Great kid, that Nellie. As Laura reaches out to touch the doll's dress, Nellie snatches it away, says, "You keep your hands off my doll, Laura Ingalls." Mortified, Laura spends the rest of the party looking through a magazine that Mrs. Oleson gives her. But not forgetting.

Later, in one of the best revenge scenes ever, Laura holds her own "Country Party," and uses her friend Plum Creek to get back at Nellie. Wading in the clear gravel, Laura first lures Nellie to where she knows a crayfish will be lurking, which scares Nellie into the mud, from which she emerges with "bloodsuckers sticking to her feet and legs." It's pretty horrific. And also perfect.

I didn't read the Laura Ingalls Wilder books when I was a kid because I thought they were about girls. So instead I just lived the pages of *On the Banks of the Plum Creek* without ever knowing it. The bloodsuckers in the mud? That mean crayfish? That was my childhood.

On hot days, Heidi and I followed the gravel road that ran past our house down the hill to the bridge that crossed a little "crick" we didn't know the name of to wade in its waters. Inch-perfect to *On the Banks of Plum Creek*, there were gravelly parts that cut clear and fast, and stagnant, silted parts where we got leeches—Heidi actually called them bloodsuckers—between our toes.

Later, I would wander the crick alone, tracing it back from the bridge toward its source. I was young enough to make a mental trail of breadcrumbs in order to find my way back: the marshy area in the old pasture with "camel humps" surrounded by sucking mud, then a bend to faster water and another bend back into a long straightaway, near the end of which a strong current entered through a tile outlet and sparkled over a gravel bed where something flashed silver in the sunlight.

Minnows!

I hurried back to tell Dad who at first just pursed his lips and nodded but then said we should get a minnow trap.

"A minnow trap?"

"Yeah, then whenever we want to go fishing, we can just pull minnows out of the crick and go."

A week later, Dad came home with a cylindrical metal cage with inverted conical ends leading to small holes. Minnows would swim down one of the funneled ends into the middle part of the trap, Dad said, then not be able to find their way back out. We drove out and dropped it in the crick just at the tile outlet.

After that, I walked the crick at least twice a week to check on the trap just to see its wildly flapping treasures. Opening its middle hinge, I found ancient sticklebacks with spiked dorsal fins, small bullheads, and crayfish with—as Laura said—beady, glaring eyes and fearsome claws that seemed to be raiding my hoard. I mashed them to a green paste on the bank.

And once, in the deep pool beyond the minnow trap where a couple of gnarled ash trees were trying to get started, I surprised a brown animal that dove when it saw me, swimming the length of the pool before disappearing in a hole in the bank—beaver!—a creature I could almost imagine to be sentient, like Mr. Beaver, of *The Chronicles of Narnia*.

The crick was revealing itself to me, was taking on personality. It made me think for the first time about where we lived. If you owned a section of perfectly flat land that you planted in straight row crops, who the hell cared? No, the crick with its twists and turns, its unfarmable soil banks and mud holes and rocky knolls, gave the place life, personality. The crick—Champepadan Creek, a name I wouldn't hear for thirty years—was the heart of our farm. Like Plum Creek for Laura, it also became solace, friend.

JUST AS I was discovering the crick, economics intervened.

In 1983, seemingly out of nowhere and before the real farm crisis hit us in southwest Minnesota, Dad sold his dairy cows. Like a good Calvinist, the part of the story that Dad most likes to recount is the inscrutable "act of God" part. Dad's dairy herd, on an exemplary dairy farm for the time, got infectious bovine rhinotracheitis, common name "Red Nose," but the Slayton vets didn't catch it. In a matter of three years, Dad had X amount of stillborn calves, Y amount of milk cow deaths, "and a $24,000 vet bill." That's the chorus in the musical version that rings in my head, "and a $24,000 vet bill!"

But it turns out Dad's experience was pretty typical. The wider economic story starts with Earl Butz, secretary of agriculture during the expansive seventies. Butz was the demagogue who told farmers, "Plant fencerow to fencerow" and "Get big or get out." It was just the latest chapter of American agriculture in the twentieth century, of conquering the West, from draining the swamps to straightening the rivers to condensing and confining the livestock, to farming every square inch of the American continent, and Butz was its mouthpiece. In the eighties, Ronald Reagan took up the call, declared that he could not "protect farmers, either from themselves or from inevitable changes in technology and the marketplace." It was time to shake out the "bad operators"—the administration's actual term—in favor of the efficient ones, the big ones, who were to bless all the others by driving them to ag service or blue collar jobs in the city.

They used science to do it, of a sort. Dad had always been a friend to both technology and science. An early adopter of a state-of-the-art Surge milk machine, Dad welcomed the milk tester and prided himself on having a clean parlor and milk with low bacteria counts.

But they went over the head of the milk tester, Kevin's dad, and went beyond science. New regulations said that if a parlor was deemed too old, bacteria count be damned, they downgraded you to Grade B milk. Because Dad milked in a 100-year-old barn, some bureaucrat declared that Dad produced Grade B milk, which meant a lower price and a depleted cash flow. He would be forced to build a new parlor. But because the banks were reining in inflation, no one would lend Dad the money.

So, in what may have been a manic decision, Milt Schaap, former Young Farmer of the Year for the state of Minnesota, auctioned off his dairy herd. It was the first domino and typical of the widespread foreclosures of "the Farm Crisis." One thing went wrong and the rest of the dominoes toppled. Undiagnosed Red Nose meant Dad missed the window for building a new parlor meant he was kicked off Grade A milk which cut into his cashflow and caused him to sell his dairy herd in March 1983. Had he held out for two years, he could have been part of the "dairy buyout" built into the 1985 Farm Bill and he'd have come out, in his favorite cliché, "smelling like a rose."

HEIDI'S SKEPTICISM rings in my ears, that I've once again swallowed Dad's story hook, line, and sinker.

But already a century earlier, Charles Ingalls had established precedent and pattern.

For Charles, the first domino at Plum Creek was also an act of God, a locust plague of straight-up biblical proportions. In the climax of *On the Banks of the Plum Creek* locusts descend in layers upon layers on the Ingalls's wheat and everything else, blacking out the windows and crawling up each other's backs and flying in Laura's hair and crunching underfoot. For two straight years they completely devour the Ingalls's wheat crop. Even in the book, it's clear the family faces stark poverty, so Pa sets out east in a pair of broken-down boots to try to find work elsewhere during harvest.

What grabs my attention is the rhetoric as laid out by Caroline Fraser in *Prairie Fires*. While Charles Ingalls got some aid from the county in the form of flour so his family didn't starve over the winter, the state's response is familiar. After the grasshopper horror, Governor Pillsbury is on record as saying, "Poverty and deprivation are incidents of frontier life at its best." It's an almost kind statement compared to that of the *St. Paul Pioneer Press*: "If anybody chooses to lie down and be eaten up by grasshoppers, we don't care much if he is devoured body, boots, and breeches."

IT WAS A GRAY day when we sold the cows, but the presence of so many men and a few women in the old freestall barn made it cozy. Assorted metal gates and panels had been made into a makeshift ring thirty yards across, wood chips strewn in the middle. Men in feed caps and cowboy hats stood behind these barriers. I stood in our feed bunk, where my boots kicked the leftover dry silage, like corn cereal for cows. A few feet to my right, the auctioneer with a handheld mic and cowboy hat introduced the sale, then began his cadence as the first cow entered the ring.

They sold the tech separately: the Surge milk machines, the frozen bull semen for artificial insemination, and a computerized self-feeder that doled out feed according to each cow's needs.

The rest of the day was spent parading the cows through the ring one by one, guided by the voice of the auctioneer. It all went smoothly, as you would expect from an operator like Milt Schaap.

At some point I heard the Bobcat start up, in the back of the holding area, adjacent to the shed where we stood. A last, young, spiritless bull appeared in the ring with Dad behind it in the Bobcat, which he pivoted on point and parked, conjuring one last time the glory days of King Solomon.

After all the cows were sold and everyone was gone, Dad felt the silence. We all did.

WITHOUT COWS in the pasture digging it up with their heavy hooves, the creek came to life. I hunted crayfish the whole length of the crick with a long stick and the dip net, killing them and taking their claws as souvenirs.

The iron schedule of Dad's days also opened up. He did the work to transition us to hogs, but once the system was somewhat up and running, Dad looked around and found he had extra time. For the first time his work week went below sixty hours. With the ball and chain of milking suddenly gone, we could now go fishing more easily.

So one late April afternoon, Dad asked, "Ready to go fishing after supper?"

I couldn't believe it. We never went fishing midweek.

"To Shetek?"

"Hadley."

"But where will we get bait?"

"You know the minnow trap?"

The air was cool and moist, the ditches green, the fields starting to turn black as farmers began spring tilling. We took the Chevette, about the smallest car made at the time, and Dad had to wedge himself in.

As we pulled off the yard, our neighbor Mert, Florence's son, went by in a tractor. "Wonder what Mert's doing?" he thought aloud. "Too wet to do anything, ain't it? Oh well. . . ."

As we reached highway 91, Dad said, "I guess we're leaving late, seven o'clock, but that's six o'clock sun time. It's not dark till eight. That's only two hours, but that's worth it, right, Pal?"

Of course it was worth it. That extra hour of sunlight was a trick on time itself, like Moses getting the sun to stand still. At the lake, you had to feel like time was a wide plain that would take so long to cross that you didn't need to think about what would happen on the other side.

But I knew what was happening. Because time was short, we went to Hadley. Because fishing midweek was suspect, we went incognito, in the Chevette.

All the handful of places Dad took me fishing were magical, and Hadley was no different. We drove around to the north side of the lake, around the backside of a mysterious old building, a creamery, Dad said, where they used to make butter, now standing empty.

It was a large brick building partly covered with ivy, still quite beautiful, stalwart, like it meant to stay. With its many tall, narrow windows, it seemed like a place where you let in the sunshine while you did meaningful work, or like a stately home, where you lived with the butter. It was a building that interacted with the world around it, in the ivy, in a carport for delivery in the rain. It certainly came out of a different vision of what it meant to be Midwestern and a farmer—to transform what happened to commodities on our terms. Even abandoned, it made the tin and concrete hog confinements seem like tents to what this creamery was: a temple. The town baseball team in Hadley is still nicknamed the Buttermakers.

We parked in a gravel patch on the far side of the creamery where we could access the lake through the grass and reeds that fringed it.

"I'm not sure if this is private property or not," Dad said. "We'll hope it's not. They can always tell us to move."

I took the spot next to a small tree on a point, the prime spot, and casted.

When you first cast out your dobber, you always think it will go down immediately, that you'll whip the fish out one after another in a cartoon frenzy. Then, thirty seconds in when you don't have a bite, reality sets in.

But the dobber went straight down on this night, and it was like the finger of God. Before Dad even had his line out, I set into something with the Zebco 33. Dad was hoping to catch a mess of crappies, the panfish that spawned along the fieldstone that fringed so many area lakes, but this was a walleye, a couple of pounds, worth five crappies in size and a hundred in prize-worthiness.

"Doggone, wouldn't you know it?" Dad thought aloud. "That is a beautiful walleye! Why don't we catch them like this during the season?"

"Can't we keep it?" I asked.

He shook his head. "It's not the season yet. Gah!"

He lifted the fish, held it up for a moment to feel its weight, looked around, then pried the hook from its beautiful mouth and dropped it carefully back into the water.

When you catch a fish in a certain spot, it becomes a target. I was full of adrenaline and missed the spot on the next cast, let it sit for ten seconds, then recast. Then recast again.

When I was finally satisfied I was on the spot, my dobber indeed went down again, a down periscope bite. This time it was a crappie.

"Way to go, Pal," said Dad. "They're biting. Wouldn't it be nice to go home with a slew of these! That's what I was hoping—"

When I casted again, it was off, but I left it and within ten seconds, down it went—straight down. I set into it and felt the weight at the end. I cranked and cranked, the drag sang. Near shore, Dad saw it flash before it ran—"Another walleye—a huge one! Now take your time." When it came up to shore, turning on its side with fatigue, Dad stepped with his Chuck Taylors into the water and lifted it out with two hands. It was a beautiful fish, long and thick across the back, the bars down its sides dark in color from the cold water of spring. These were our first walleyes since that day on Lake Shetek.

Except it wasn't the season.

"Damn the luck!" he said. "Would you believe it!? I'm going to—"

He took off the light jacket he was wearing.

"Ordinarily, I wouldn't do this," he explained, "but—Gah!—we catch walleyes like this so rarely. If I just throw this one in the car.... One fish ain't going to hurt anything, is it? Anybody looking?"

He wrapped the fish casually in his coat and carried it over to the Chevette, like a shoplifter, hoping the Great Cashier in the Sky, tending to another customer, might not notice this one time. He opened the back door of the Chevette and tossed it in, then bent over to secure the coat around the fish.

We went back to fishing, but whether we were so jittery we actually missed our spots, or whether the window on the bite had really closed, or whether the Cashier had of course noticed and hit the buzzer to kill the bite once and forever, the lake went dead.

"Stupid!" Dad said under his breath. "Suppose I shouldn't have done that."

After that, he couldn't really concentrate anymore, couldn't stop from muttering.

"If you catch any more, we won't keep them, OK, Pal? We'll throw them back."

Twilight deepened.

"We shouldn't have kept that one. I suppose I did the wrong thing. Again."

This is also what the world post-dairy cows brought: a different kind of down time. With time for introspection came time for second-guessing, which brought regret. And with regret came doubt, came listlessness, came despair.

Down time. Time to be down.

We caught no more fish that night, had no more bites. Something had changed. Someone *had* been watching, and he was going to make us pay.

Usually, I watched Dad fillet the fish on the basement table covered by a plastic Nabisco table cloth, asked to see what was in the stomach, a trick he had showed me on one of our first walleyes—slit the stomach and you could find out what a fish had been eating, minnows, perch, baby bullheads. On this night, he filleted the fish alone, clandestinely, while I went to bed.

It will be ten years before we catch another walleye in local lakes. We will catch exactly two walleyes before that time, in lakes at least four hours north, as if the word took time to catch up to us in a different area code, before the interdict would clamp down on us once again.

Calling this "the interdict" is not too strong. Excursion after walleye-less excursion, it became clear something was up.

"I suppose this is what I get for keeping that fish before the season," Dad would mutter after another fishless outing. Mostly, he attributed our inability to catch walleyes to the fact that we needed a boat, that all the fish were out in the middle of the lake, where we could see boats congregating like tents of the Bedouin. But later, when we got a boat, it didn't matter. Pulling off the lake, skunked again, we'd ask fisherman after fisherman, prodding for failure, "How'd you do?" "Guys have any luck?" or the loaded, "Pretty dead, huh?"

And time after time the answer came back.

"Oh, we got a couple."

And they'd flip open their live wells to reveal the white bellies of walleyes, the slightly pink gills where life still pulsed, pectoral fins testing for balance in the thin air.

"Doggone!" Dad would say in the pickup. "Why can't we catch 'em like that." Eventually, we almost forgot, dropped the object of the preposition: "I suppose this is what I get for—"

At Mayo, Dad's still stuck on the Bobcat. He can only see one step ahead, and it's too tempting for me not to finish the thought, an alternate history for us both, one where I get to run the Bobcat.

"Come on. Let's go!" he demands.

"You need to clean the hog house? Already done."

"What?"

"I did it. Before I came. Yeah—I can run the Bobcat, too, you know."

"You gotta be shitting me," he says. He's irked, knows something is up, that he's being played.

"And I already got chores done, too," I say, playing out the fantasy, as the son who takes over.

"Then how is it that you're here?" he slurs. Considering he has no idea where here is, his logic is pretty sound.

"Don't worry about it." Then, digging even deeper. "Kevin's going to watch it this weekend."

He doesn't know what to say to this. He still wants to get out. He grabs onto the bar and pulls.

"Just relax, Dad," I say. "We've got it taken care of."

More than my words, the six-inch bar is too much for him. After a moment's struggle, he falls back onto the bed.

"Yeah, you're a helluva kid," he says. It's among the hardest words he's ever said to me.

"Now we have time to go fishing," I say.

6

Walking in Water

THE LIPS ARE by far the most disaffecting thing. They're constantly pursed but without any muscle control. They make Dad look like a different person, a caricature, a yokel. It's completely unnerving, like something from a cartoon. He's pulling so far down within himself that it feels like we might be left with just this, a shell of a man with pursed out, crazy lips.

It's clear after the first weekend at Mayo that we're in this for the long haul, and so we begin to divvy up days. Heidi and Lisa leave for home with plans to return later in the week. Carmen will be on duty for the first couple of days. I'm teaching three classes on a Tuesday / Thursday schedule and finishing up a master's degree the rest of the time. I'll spend the weekends with Dad, then travel back Monday night for class on Tuesday.

But with the promise of doctors rounding, I stay into Monday evening. The doctors travel in packs at St. Mary's Hospital, and when they come into Dad's room, the lead is a dark-haired, dark-eyed doctor of vaguely Southwest Asian descent, Dr. Nassar. She speaks directly and unblinkingly, a direct bedside manner for serious situations without any hint of a customer service demeanor.

She stands near Dad's bed, asks him a few questions directly, but he's been asleep. He looks up at her, attempts to slur an answer, but he's nowhere close, so Mom fills in for him. Dad drowses, with those mad, maddening, yokelly lips. Doctor Nassar turns to us.

"So we'd like to get another MRI of Milton's brain. The antibiotics should be clearing up the urinary tract infection, but the fact that Milton is still having tremors and muscle weakness and is still delusional tells us something else is going on. So then we'd also like to get a spinal tap after that, probably tomorrow. The idea would be to check for any Lewy bodies in the spinal fluid. If we don't find any Lewy bodies, that might lead us a step closer to Hashimoto's encephalopathy, which is a kind of negative diagnosis, but we'll see."

Carmen and I look at Dad to get our bearings, but he's started smacking those crazy lips.

This is the first time we've heard the term "Hashimoto's encephalopathy," and so we hear it the first time as gobbledygook. This might be a gibberish skit where the actors have to make up conditions: "tekloclomatose barfistophany; bulwinkle's cartofasmaplasty; Hashimoto's encephalopathy."

Carmen the nurse has many questions, but the problem is to order them.

"So Lewy bodies—that's to look for dementia?"

"Yes, Lewy bodies in the spinal fluid would signal dementia."

"Ok, that's interesting because he hasn't really had many symptoms of that."

"At Milton's age and with his delusions, it would be consistent."

"Yes, I just—we just have to reorient our thinking a little bit. We've been thinking lithium toxicity. . . ."

"Well, he came in lithium toxic, but now as the lithium leaves his system, he doesn't seem to be responding, which leads me—leads us—to consider other things."

"Such as the Lewy bodies."

"Such as Lewy bodies which would signal an underlying dementia."

"And the spinal tap—will that work with his tremors and his . . . condition?" I ask.

"Well, we have to try it. It's really the only way to see, if the MRI doesn't show us anything new, what might be going on."

"Can he be sedated for that?"

"Well, no, not really, because we'll need to adjust his body while he's awake in order to get into the spinal area."

"Oh boy."

"Well, that's where the family is very important. He seems to listen to you very well."

"And the Hashi…?"

"Hashimoto's encephalopathy. It's an autoimmune disorder where the immune system attacks the brain and leads to similar symptoms to what Milton is experiencing—delusion, tremors, weakness, and lack of coordination. If there are no Lewy bodies, then we would probably treat him with steroids to see if he responds to that."

"But you suspect the Lewy bodies."

"With Milton's age and symptoms, I would suspect some Lewy bodies, yes."

Dad puffs out his lips. He is slipping away: the broad-shouldered bale-stacker, the cross-dressing jester, the patient fisherman, the trumpet aficionado.

Dad was the music in our lives, and he is fading in front of us.

DAD TOUCHES a different time, when the earth was young.

Dad learned to swim—impossibly—on the west branch of Champepadan Creek when it ran so deep he could dive off the bridge a mile west of our place and not touch bottom. Now, that same creek stagnates by late summer; the deepest I ever remember it being is eighteen inches.

Dad made little secret of the things he loved. Hunting. Fishing. Swimming.

On visits to Carmen at college, Dad would swim with us in the hotel pool, his thick white belly and ironed-on farmer's tan lithe in the pool. He would dive and hold his breath under water, gliding like a whale, and though we clung to him and tried to wrestle him, he was immovable yet impossibly gentle.

Dad could mimic a crow call, a skill he learned growing up in the forties hunting them for bounty with his .22. He'd call in the scout, the first bird on site whose job it was to check for danger. If he could wing that bird, it would bring in the rest of the murder for Dad to plunk off one by one.

Dad's the closest thing to a crack shot I know. When Uncle Hein from Chicago missed pheasants with the .410, Dad plunked them out of the air with the .22, a story Uncle Hein tells every time they're together. And Cousin Gary recounts Dad stepping outside with the same gun and picking a pigeon off the silo at 100 yards.

Speaking of those Chicago cousins, to them Dad is prankster and crazy uncle. When Doug and Gary came out to work for the summer, Dad scared them with firecrackers while they thought they were sneaking a smoke in the barn. When they were stuck behind a slow car on highway 91, Dad passed it on the s-curve—through the ditch. When Doug challenged Dad to test out his new karate skills, Dad picked him up and set him in the kiddie pool. When Gary stayed out all night at Valhalla Ballroom on Lake Shetek, Dad rigged a pail of tin cans to the stairway door so that it dumped all the way down the stairs when Gary tried to sneak in.

Dad is a '55 Chevy, regal turquoise and India ivory hardtop.

Dad had literally outrun cops—or knew people who had; the difference became indistinguishable in his stories. The cops in their '49 Fords would turn on their lights to pull you over, and you'd slow down like you were complying, then when the older car was shifted down, the newer '55s and '57s would work through their gears and leave the older car in the dust. We pointed out old Chevys on car trips but just the ones from the '50s. The '60s and '70s don't exist for us.

Dad is Brylcreem and Chuck Taylors. He wears his hair in a flat top, all perfectly pitched up with Brylcreem. Sometimes, when he comes outside to play catch or shoot hoops, he laces up the Chuck Taylors—the actual Chuck Taylors he wore as a senior in high school in 1955. He wears them down to the garage where the basketball hoop is nailed, and he steps to the place about where the free throw line would be between the gravel ruts and chickweed and shoots an honest-to-God Rick Barry granny shot.

One of his stock stories is about playing basketball one night in Ellsworth, a half hour straight down highway 91. Dad couldn't go to the game, the story goes, because he had to go home to do chores, his own and Uncle Bill's, who was gone somewhere.

When the coach heard about it, he told Dad to get going home after school and they would pick him up in the bus on the way, right on highway 91.

So, at the final bell Dad hightailed it for home, milked twenty-odd cows, fed and watered and cleaned up, then did the same at Uncle

Bill's before grabbing his duffel bag and sprinting the quarter-mile to 91 where the bus was waiting.

"When I got on the bus, you can about imagine how I smelled," he says. "No one wanted to sit within a mile of me." There's still hurt in the telling, in the unbending law of Grampa Hank that put work over everything. There's also pride, in the way he got it all done.

"First thing I did was shower during the JV game."

And then the varsity game. The first play, Dad gets kneed in the balls so hard he goes to floor, calls timeout. The coach is upset at wasting a timeout this early, but Dad tells him what happened.

"And the coach said, 'If that's how they're going to play and if the refs aren't going to call it, then go ahead and take it to 'em, boys.'"

Cut to the inbounds play: a forward passes it in to a guard who passes it to the other wing who feeds it to Dad.

"The next time I got the ball, I elbowed the guy hard as I could in the ribs and went up for a layup. I scored twenty-six points that night, and when I got on the bus everyone gave me a standing ovation, the cheerleaders and all."

Dad is a fifties tune, pre-Elvis, maybe "Summertime," which he'd belt out at the lake in his deep bass.

Dad is marching bands and Herb Alpert. He would have me put on a John Philip Sousa record or *Theme Songs of the American Military* and would hold his finger and thumb together as he followed the articulation of the trumpets, and something of the rhythms would enter my veins, too.

Dad loves piano, insists that we all take "music lessons." During the torture of these lessons as I try to make so many fingers hit so many notes, Dad sits down at the old upright, plays a few bars from memory. It's just what he remembers from "Heart and Soul," but I've never heard anyone play "Heart and Soul" like that, ever, with pop and verve, like the keys are alive or electric, a hot stove he has to pull them off quick, his back wide as a wrestler's but moving like a dancer's. It's alchemical.

I laugh, and he thinks it's at the wrong notes he hits, but it's from sheer wonder at his ability, that he could breach my definition of manhood so easily.

"My fingers aren't used to it anymore—they're too fat to play, but I used to could."

I don't doubt it.

This, the musical Dad, was Dad at play, Dad transformed and easy in the world, Dad untouchable and timeless.

THE ORIGIN story of Dad and the trumpet is also peak Dad.

The house Dad grew up in was joyless. His brother Howard crying at the table on the way to the Army. "Hurry up *een beetje*" from Hank as constant chorus at five o'clock milkings. Never money for the fair. Never showing up at Milt's school activities.

But it wasn't music-less. Gramma Mary played the piano in their otherwise silent house, played and sang hymns in her warbly alto. Milt found shelter in the warmth of his mother's music. And after she crossed the abyss of losing Howard, she found comfort in Milt's love of music.

For high school, Dad went to Chandler Public, where his favorite teacher was easily Charlie Smidt, the music teacher, who announced in 1953-54 that Chandler High School would be starting a band the following year, when Dad would be a senior. Dad asked his mother if he might get a trumpet, and she conspired with him. Where would they get the money? Gramma would save egg money, a pittance of income that Grampa Hank couldn't begrudge her.

Cut to montage: week by week, quarters mount in a quart jar: the first two coins Gramma Mary lets Dad drop in; the daily egg chores followed closely by the ever-clinking quarters; a few pulled out for a fender bender on Grampa's pickup; the last two with a meaningful look between mother and son.

Finally, Dad brings home an alligator skin case, pulls out a brass trumpet, fits the mouthpiece and blows his first note.

The year is 1954 because the line in Dad's story is, "I had it mastered in six months."

Milt practices nightly. In Chuck Taylors and a crew cut—I'm imagining again—Milt retires to the parlor, to the smell of wet cement and stainless steel, the sweet acidity of cow manure. He practices scales to warm up, stretches his range into the high notes, his lips reddening.

Then he sets a song up on a music stand he's borrowed. There's no one to hear so he gives it everything. When he stumbles over a run, he backs up and runs it again. Then he runs the whole song once it's all ironed out. It is like ironing, or like any art. His tone becomes clear and centered. A thing emerges and that thing is alive. Milt is seventeen. This space is what he always wants to live in, down the yard from Hank who sits in the house in his chair, mulling over ledgers and church business.

Gramma Mary wanders down to the barn. This is it for her. Her oldest daughter is married to a man who overshadows her; her second daughter, to a Chicago businessman, escaped from Hank but not from a constrictive Calvinist world. And far away.

And Howard.

She finds a seat on an old milk can and listens. When Milt's done with a song, she proposes playing a duet, she on the piano and he on the trumpet. The next week the trumpet moves into the house. Mother and son practice when Hank's not around; finally, they're good enough, and their end game—playing in church—is pious enough that they play when Hank *is* around. He fights his nature until he can't help himself, "That's enough now! I'm trying to read the paper!"

They play through the song twice more as if they don't hear him.

When the time for the duet comes, it is a beautiful thing. They're playing the same duets that people are playing everywhere, among them, "The Holy City."

Dad's story, when he tells it, is about the duets, about how good they were. The story is about Charlie Smidt who could walk on water. The word about the trumpet, never varying, is "mastered." The image is Dad in the parlor with a big cat and a whip, with a Holstein bull and a red cape. Controlling his own fear, taking his licks, getting a few scars, attaining the respect of the thing. He gets playful, then risky. He runs high and the tone remains pure. He double- and triple-tongues, sweat gleaming on his forehead. He asks Mr. Smidt for harder music and gets it and plays it.

The story culminates in the idea to run away to join the army band. It seems to be Charlie Smidt's suggestion, but again I have to imagine the details.

It's the spring. All of this—buying and learning the trumpet for only one year of high school—has been a whirlwind, but graduation looms. Mr. Smidt notices his first chair has plateaued. Just that fall, Milt had seemed almost a prodigy, but now Mr. Smidt can read Dad's concern for the future, can read his story: a difficult, even backward family life where he works hard. Milt's back is broad now, freakishly strong, but that will go. It's rare that someone can bend that bodily strength into art, but Milt can. It comes out of his trumpet in both power and control. He's destined to farm with the passing of his brother in Korea, but imagining a future under his father's thumb is starting to affect the music.

"So Milt, I've been thinking," Charlie Smidt starts one day after practice. "What's the future of you and the trumpet?"

"Oh, I plan to keep it up, Mr. Smidt," Dad says earnestly. "I play duets with my mother in church now and I'd love to keep going. Can I still get music from you once I graduate?"

"One thing that you could do is join the army—the army band, I mean," Mr. Smidt says. "It's some of the best trumpet music in the world. And it would keep you out of combat."

Milt's bright brown eyes look hopeful. "But how do I do it?"

"The recruiters will help you with that," Mr. Smidt says. "There will be tryouts and it won't be easy, but you're ready, Milt. You're as good a trumpet player as I've seen."

"Gee, Mr. Smidt"—this is the movie script version, I don't know how else to imagine it—"you really think I could do it?"

Central to the mythos of a father is exactly this kind of story. His secret love. An alternative history. A genius that would have remade him and the figure he cut in the world.

THE STORY had its effect. When it came time to choose an instrument in fifth grade, I chose the trumpet, hoping I would take to it naturally.

I did not.

As the eighties dragged on, the music slowly drained out of Dad's life. The few bars of "Heart and Soul" seemed like a dream. The few times he picked up my trumpet, blowing a few powerful notes only to fizzle out by high C, made the trumpet story seem fabricated. After Carmen graduated from college we didn't go back to hotels with swimming pools.

Music was replaced by the hard realities of economics, measurable by the way Dad talked on the way to the lake.

Almost inevitably, as we drove toward highway 91, we'd see our neighbors from across the road, Mert and Florence in her kerchief, picking rock. At first, Dad offered pity: "That poor kid works hard. *Man*, does he work. We should take him fishing some time."

After the cows went, that changed. "I suppose I should stay home and work. That Mert—you never see him go fishing. Maybe that's why he's successful."

Then, when "net value" had become "cash flow," came the F-word: "There they go again, picking rock. That's why Mert's successful. But I'm a failure."

The lake could still make him forget, except if we sat within calling distance of another fisherman, in which case after some friendly, contextless banter, Dad would drag him into it.

"And then my cows got Red Nose . . . and I was stuck with a $24,000 vet bill."

The other fisherman would nod, whistle, agree it was a pity and the conversation would grind to a halt.

One Saturday in late June was different.

It was a sunny day, approaching hot. Lake Shetek had not yet turned over, but the good fishing was done. We sat on the north side of the second dike and nothing bit. I kept moving up and down the dike, trying to find fish. A large rock protruded from the corner of where the dike met Valhalla Island, "Uncle Albert's rock," Dad called it, underneath the trees and still in the shade. I had danced out to this rock on a couple of stepping stones and pulled out a crappie and then a small walleye, just too small to keep. After that second fish, I ran down the dike to the full sun where Dad sat and convinced him to join me.

Then the fish stopped biting.

And we realized just how rocky it was. I lost a lure, then another one. This venture was quickly getting expensive, and I was feeling guilty. I could get snagged on rocks every time I cast unless I reeled fast enough to pull the lure just under the surface, in which case I wasn't getting down to where I was sure the fish were, holding behind the larger boulders or resting on the cool of rock piles.

"Dang! Another snag!" It was one of those snags seemingly beneath your feet, that you can't believe won't let loose though you can circle it with your pole, pulling this way and that to pop it free. Dad said, "Better go get it."

"What? In the water?"

"Yep, it's not that deep. You can do it."

"Like, take my shoes off?"

"Just keep 'em on—those rocks can be sharp. Your shoes'll dry out."

So I pulled my jeans up as high as they would go, stepped down into the murky water, reached down to where the lure was wedged between two rocks, and freed it. Then, back up to Uncle Albert's rock.

But the problem repeated itself, a little farther out.

"Go ahead," Dad encouraged. "You're already wet." So I got down again. The slow slog. Water creeping higher up my legs.

"Da-ad!"

"It's only water—you'll dry out." My pants were wet nearly to my crotch, the bottom of my T-shirt and arm were both wet from reaching down to get the lure.

By this time we'd seen enough fishing magazines and TV shows to realize that there was a whole world of fishing equipment that could make our fishing lives better, like waders that would allow you to walk out to depths of three feet or more, sending your casts out that much further to where the fish *really* were, beyond us sorry shore fishermen.

But we didn't have waders, and it was hot, and our lures kept getting stuck. As I walked out toward another snag, I stumbled against a large rock and wet myself to the waist. I gasped from the shock. Dad laughed.

"May as well stay out there now," he said.

On his own snag, Dad lost his balance and stepped off his rock into the water with me.

We started moving down the bank. Turned out the entire shoreline was littered with rocks—little ones and massive ones that you couldn't account for with careful steps in the dingy water.

"Kinda shallow all through here. I'm waiting for it to drop off," Dad said.

We tried moving farther out, but then our lures just got stuck deeper. One of my casts got stuck in water more than waist deep.

"Here, bring me your pole. Then dive and get it."

I handed it to him, then started following the line out to the rock.

"Dad!" I said, as the water reached mid-chest.

"You're OK—just be careful."

"I'm going to have to go way under to get it," I said.

"That's alright—I'm watching you."

With one hand holding my line, I submerged myself, followed the line down with my hand toward where it was stuck, but it was too deep. I came up for air.

"I can't get it."

"Should I try?"

Until that point, he'd been the drier of us, wet to mid-thigh. Now, he walked toward me with both our rods.

"Ho—that water's chilly yet," he said as it reached his privates. When he got to me, he handed me both rods.

"You sure you can get it?" I asked, meaning, "Are you sure you want to do this, a grown man diving for fishing lures in full clothes?"

He made a big show of closing his eyes and holding his breath, then submerged slowly. I saw the bubbles come up from when he exhaled. After a few seconds, he came up in the same way, slowly, eyes pressed shut. At the surface, he blew out his remaining air into a big smile and a laugh and handed me the lure.

Eventually, by a yellow cabin almost at the end of Valhalla Island, we ran out of shoreline and waded up the bank by a sign that said "No Trespassing." As we stood there dripping, a woman came out to talk to us.

"Sorry about this," Dad began. "We were just fishing along the shoreline here and—do you mind if we walk back to our pickup?"

"I was just afraid you were going to drown," she said.

I saw us then as she must have seen us, this middle-aged blond woman behind her oversized sunglasses: a grown man and a boy, fishing and swimming in their clothes, transgressing property lines and public decency lines and that impermeable line between child and adult.

I didn't know another father who would have done it, plier pocket, wallet and keys and all. You might say there was mania in it.

Or you might say there was music in it. The rhythm of casting and retrieving, the wading and diving, talking and sputtering and laughing. Leaning into that music, dancing to a tune that only we heard.

THE TRUMPET story always ended with something like, "But I needed Hank Schaap's signature in order to join, and he wouldn't give it to me."

I'd always pictured a scene at the recruiter's office, Dad waiting nervously, a distracted secretary, a man with a high and tight coming out to talk to Dad, and then after a few minutes in his office, the camera positioned outside the large, plate glass window, the man shaking his head, offering Dad a handshake, Dad's face falling.

The truth is, Dad never actually took it that far. He heard that he would need Grampa's signature so he thought there was no point in trying. He never went as far as asking a recruiter, actually trying to leave.

Both Lisa and I played the trumpet, Lisa achieving first chair in high school. I found it to be a lot of work without a lot of reward, and I botched the one solo part I ever got. Mostly, I discounted Dad's claims about double and triple tonguing.

Then, once, cleaning out the square end table that was a permanent fixture in the living room, I came across some of his trumpet music. Here was "The Holy City" and other pieces. One of them was impossibly full of black tracks for the trumpet line, sixteenth and, I swear, thirty-second notes.

CARMEN HAS the idea to try to hang the room with pictures for Dad. "And what about playing trumpet or marching band music?" she suggests. "Old hymns? Could we play some of those for him? Some music that he likes."

Mom says she could bring some CDs from home. She'll make a trip before the spinal tap to refresh clothes.

Dad's eyes are pushed closed, his head rests on his chest. He's not sleeping but looking deep within himself. His lips, those lips that mastered the trumpet in six months, fall outward, as if some invisible wind sucks the life out of him.

Once, the time we had him committed and he ended up in the state hospital, Dad was medicated into something docile. When I visited him, he was just bemusedly pleasant, relaxed. He didn't know what day it was, necessarily, couldn't care less about the outside world. I couldn't imagine him doing his voices in that condition, or pestering you until you were breathless. He was just in neutral, like he was high. I thought then that we'd hit on the Dad we all wanted, a clueless Dad, who wouldn't care when he passed Mert and Florence picking rock or a neatly mown farm, who wouldn't rub his head and whisper to himself in his chair, "Jack of all trades and master of none."

But that docile Dad also wouldn't wade into the water with me, submerge himself, full-bodied and come up spitting water, a smile all the way to his eyes. That Dad heard no voices; he also heard no music.

Now, in the bed at St. Mary's, eyes closed, lips pursed, Dad is submerged again, somewhere deep inside himself. But we won't let him go. We will pull him up from the depths for even one more glimpse of that smile, to share just one more bar of the music that is his life.

7

Cross Lake

I HAVE TO GET back for classes. Carmen will stay with Dad at Mayo through Wednesday, Heidi will take Thursday, and I will return Friday. As luck would have it, I'll miss the upcoming procedures, both the MRI and the lumbar puncture.

And I'm thrilled to avoid it, all the coaxing and prodding and cajoling it will take to get Dad through it. So as I leave Rochester I'm the one on jailbreak.

Carmen's request to hang his room with pictures to help anchor him to reality has me thinking.

I have just the thing. Last spring, I took my two boys to the Rock River in northern Pipestone County, really a creek in a cow pasture, and we hit it big. I have a picture of them each holding a northern pike, with smiles that borrow pieces from Dad's own smile, the fish big in their hands. I'll posterize it for him, so it will hang large in his room, and I can say, "Look, Dad. Your grandchildren. We made it."

There's one minor problem. They're not walleyes.

I'M NOT SURE when the walleye became totemic for us. In the early days northern and walleyes and even crappies were almost equal for me, with northern and walleyes slightly ahead because they were both predators. Predators were pretty. And awesome.

I remember the first walleye I caught with my Snoopy pole, under the creosote bridge on Lake Shetek's second dike. It was silver in the cloudy light but not necessarily beautiful, with a slightly hooked chin and those all-seeing eyes.

The second two, the miraculous catch of fish on the culverts of the first dike, were more golden. Once, when I went shopping with Mom and Heidi to Sioux Falls, Dad went fishing without me to Hadley with a friend of his, Casey Lolkus, and brought back two beautiful walleyes. I was so mad at him. Those fish were more green, with the characteristic green bars or saddles on their sides, the equivalent to stripes on a tiger for a fish in a shadowy, green, underwater world. Then the interdict fish.

For Dad, something about taste and fillet-ability entered in. Northerns had y-bones that you had to systematically remove when you ate, walleyes didn't. The meat on walleyes was perfectly white and flaky. They became Dad's favorite simply because they were easier to clean and they didn't "taste fishy," as my family was fond of saying.

But they weren't easy to catch. Walleyes are notoriously finicky, elusive. Mysterious. Talk about fishing in Minnesota for long enough and you'll inevitably hear the phrase "walleye mystique," which we read about in the magazine that influenced us toward walleyes more than anything else: *In-Fisherman*.

THE FIRST centerfolds I ever saw came from Dad's subscription. Every month, page after page of glossy, sleek, perfectly poised, impossibly protuberant images. Sure, they were distorted by perspective, even airbrushed, but you knew they also had to be somewhat candid—which made them all the more juicy.

In-Fisherman.

As a means of ending the walleye interdict and accessing our birthright as Minnesotans to the official state fish, Dad subscribed to *In-Fisherman*, the gentleman-fisherman's magazine started by the Lindner brothers, Al and Ron, they of the Chicago-Nordic accents and fishing gear empire. *In-Fisherman* fed both our fantasies and our thirst for knowledge.

Did we want to catch monster pike? We should consider the time of year and presentation and visit such and such a lake up north where—look!—the Lindners had caught trophy after trophy.

Did we want a stringer full of crappies shedding water jewels in the sunlight? We should use exotic-sounding reel brand on periodic table-referencing rod brand while fishing funny-named tube jigs above submerged weed lines near the resort name that conjured clear water and towering pines.

Did we want to be laden with walleyes almost too heavy to hold, with perfectly arched dorsal fins and clearly delineated dark bars down their golden sides, eyes ghostly as the light caught their translucent lenses? Why, we should buy Lindy Rigs and Roach Rigs and Rapalas and troll them from a Lund boat with Mercury motor and Minn Kota trolling motor and Lowrance Fish Lo-K-Tor and plan a trip today to Rainy Lake, Lake of the Woods, or God's Own Private Lake, Manitoba.

Fish porn.

I looked through every issue right when it came. Even read some of the articles.

Then again, our experiences fishing had always been colored by the Minnesota ideal, even before *In-Fisherman*.

Consider holidays at Lake Shetek State Park. We spent every Memorial Day and post-acquiescence Fourth of July at State Park on the backside of Lake Shetek: campsites, picnic areas, walking trails, interpretive center, and swimming beach whose overarching burr oak, ash, and maple could trick you into thinking you weren't on the flat of the prairie but in the arboreal Up North.

On these holidays, we'd pack up the tripod grill and charcoal matches and lighter fluid and paper plates and buns and hot dogs and hamburgers and salt and pepper and ketchup and chips and watermelon and head to State Park. It was always windy, cool or downright cold on Memorial Day or stiflingly humid on the Fourth, even with the wind. No matter—even in May's fifty-five degrees, we'd run to the beach house to change and swim in the dingy waters, then shiver in towels while we ate a burger and chips and all agree: this was paradise.

In the afternoon, Mom and the girls might walk to Loon Island or the interpretive center. I remember the fetus of a fawn in a bottle I saw there, like I imagine they preserved Lenin's head, only prettier, complete with tiny white spots. The presentations at the interpretive center were enough to interest you in the world. Heidi fell in love with flora there, for instance.

I came to State Park for one thing: to fish. Of epic proportions to me was the time I took my cousin Drew along. Dad and one of his friends were going to rent a boat from the marina on Valhalla Island, but it was too small and too unsteady for kids, which was why I was bought off by taking a friend.

Drew and I found our way to a sandbar that jutted out perfectly into the channel between the north and south parts of the lake. Casting and recasting our bobber into the stiff south breeze, I was thrilled when I set the hook into not a bullhead but a northern pike—a game fish!

We kept it, though by the picture in Mom's scrapbook, it's too small to be a keeper.

It was still more than they caught in the boat.

When I got older and proved to have an iron will when it came to fishing, I got to go out with Dad. Dad's pride and joy was a six-horse Johnson outboard motor that he kept in the basement "to save him some money" on these boat-renting days. We'd rent a fourteen-foot aluminum boat from Pete with his big belly and captain's hat, like Skipper on *Gilligan's Island*, and Dad would hump out the Johnson motor and mount it to the back.

The Johnson would never want to start. Dad would pull and pull, spend ten minutes just to get it started, only to have it choke as we pulled away from the dock. But finally it would catch and he'd gun it out of Pete's inlet into Lake Shetek in herky-jerky motion with a sketch motor. This began the exercise in futility that was fishing Lake Shetek in a rented boat.

What problems did we have?

Wind. Central to the narrative of boat fishing was the time Dad invited Lisa's husband out with him on the Fourth of July and they were almost driven across the breadth of Lake Shetek by a stiff south wind. From that trip on, Dad dubbed these boats "tin cans" and "bathtubs."

Control. We'd troll and he'd tell me to cast toward shore but we would be going too fast and the lure would end up trailing behind the boat. So we'd back troll to slow us down a bit, but then we'd get turned around by the wind and Dad would curse. Or he'd have to tend to his line with both hands meaning he'd take his hand off the motor so we'd get off course, and he'd curse. Or, everything finally in line, we'd snag and have to go back to get it loose. Sitting on the flat aluminum benches and twisting backwards to turn the motor, he'd complain of the backache these tin cans gave him.

All this as we watched the Lunds buzz by.

"They've got livewells right on them boats," Dad would say, "and you just put the fish in them and keep 'em just as fresh as you can believe."

Or we'd watch them troll a path along Loon Island's rocky shore, the front fisherman elevated on a casting platform, controlling the boat's direction with a foot pedal.

"They've got depth finders on there that you can see right where them fish are at—what depth."

But there was always hope, always a new plan.

"Let's go over to those cattails and see if we can catch us some crappies."

"They say there's a rock pile off Loon Island a ways. Let's see if we can find it once."

"Let's drift this now. *In-Fisherman* always talks about 'drifting the flats.'"

Finally, fatigue setting in, we'd scramble for chocolate milk and donuts, as long as they weren't sodden from the water that inevitably splashed or seeped into the bottom of the boat.

One year, trolling my favorite lure, a Daredevle five-o-diamonds, I caught a crappie and a northern in a five-hour jaunt. It was a wildly successful trip.

But no walleyes.

"WALLEYE MYSTIQUE" predates white settlers. For tribal people of Wisconsin, it was the eyes. According to Larry Nesper's *The Walleye War*, the old man Akiwenzii founded the spring spearing tradition among the Ojibwe by stalking fish at night, burning white pine pitch in a birchbark dish, drawing the fish to the light. Among the various fish he could spear this way, *ogaa*, walleye, were Akiwenzii's favorite, partly because their eyes lit up, making them visible for spear throwers poised at the front of torch-lit canoes. Akiwenzii passed on this secret to Winaboozhoo, the famous trickster, who passed it on to the Ojibwe. True to much tribal philosophy, though their eerie eyes may have made walleyes the stars of the spring show, the walleye seems to be one among brothers for the Ojibwe.

DAD WON THE Young Farmer of the Year Award for the state of Minnesota in 1965, the same year the walleye became the state fish. You might say he and the fishing industry were destined for each other, even if he was a late adopter.

Holden Illingworth invented the spinning reel in 1905; Dad got one in the early eighties. And hated it.

Carl Lowrance invented the Fish Lo-K-Tor in 1959; Dad got one in the mid-eighties.

When he got it, we knew our fishing careers were set.

The Fish Lo-K-Tor was sonar in a little green box. It had a simple, circular readout. Tuned to the proper frequency, that circle showed one red line at zero and one red line wherever the bottom of the lake was. Any other blips in between those two lines meant there were fish between you and the bottom.

And then we tried using it when we rented a bathtub the next Fourth of July.

The circle of the Fish Lo-K-Tor measured sixty feet of water and could double its circle to 120 feet. The lakes that we fished in southwest Minnesota almost never measured more than ten feet deep, using only a fraction of the circle. Turn the readout up too high and it would send all kinds of red blips all over the place. So Dad would adjust it and then say, "OK, now, according to that there are fish right there—fish at eight and now five and now three."

"No, Dad, it's flashing all over—it's still up too high."

"OK but if I turn it there then—OK, so that means there's fish at six. I don't know if I believe that—you?"

Our biggest problem with the Fish Lo-K-Tor was literally a problem of belief: we doubted that there were that many fish in the mud lakes we fished. And that we could make little red lines bite.

Europeans did their best to classify the mystique out of the walleye.

The Latin classification for walleye, *sander vitreus*, though it focuses on the "glassy" eyes, doesn't do much for me in placing the walleye. *Tapetum lucidum*, however, the term for the light-gathering layer in their eyes—literally "bright tapestry"—is much more poetic.

The English word "walleye" also focuses on the fish's primary evolutionary feature, those all-seeing eyes. I blame the British for screwing up their Carolus Linnaeus in dubbing the fish the "walleye pike" since it's in fact in the perch family and not a pike. Apparently the Canadians still call it a pickerel in some places, which shows how closely connected "northerns"—colloquial in southwest Minnesota for "northern pike"—and walleyes remain in popular consciousness.

But my favorite term comes from the French who went off impulse, color, impression: *doré*, the French called the fish, golden.

The gilded fish. Yes.

The walleye as the riches of North America.

When your state is nicknamed "Land of 10,000 Lakes," when beer commercial jingles recall the "land of sky-blue waters," when your state's name is synonymous with pine trees and clear lakes but you live in the treeless part of the state with only mud lakes and can't manage to catch your state's state fish, it can turn into a kind of psychosis. The lake is always bluer on the other side of the state, in this case quite literally. To really enter into the bliss that was our Minnesota birthright, *In-Fisherman* made clear, there was only one answer. Up North.

And we needed a boat.

As the walleye interdict extended, and financial trouble mounted, and as we sat for hours on end on the uncomfortable rocks of Lake Shetek, the ideal of a boat only grew.

"Now if we had a boat, I'd like to try around Loon Island and Keeley Island," Dad would say, looking out towards where the boats were congregating. "And I'd like to go up to Bloody—try it there—and Lone Tree. Quite a few guys talk about Lone Tree."

A boat equaled freedom. In a boat—a real boat with a real motor—you could access not just the better-named landmarks on Lake Shetek, but also the lakes that didn't have public shorelines, Lake Sarah and Dead Coon and Round Lake and East and West Graham and Talcot.

But here we were, with sore asses, marooned.

AMERICANS MADE the walleye totemic. After World War II, when men with disposable income came searching for a trophy in the pristine world of Up North, Minnesota gave them its most filletable, most photogenic fish: the walleye.

Consider some head of industry seeking an experience in the natural world, seeking conquest. He goes to the Big Woods of Minnesota, "roughs" it. Going out on day one, our man gets into some walleyes, fillets them out, samples some of the purest fish flesh known to humanity. I can do this, he thinks, nature at my beck and call. It fits his narrative. The next day he goes out to the same spot: crickets. So now our man has got to work, got to think. This is just what our man likes. He tries a different approach but it doesn't work. That whole day, nothing. So he goes back to the cabin, brow knitted, interest piqued. He works that next day for a few fish, and the next. Last day, he gets into them again and tells himself that not just anyone could have done what he's done, that it's by his own genius he's gotten his quarry, the mysterious walleye of the north.

He goes back, tells stories. For all the men he evangelizes, the walleye becomes the snipe, the white stag. Next year, those buddies schedule vacations to the Big Woods. The walleye becomes the trophy of Minnesota, the Holy Grail of northern fishes. The next year, the wives will be damned if they'll be left behind with the kids. Resorts are spawned. World's Largest Walleye Statues made. State fish status endowed.

"Walleye mystique," then, comes from a combination of things.

From being an apex predator—though both northern pike and muskies are larger and much better fighters. From its strange beauty—a walleye can be *doré*, golden, can be green with darker bars, can be a warm brown, with a coxcomb in its arched dorsal fin and those all-seeing "marble" eyes. From taste—with some of the purest light flaky meat imaginable. From unpredictability—connoisseurs of bait, walleyes will send a meal back, spit it out, walk out slowly without saying a word. Or paying. You have to be skilled to catch them regularly, stalk them in their precise habitat, present just the right bait at just the right tempo, sense their light bite before setting your hook into—ah!—satisfaction. Fishing walleyes is chess compared to which everything else is checkers. Or Old Maid.

WE MADE IT Up North to a lake vacation when I was about ten, and the opportunity came as Dad knew it would: through marriage. Carmen, true to Dad's advice for her, had evaded local guys and found a husband among the Scandinavians, a city guy whose family had a cabin on Cross Lake, in Crow Wing County, the fishing bullseye of Minnesota. And Carmen got us an invite. Dad and I were elated. Finally, we'd fall into our Minnesota fishing birthright.

But at the bait shop in Crosby where we rented the bathtub to go with Dad's six-horse Johnson, the guy didn't say anything about walleyes, at least not in Cross Lake.

"You can catch northern in Cross Lake. They bite on these." He showed us the largest orange Rapala I had ever seen, an easy eight inches from tip to tail.

"Alright, give me four of them," Dad said, to my surprise. I gasped at the total cost—over thirty dollars.

Cross Lake was a long, thin lake, clear but shallow, with weedy shorelines that we thought must hold walleyes.

"We'll fish the weed lines, just like I did with Casey Lolkus on Hadley," said Dad on our first outing. "Those walleyes come up into the weeds to feed at night."

But it was as the bait shop guy promised. We trolled the weed lines and the big Rapalas worked, waddling side to side in the clear water, lazy and languishing, drawing northerns from the cabbage weed. In the clear water, as you let out line slowly, you could often see them hit. Most of them were hammer handles, barely bigger than the lure itself. But seeing is believing. We did that all day, trolling around and around the lake, occasionally reeling in northerns that were big enough to fillet. We ate a meal of fish this way and felt like providers, picking out the Y-bones as we ate.

We caught no walleyes.

"If you want walleyes, you have to go up to Whitefish," the bait store guy said. "If you go through Cross, you can get into Rush and then into Whitefish. That's where the walleyes are."

Whitefish was big and bulbous on the map, with two lobes, North and South Whitefish. It would be an epic trip in the bathtub. And Whitefish was so big, any wind would blow us right off.

Dad had a better idea. "Do you know of any guides?"

I DON'T remember a time when money wasn't a hardship. Stuff cost too much and it was better if you could go without, best if you just didn't ask. Dad was open-handed with money, but we knew that "bookwork" stressed him out, especially after the cows went and money wasn't coming in regular from a milk check. We couldn't be the kind of kids that nagged for spending money for unnecessary shit because Dad would give it to us and that would draw down whatever thin reserve we had that kept us from Joading it for California.

So we didn't ask.

Vacations were the worst. You wanted to do stuff, to try stuff, to eat out, but you knew that you shouldn't even be on vacation.

So when Dad said "guide," you almost coughed up your heart. Dad got a number from the bait shop guy, called for rates. Three figures for even half a day.

I figured that was that. No doubt Dad's conscience itched. It was money we didn't have. Then there was the specter of Grampa Hank, with not just his simple tastes but his religion of simple tastes. But this was fishing. No doubt Dad shouted down Grampa Hank in his mind, then scheduled a half day with the guide.

The next morning we were early at the appointed dock, and when the guide pulled up, it was not just in a fishing boat but in a fishing machine. It was maroon with gray carpet floor, not as deep as Dad liked, who favored deep-hulled fishing boats for protection against the wind. This was a bass boat, with a shallow hull made for speed, a huge, 225-horse motor on the back and a trolling motor on the front.

The kid who was the guide was nineteen years old and he's faceless in my memory, maybe because I was so damned jealous of him, paid to catch fish.

The place to catch walleyes was in the upper part of Whitefish, the guide affirmed. He hammered it down and we were off, Dad rubbing his hands. We got as far as the second lake, Rush, going balls to the wall, spouting white water behind us, before the kid's motor broke. Completely died. He fiddled with it a little, but it was clear he didn't know the first thing about motors. He contacted someone over a walkie-talkie, but there was nothing to do. He put the front trolling motor down and began pulling us back toward home at five miles per hour.

The interdict had found us. In his green swivel chair in Leota, Grampa Hank laughed.

Neither Dad nor I could believe our luck, and we tried any way we could to get something out of it. Dad grilled the kid about equipment, techniques.

What did he think of these spinning rods, these upside-down, prissy things?

Only way to fish, the guide said.

You couldn't beat a Zebco 33, could you?

Put it this way: with a Zebco, the guide said, he'd land the fish as fast as he could. With spinning reels, he'd fight them all day, wouldn't worry about losing them.

Is that right, Dad said.

They talked about Mr. Twisters, about jigging and what that meant, about bottom-bouncing and Lindy Rigs, all the *In-Fisherman* techniques that now Dad could hear about from the expert.

It took forever to get back. He didn't charge us.

The next day we took the tin can boat up to Whitefish. Took an hour to get there. We got on the big lake and Dad found one of the drop-offs in the lower lobe with his Lowrance. On our first drift through I had a nibble. On the second pass my brother-in-law Thor caught a walleye. The water was clear and you could see the fish come in the whole way. I netted it carefully from underneath, like Dad had told me, and it shook its head wildly trying to toss the hook. By the time we boated it, we were in 100 feet of water. We went back one more time but may have moved off the spot, it was hard to tell. We needed one of those buoys you could throw out in the water when you got a bite, Dad said, then you could return to the exact spot where they were biting. Then the wind picked up and drove us off the lake. Still, we felt justified that in a little bathtub boat with a Zebco 33, even we could catch a walleye.

If we had the right equipment, Dad said, who knows, maybe he could have been a guide, too.

Wasn't it pretty to think so?

THERE ARE four lakeless counties in Minnesota. Rochester is in one of them: Mower County. Olmsted, the next county I will drive through on the way home, is another. I now live in one of the other two counties, Pipestone, and a mile from the fourth, Rock. It's by absence that you come to know a thing, or become obsessed with it.

What do our fishing pictures over the years—the actual ones, grainy Polaroids and faded Kodacolors, with arms in casts and wearing seventies clothes, as well as the ideal ones, whether posed and air-brushed by *In-Fisherman* or by the sepia tones of memory—reveal about us?

Something about the way we've organized our lives, the furniture of our minds and the symbols we cling to.

Let the Al Lindner centerfolds stand for the glossy ideal of Up North dreams.

Let the rocks beneath our feet, in Moulton Township or on the dikes of Lake Shetek, stand for the lakeless counties of Minnesota, for the immigrant world of Grampa Hank, and thorny theological contradictions.

Let the boats in the background, whether bathtubs or Lunds or broken-down fishing machines, stand for the middle class, the false kingdom of God.

Let Cross Lake be the crossroads that it was, a departure. When we left Cross Lake, we committed to the far shore. Dad bought me my first spinning reel and set himself on getting a boat and a new depth finder that would show bottom structure, that would picture the size of the fish beneath you, taking belief out of the equation. And imagination.

Let the Fish Lo-K-Tor stand for all the ways we attempt to shine technological power into the dark corners of the world, and of the mind, to see more clearly the lurking monsters we half want out in the open, half want to leave undisturbed. Let it stand for the MRI that Dad will undergo—just another kind of sonar trying to find bottom, to see the structure of our subconscious, and something beyond, perhaps unknowable.

But both the pictures we'll hang and the ones that are only memories tell a different story: Dad with his friends Don DeBoer and the unshaven, chain-smoking Johnny Hofkamp, each holding a salmon caught in Lake Michigan; Dad and Lisa with the ten-pound northern she caught up north in a tin can; Dad and I with the miraculous catch of fish, a Polaroid now long lost from the brag board of Pete's Corner; Dad leaning back into Carmen's hug as he's reeling a Zebco 33, his square-framed glasses still tinting dark in the evening sun, his smile radiant. Let these pictures tie Dad to real things, to real stories, as they were, so much inferior to the *In-Fisherman* ideal.

And so much better.

8

The Long Winter

MY LUCK HAS run out. The call comes back from Mayo. Because Dad is on Plavix for his heart and Mayo doesn't want him to bleed out when they poke him, they back up his lumbar puncture. He's now cleared for it Friday morning, when I will be the only sibling on duty. When Dad is most likely to turn into Patient Fiend.

This is always the way it happens. Things extend. They get extended. You have to wait longer than you ever thought possible. Life on the prairie is mostly a long wait. Waiting for the wind to stop blowing, for the weather to turn. Waiting for the January thaw, then spring. Waiting out winter.

IN NOVEMBER on the Buffalo Ridge, you can feel the earth tilting, the dusk coming earlier. December gives you some of the most beautiful sunsets, softening the horizon in pastels to impossible heights. There are no hard contours on the prairie on a soft, windless, pastel dusk in early December. Then, by January, you realize how the darkness has shut down over you. By 5:00 you're in pitch dark, and when the northwest wind starts whipping, to step outside unprepared means facing your own mortality. Every moment, you are aware of your fragility. And the sun only crawls back up the horizon imperceptibly, hidden in the longest winters by continuous clouds, continuous snow drifts building around your feet and drawing your eyes downwards.

You spend winter keeping winter at bay.

There were two kinds of winter days on our Moulton Township farm: days when the northwest wind blew and days when it didn't. Up on the ridge, the wind always blows more and the roads are always worse and that is not hyperbole. The growing season is two days shorter on the ridge than off it, a big deal when the growing season is less than five months.

Winter on the Coteau des Prairies—the name French mapmaker Joseph Nicollet gave the wider geographical feature of which Buffalo Ridge is the Minnesota part—is the season of the worst kind of declarations. Declarations from God or from nowhere. There is a wind chill advisory. There are road closures. It is not safe. Thus saith the Lord, "Let there be winter." There it is and will be.

When the winter really gets going, the northwest wind on the ridge is as much a force as any famous wind anywhere. In normal, non-sadistic winters, Alberta clipper systems dropping down from Canada race down the ridge in a matter of hours, drop an inch or two of snow with thirty-mile-per-hour winds, and leave the landscape calm. But when the jet stream is right, those clipper systems drop four-to-five inches of snow and move through every two to three days or stall out and suck moisture from the south, as far as the Gulf of Mexico, with a strong northwester building and building behind it. With snow cover remaining powdery and the wind regularly running twenty to fifty mph, they can't keep the roads open. Winter is snow blowing across prairie roads: running in sprite-like wisps, or pouring like floodwaters, or stampeding like buffalo.

Winter is mainly waiting. Always waiting, waiting without despair. Waiting out the northwest winds for something southerly, for the tipping point when the angle of the sun will win, when you will feel all the freaky old sun rituals rise in your DNA, and you can barely prevent yourself from offering your naked body to it the first time the temperature hits forty degrees.

THOUGH I'M perhaps most qualified (as the golden boy) to talk Dad out of Patient Fiend mode, I dread it beyond anything. It's entirely duplicitous, playing on shared memories and affections to find the reflex points of his mind in order to control him.

Worse is how intimate it is. Just him and you. Like it used to be on the boat, when the hard questions and revelations would come.

But no. This is what you were made to contend with—your name itself traces back to Norse where it translates as "High Guardian." You're Howard the High Guard.

In college, I'd first come into the role when I'd been called in after Dad's double knee replacement. Why do one at a time when you could save time and money by just doing them both, bada bing, bada boom? That was what Mom and Dad had decided. Just do it once and get it over with. Plus, Dad was a bad patient, so why put him through it twice?

Immediately after surgery, however, there was great fear that Dad's supervillain would appear—Patient Fiend—basically the Incredible Hulk in a hospital gown, who rises post-op, eyes bloodshot and totally disoriented, to mangle side rails, rip out IVs, and pull cords sparking from the walls. Patient Fiend then cuts a path of destruction through concrete block and out into the street where the bad guys can't touch him with bullets or the good guys with tranquilizer darts. He wreaks havoc across the country, would destroy the White House itself but for the person who can reach through Patient Fiend brain just in time.

Me.

And always the last shot: Patient Fiend walks off into the sunset with his loose hospital gown revealing his bare back and ass crack.

In general, there's not much to managing him. You engage in the conversations he starts, no matter how nonsensical.

"I've got to go—I've got to cultivate Haze's. That corn's gonna be too tall."

"I already took care of it."

"You did?"

"Yeah, don't you remember? You had the 4010 all ready to go for me."

There's also managing his impulses.

"Where am I?" he asked after the double knee.

"The hospital."

"Help me take these things off. They're damn hot."

Post-op, Dad had on full-cloth leg braces, from mid-thigh to low calf. He fiddled with them immediately when he came to, and we asked a nurse if we might take them off. No, she told us, it was imperative that they stayed on.

Here, then, was the task of Howard the High Guard: to keep those braces on.

"No, Dad, you've got to have those on."

"You gotta be kidding me."

"Sorry, doctor's orders."

"I got to get them off, just for a minute."

"Dad, leave them alone. Corn looked great this time through. Won't be able to get through it again. Way past knee high by the Fourth of July."

"Oh, come on. . . . Can't I take these damn things off?"

A night of waking sleep followed. Every time he agonized or fiddled with the Velcro, Howard the High Guard redirected. Finally, in the morning, a new nurse.

"How was his night?"

"Terrible. He wanted to take those braces off—his legs were so hot—but I got him to keep them on."

"Oh, he didn't need to have them on," she said.

This is Howard the High Guard's flaw. He doesn't double-check, doesn't assume alongside Patient Fiend that medical protocol is mostly bullshit. Howard the High Guard smiles and nods, absorbs the mistakes of others in outsized magnanimity, leaves Patient Fiend to suffer through the night.

I DIDN'T INTEND to read Laura Ingalls Wilder's *The Long Winter*. There's nothing less interesting to someone from the upper Midwest than a book titled *The Long Winter* when you suffer through one yearly, sometimes for seven months of the year. Then Caroline Fraser called it Wilder's masterpiece.

And gave the context for the book.

After ventures in the Big Woods, Plum Creek, and Indian Territory ended up under water, Charles Ingalls lit out for the territory once again, this time to Dakota Territory, settling outside De Smet, South Dakota, on the promise that it was prime wheat country.

It wasn't.

And of course the promisers said nothing about particulars, about the prairie Coteau, or the winters it could produce.

The De Smet winter that Laura Ingalls Wilder describes in *The Long Winter* sounds impossibly harsh, even by Upper Midwest standards, with blizzards roaring through twice a week for the entire winter. Then you quick google the winter of 1880-1881 and you realize, oh damn, *not* impossible.

The typical Wilder anecdotes are of another urgency in *The Long Winter*: barely making it home out of blizzard after blizzard, twisting hay to burn for heat, slaughtering the last of the stock with months of winter yet to go, eating seed saved for spring planting. Wilder narrates this slow slide with the darkest possibilities left unsaid, all while the family tries to outwait winter by playing parlor games. You can feel the mastodon of starvation moving beneath your feet as you read. It's horror masquerading as children's literature in that true-wonderful way of fairytales.

Turns out *The Long Winter* should be required reading for anyone living on the Coteau des Prairies, the great slide of land running across three states in the exact path of the predominant winds of winter. While we live on the eastern part of the Coteau, De Smet sits on the western part, perfectly set up to be cut off from the East and its supplies by the storms of winter roaring down the chute that is the Coteau. In the winter of 1880-1881, that's exactly what happened.

OUR LONG winter had a long run up. Already in the late summer of 1986, shit started to hit the fan. Dad stopped doing bookwork at the particleboard desk with the small fluorescent light because it "fried" him. Dad had meetings at banks from which he came home quiet. Mom and Dad increasingly talked in low voices in their bedroom, from which floated the word "California." That fall, for the first time Dad took a day job to try to supplement our income, running a backhoe for a neighbor, Dick De Jong.

The De Jongs had a big farm operation—the biggest equipment, a perfectly groomed farmstead complete with landscaped sign—that was also in financial trouble. So now Dick was trying to get into the earthmoving business to stay afloat, pairing a backhoe with his son's tiling machine, which everyone knew was the real moneymaker in the family.

In between trying to take the crop out, Dad spent days that fall running Dick's large backhoe, a "track excavator." In the evening, he told us tales of his work: how people remarked on his perfectly straight ditches, or how he almost buried the machine in water he had no business being in, or how he was digging ponds with islands in the middle expressly for nesting ducks—the money some people had for things. Dad took pride in ditch digging until early December when the frost set in and closed down operations till spring. Then he wandered around our empty farm buildings with banging doors and scuttling animal life. At night, he listened to the promises of California preacher Chuck Swindoll on his clock radio. We could hear it blare from their bedroom, punctuated inevitably by Dad's snores.

I don't remember selling the hogs but by the fall of 1986 they were all gone save a project or two to raise and slaughter for our own meat. Winter was always a problem for Dad's moodiness, but livestock had long ameliorated it. Grampa's answer to any kind of sickness had always been to just go to work. For Dad, the regular demands of milking probably did pull him through the hints of bipolar that had been there all his life. No matter if he was up or down or if the sun rose at 8:00 and set at 4:00, Dad had to milk. Hog chores were simpler, but they still had to be done. Now, with the animals gone, winter settled down around him.

That year Dad receded from Christmas. Mom was always the orchestrator of Christmas, of course, but Dad was the benevolence behind it, the Santa Claus with a belly laugh spreading good cheer. Before, there had always been a running joke about what I would get for Christmas, from Barbie dolls to a moldy fruitcake. Everybody got in on it, even Heidi. The night we opened presents, there it was, a traditional and partially eaten and solidly leaden fruitcake.

During the hard years, we agreed we had to do something else for Christmas, that Mom and Dad—and Lisa and her husband, who also farmed—could not afford regular gift giving. One year we set limits on what we spent, the next year we made gifts. I ended up "making" a birdfeeder for Thor, which meant I bought it and put it together, but still a gift I remember more clearly than any other one I gave between the ages of, say, 5 and 32.

After Christmas, in the dark days of January, when six o'clock might as well have been midnight, with no physical work to do, things really got dark for Dad.

So he turned where he always turned for hope: fishing.

OF COURSE, Patient Fiend predates Howard the High Guard.

"Are you scared of needles?" a nurse asks in the founding story of Dad in hospitals.

"Oh, deathly," Dad says. He's not, of course, but the nurse doesn't know this. He's got this falsetto shriek, part pheasant cackle, part crow-call. Dad's laying in the grass for her. The needle's going in; this is a big man, hands like a stone idol's; she can't read him.

He shrieks and she jumps, lifts off the seat opposite him. The needle comes out of the vein, the syringe clatters to the floor. Blood-spray. She turns away to compose herself over the sink. He knows he shouldn't have done it but God it was funny, God what a story it'll make.

Most recently, five years before Mayo, at the St. Joseph psych ward—after the seventy-two-hour lockdown in Worthington, after the nightmare stay at the state hospital, after he tried to pound his way out at St. Joe's—I spent a night with him. Everything had gone so badly that they had agreed to release Dad to Mom if he didn't have another episode. Carmen had been there; now it was my turn, Howard the High Guard, to walk him through the final stretch.

I had become scared of possibilities. He had never not listened to me, but I realize I couldn't take it if he didn't listen—if despite my stories to jog his memory, he tried to pound his way out again, to be gang tackled by men in white uniforms as I watched, helpless.

At 2:00 a.m., he stirred.

"You OK, Dad?"

"Howard. You here?"

"Yep. Go back to sleep now, OK?"

Instead he sat up in his tighty-whities and underwear tank top, grabbed his pants.

"Where you going?"

"It's time to get out of here."

"No it's not, Dad. It's the middle of the night."

"Well, you can stay here. I'm going."

"*Where* you going? There's no place to go."

He kept dressing.

"Dad, for real.

"Dad, you gotta stay with me, OK? I'm tired—I drove all the way up here and now I need to sleep. If you go, I gotta go with you and I am worn out."

"You don't gotta go with me."

"Yes, I do, Dad. You go, I go—and I don't wanna go."

He kept fiddling with his belt.

"I promise, in the morning I'll go with you, OK? But I'm tired now."

He yawned.

"See, you're tired too. In the morning Mom's coming and then we'll get out of here. Go fishing or something, OK?"

It did feel like a fishing trip, one that was ill-planned and overly hopeful, when Dad woke early and his putzing around had wakened me, and we would eat a hurried breakfast and then go.

He undid his pants to go back to bed.

"If you weren't here, I would go. Right now."

"Well, I am."

He laid down and was soon asleep.

I had won again.

But barely.

I didn't want to win anymore.

WE HAD NEVER been bitten by the ice-fishing bug like some people. I know fishermen who prefer the ice-fishing season to the regular season. Mostly, these men have wives that they prefer to be away from in the long darkness of winter. Ice houses may be the original man cave: a box set on the ice with a heater, a few folding chairs, some beer, and a deck of cards. You play cards and drink beer until the fish start biting, the paradise of *Grumpy Old Men*.

We didn't have a fish house, so it was just cold and miserable. Dad and I only went ice fishing a handful of times and fished out in the open, freezing our fingers and feet and starting the Scottsdale for warmth. I think we caught a grand total of two four-inch perch on these excursions.

So Dad tried another option. For two winters he worked with a commercial fishing operation run by a Catholic from Currie, Donnie LeClaire. When the ice got thick enough, LeClaire and his crew drilled holes around the perimeter of local lakes. Then, they dropped thousands of feet of net down one of the holes and moved it in a dot-to-dot pattern from hole to hole, lead line on the bottom, floats on top. With a huge perimeter circled, LeClaire's crew would hook the nets to an engine and start dragging it in beneath the ice. Near the shore, they'd cut a large hole where the final basket of the net would come through with, in theory, tons of fish.

Dad was hired to be one of this crew, earning minimum wage to help with various tasks related to setting and pulling in the nets. It was a big project, so big that it couldn't be done more than twice a week, and Dad was the low man on the totem pole of what was primarily a family business. It didn't do much more than add a little spending money to our family finances and get Dad out of the house.

But it was really cool.

Southwest Minnesota, with its shallow, flat lakes and high population of "rough" fish—carp and buffalo that stir up the mud bottoms and make life miserable for game fish—was perfect for this kind of fishing.

Dad got to wear a yellow rubber suit and waterproof gloves. He ran around doing odd jobs, from untwisting the net as it went into the water to passing the lead line from hole to hole. Once, using a heavy ice pick to reopen a hole, Dad broke through unexpectedly and lost the pick. He got swore at for that, he said. Another time a hole had gotten covered by snow and Dad went down, catching himself but not before he was wet to mid chest and cold to the bone. He spent the day warming up in a trailer they pulled on the ice for just such a purpose.

The days when it worked, when the nets didn't get hung up on rocks or tree branches, creating gaps for fish to escape, were amazing.

You could see the huge bodies of the carp underneath the ice as they accumulated into a tighter and tighter space. Some fish would trickle in throughout the day but then the last "bread basket" would finally come through and the net would be full to bursting with thrashing five-to-thirty-pound fish, a real miraculous catch of fish. Then the task was to remove the game fish with hand nets and return them to the water, sometimes with a DNR officer taking quick measurements. Once, on Bloody, Dad pulled out a 22-pound northern this way. "Boy, you should have seen that fish—it wrapped completely around me, all the way around my waist," Dad remembered. Afterwards, he always wanted to fish Bloody with the express goal of catching that fish.

Finally, with thousands of pounds of big-bodied carp and buffalo left, the LeClaire crew used a backhoe to scoop them out and put them on trucks headed for Chicago and the East Coast where, the rumor went, they were made into fish sticks.

But then, in mid-February, as the higher angle of the sun changed the quality of the ice, seining season ended.

That was when the first confession happened. We were having breakfast, just him and me. Mom was working her Saturday shift at Huisken Market in Edgerton, and Heidi was holed up in her room. I heard something and looked over at Dad. He was crying in his Cheerios.

"Oh, Howard—" he said, head in both hands, and sobbed once.
"What's wrong, Dad?" I asked.
"I'm—so—sorry," he gasped.
"For what, Dad?"
He couldn't speak.
"It's OK, Dad," I said. "Love you, Dad."

That winter Mom convinced Dad to see Dr. Becker, who gave him the bipolar diagnosis and put him on lithium.

Then, of course, he stopped going. It cost money, and anyway it was all in his head—all he needed was to go to work.

Problem was, there was nothing to do.

Howard the High Guard can't anticipate what the spinal tap at Mayo will be like. It's like labor and delivery, like a birth. A young blond doc has a syringe with an impossibly long needle. Dad lies on his side curled up in a ball. Mom and I stand at the head of his bed, call up consciousness in Dad's vacant eyes.

"They're going to take some fluid from your spine, OK, Dad? To see what's going wrong up in your brain. So you won't fall. So you can get your balance back."

"OK, this is going to hurt a little bit, Milton," says the Doc.

"Ow. Ow. Ow ow ow. Ouch! Ouch!"

"It's OK, Dad. Just hold still, OK?" I say. "It'll be over in a minute."

Except it won't be. The doc is fishing, casting and retrieving the needle, trying to find the clear water in the spinal column. He can't find it.

"Nope, that's not it."

"Oh! Ouch! Oh, Howard!"

Mom and I make vague promises around words like "sick" and "better" as he cringes, weeps.

"Hold still, Dad, almost got it."

"Oh that hurts! Why why why why?"

"Dad you're doing great—this is going to help you get better, OK? So we can go fishing again?"

"I need you to curl up just a little more, Milton, can you do that?"

"Dad, pull your knees up just a little more, OK?"

"I can't seem to—I'm going to try a longer needle."

This is getting medieval. Like an old-time extraction. Or exorcism via needle. Like we're trying to draw out the thing that feeds on him.

"OK, you're going to feel a little pain again, Milton."

"Owowowowowowow."

"I know it hurts."

"Why are you doing this?"

"OK, Milton, I need you to roll up just a little tighter—can you do that? Can you pull those knees up?"

"Dad, we need you to pull your knees up. You can do it. Almost done. I promise, OK?"

"I can't I can't I can't."

"Just a little bit—you're doing great."

"I'm sorry, Howard. I'm sorry. What'd I do? I'm sorry I'm sorry I'm sorry."

I don't know what else to say. I look to Mom, then the doctor. I want to call it off.

"Why, Howard, whywhywhywhywhy?"

THAT LONG WINTER of the first confession, the blizzards that buried us were psychological. As the days lengthened imperceptibly, Mom and Dad floated the question of how would we like to move to California? The plan was for Dad to go there to work for a season. They needed money and there were jobs there paying unbelievable wages. The trip would be exploratory for an actual move to California. Also, Dad was frighteningly depressed and Mom hoped that him being away, working and in better weather, would improve his mood. This last was left unspoken, of course.

Actually, I'm not sure moving was ever really a possibility. But Mom let Dad think it was, to make sure the trip happened.

He left in our two-tone, stick-shift Chevy Citation with red plush interior, accompanied by our neighbor, Corky Bootsma, a small man with slicked-back black hair, who had likewise fallen on hard times. In one of Corky's schemes to keep his farm afloat, he had showed up on our yard with a divining rod looking for oil; it led him to a spot right by our fuel barrel. We once would have thought Dad and Corky an odd couple. Now they were headed together out West.

Here's what I know of the California trip: Dad and Corky slept in the Citation at truck stops on the way out there to save money. In southern California, Dad got a job with a ready-mix business owned by a former hired man of his. The size of the gravel truck he drove had tires higher than his head, a scale we could scarcely imagine, verified by the pictures he sent. At night Dad slept in a sleeping bag in a company trailer, locked behind the chain link gates of the pit, occasionally doing his business in a five-gallon bucket as necessity dictated. At least five times a week he wrote letters to us by flashlight that showed up in our silver mailbox, sometimes two at a time, in which he apologized for his spelling at least twice per letter and asked us how we were doing and referred to the stock of jokes that we'd come to know by heart long ago. He also tried to shift our thinking to living out there, imagined him and me ocean fishing and catching bigger fish than we ever dreamed. I don't remember what he imagined for Heidi—maybe reading a book on the beach.

But I remember most the sound of his writing voice, a mixture of jokey and yearning, of the same old Dad yet heartbroken, there in a trailer at the bottom of a gravel pit.

As advertised, Dad made over twenty dollars an hour driving a gravel truck, an amount you simply couldn't translate to the southwest Minnesota economy, where minimum wage was $3.10. Near the end of his stay, he flew Mom out and they walked along the beach and maybe, with the trace of lithium carried on the ocean breeze, he actually felt calmer than he did back in Minnesota. He did not convince Mom to move.

Dad was gone just six weeks the winter of my fifth grade year, right during the time they showed the films about where pubic hair would grow and as the migraines I'd been getting became unbearable.

We counted down the days to Dad's return, the story of which is now part of family lore. Instead of sleeping in the car like we expected them to do, he and Corky drove through the night, arriving home early in the morning. When I heard his voice at breakfast that day, I made it down the stairs in record time.

"You heard my voice and you took those stairs five at a time," he recounts. "You couldn't wait to see your old man—you were down those stairs NOW!"

"That's it," says the young doc at Mayo, surprised and almost as relieved as we are, as if he were saving a career. "I got it. Lay real still Milton," he says with restored confidence, "this will be over in no time now."

Mom and I can't believe he's done it—Dad, I mean, can't believe he listened to us in his condition, curled up in the fetal position, in pain, crying out. I feel relief like I've felt only one other time: when I corralled him in Pipestone, when he was off his meds, a rogue bull ready to bolt, starting the whole state hospital mess. Now, it feels like everything has been riding on this one draw from the liquid stream of his body.

And now that we have it, it feels like another promise.

I grab Dad's thick shoulder, get close to his face where the wrinkles of his agony are still visible.

"Proud of you, Dad. You did it." I rub his buzz cut, flattened by lying in the hospital bed, his head dry with dandruff. "Love you."

And I hope against hope that it's the end of this long winter.

9

Pond Fishing

YOU'RE SIX YEARS OLD and Chicago O'Hare feels like purgatory. Too many people milling around in each other's smells as they await their final destination. You're bored and tired of chairs, and your sister's flight has been delayed a second time.

You've come to Chicago to retrieve your sister Carmen, who has been on a mission trip in Belgium through her Christian college. In the meantime, you got to see Aunt Lida with her bright lipstick and dark mascara and drawn eyebrows and flashy purses and big sunglasses and oversized gestures and love—"Oh, and Howard! How's my Howard? Are you happy to see Auntie Lida, to come all the way to Oak Park, Illinois? You know, I told my friend from church yesterday, 'Yes, and my nephew Howard is coming all the way from Chandler, Minnesota, to see me, and I'm going to give him a Dutch peppermint.' And Heidi, oh, how's my Heidi?"

But you've never seen so many people as there are in O'Hare and it turns out you *like* Chandler, Minnesota, where you live like you're the only people on earth and you are.

Then, Dad disappears. You know he's found someone to talk to because he loves talking to people with his opener, "What part of the world you from?"

Sure enough, you find him down the hall on a bench along the wall talking to a man in a head wrap. He is the first real person you've seen in a head wrap, and your first instinct is to pull Dad away, but he's fully engaged, a semi-smile on his face. He could sit here for eternity.

Even at the age of six, you know that this is Dad living out his credo, that all men are made in the image of God. That this conversation is the authenticating of Dad's faith, the evidence of his broad-minded, open character.

The story immediately becomes part of family lore: "Remember the time Dad disappeared in O'Hare and we found him talking to the Arab guy?"

"Yasser Arafat in a Pizza Hut tablecloth?" you and Heidi will say, after you start watching *Saturday Night Live*, knowing nothing about a keffiyeh or what it meant. "I remember that!"

AFTER THE spinal tap weekend, I return to Mayo on Tuesday evening to find a Somali man is the aide for the night. An aide watches Dad 24 / 7 to prevent him from trying anything crazy, but so far it's been only white men and women, and seeing the man's dark complexion, hearing his accent, and betting on his religion, I jump to conclusions: this is the perfect, xenophobic storm.

The man's name confirms my fears, "Zahib," very Muslim-sounding, especially to Mom and Dad, who bit hard on the mashup "Barack Osama."

"OK, Milton, your son is here now," Zahib says to Dad when he attempts to get up. Dad remains confused yet has the impulse to get out of bed and go who knows where. Fortunately, his declining motor skills make his efforts mainly ineffectual. "Excuse me, what is your name?" Zahib asks me in an aside. "Don't you want to sit back now, Milton, and talk to H*o*ward?" he asks, accenting the o.

This can't be going well.

THE WORLD I grew up in was approximately one hundred percent white, flavored barely by Asians, two adopted Korean girls that lived just down highway 91 and a Laotian refugee family sponsored by the Edgerton church we moved to after Leota Ebenezer.

The only way I learned anything about, say, Black people, was from eighties pop culture. Michael Jackson's *Thriller* left a deep impression on the junior highers at Leota Christian, which trickled down in the Reagan eighties all the way to me in first grade. From TV, I learned that white people could take in cute Black kids, like on *Different Strokes* and *Webster*, and that as a rural kid I was just a good old boy, never meaning no harm, like Bo and Luke Duke of *The Dukes of Hazzard*.

Oh, and from basketball. I loved Patrick Ewing's Georgetown Hoyas and the gray T-shirt he wore to sweat through under his jersey. But I loved the Los Angeles Lakers more. On Sunday afternoons in winter, as Dad snored away on the couch, I fell in love with Magic Johnson's smile and playing style, his no-look passes to Michael Cooper and Byron Scott for three, his gestures that isolated Kareem in the post before a perfect entry pass that Kareem finished with a skyhook. I imitated James Worthy's spin moves on my Nerf hoop. Even Kurt Rambis could be beloved as the super awkward token white guy.

Dad's formal instruction to me about race was, as far as I could see, noble. God made all men in his image, he told me earnestly, no matter what color they were—a man was a man.

But our household language use and jokes touched an older time. As in, I remember the word "darky" being used on occasion. As in, Dad had a joke about a "fat squaw." As in, Dad teased the older of the two Korean girls, whose name was Natalie, every time she got in the school van, "Well hi Sue! How are you today?" As far as I was concerned, it was equal-opportunity teasing. I'm not sure he knew either girl's actual name, but that would not have been expected of an adult white male in 1981.

In some ways, we were probably closer to the Ingallses on race than to Civil Rights. As in, Pa dons blackface at a town minstrel show and Laura tries to figure out who each "darky" on the stage is. As in, Ma resists her neighbor's assertion that "The only good Indian is a dead Indian," but just barely. As in, Pa promises to show Laura a "papoose."

Farther down highway 91, beyond the Korean girls' house, lived a friend of mine, Shane De Jong, Dick's grandson. I had first heard Shane's name via the prayer chain. In kindergarten, Shane had gotten ridden over by his second-grade brother Clark on the family's three-wheeler, the foot peg catching in Shane's mouth, ripping out his front teeth and breaking his jaw. It took several hours of surgery and several feet of wire to put his mouth back together. Shane spent his kindergarten year sucking his food through a straw.

About the time Shane joined my combined first- and second-grade class at Leota Christian School, his family moved to the acreage just off 91 and took their three-wheeler with them. I was thrilled.

The De Jongs got stuff, from the three-wheeler to illegal fireworks to the first Nintendo in the neighborhood. Hours of my life were spent watching Clark and Shane play *Super Mario Bros.* and *Kid Icarus*.

And they tried stuff. One day, Shane took me into their Quonset to show me a can with a shiny lid that he turned off slowly to reveal a perfectly groomed field of moist dirt. What was that? Copenhagen. Blink blink. Chew, like chewing tobacco. Oh, did Shane want me to try it? No—he himself didn't chew, just Clark. OK, actually he did chew, Skoal, which was mintier.

Later, Shane would show me a *Playboy*.

Later still, when his parents were away and left us with a babysitter, Heidi, we'd help ourselves to their parents' dedicated liquor cabinet.

In the space of the De Jong house we could imagine we were anyone. Inevitably, that meant we turned to playing basketball and pretending that we were the Lakers. Shane was always Magic and I was James Worthy, sometimes Byron Scott, never Kurt Rambis.

We had no idea that Earvin Johnson was from Flint, Michigan, or what that meant. He was just American. Anyway, Flint, Michigan, could be folded into LA by coolish white guys like Jack Nicholson and his snappy-dressing cousin on the bench, Pat Riley, the Lakers coach. This is where everyone would end up, we could believe, in a glowing multicultural paradise where the sun shone down on us all with smiling white teeth.

It was California dreaming. No matter what Shane and I played, whether Nintendo at his place or Hot Wheels at mine, we were playing California, imagining ourselves in a purely sunny place.

The first movie I saw in the theater without my parents was *Top Gun*, with Shane, a parable for Midwestern boys like us: through the Armed Forces, we, too, could make it to California.

"Ho, IS THAT Z good with Dad," Mom exclaims when Dad is sleeping and Zahib has stepped out for a moment. Because the name is difficult for them, Zahib has told them to just use the first letter, which Mom does gladly.

It's true. Z is the best at handling Dad yet, forthright and manly. Dad is putty in his hands. Even if Dad doesn't understand everything Z says because of his accent, he speaks authoritatively, jokes and prods Dad in all the right ways, using details from Dad's life that he's picked up from us.

"Milton, what do you need, Milton? Where are you going, Milton? There's nowhere to go. Not time to fish now—it's dark outside. We'll go in the morning. Sit here and have a nice conversation with your son." Dad circles, grasping bars and then bedsheets before he settles back again, dozes.

With Dad calm for most of the evening, Z turns to me. We talk about education and what it means to him. He works this job to support his family, to get his children a good education, which they are, he's making sure. We talk about authors I've been reading: Louise Erdrich, Junot Díaz, Toni Morrison, Li-Young Lee.

Z is amazingly personable. There's been trouble in the Somali community in Minneapolis, young men leaving the country to join al-Shabaab. I ask him about it, about the underlying problems of Somali communities there, if he's been treated alright. It's almost a non-issue to him. Z is studying, he's earning, he expects his children to do well in school, to go to college. He believes that because of the opportunity in the U.S., things will straighten out. It's only a matter of time, he says.

Maybe this is why Dad—even Dad in the birthday suit of his subconscious—is at ease with him: Z is the kind of man Dad admires, an American success story.

SOMETIME during the spring of 1987, we quietly sold our equipment.

"Here, you drive the 44 with the field cultivator to Slayton, and I'll pick you up in the pickup," Dad told me one morning. For a few days he'd been pulling equipment there, to a consignment sale scheduled for the upcoming week, but like with all my parents' financial dealings, we kids had to piece together the bigger picture: we were selling the equipment but would keep living in the house, essentially cut off from the land around us, unable to till or plant or harvest. So I climbed the steps of the 44, started it up to a sharp spout of smoke one last time, and down the road I went, the wide field cultivator winging behind me. Just before Chandler Hill, a semi passed me as I went by a mailbox. Afraid the semi would clip me, I opted instead for the mailbox, raking it off its post. When Dad picked me up in the Scottsdale, he'd been crying. I pretended not to notice, thought about that mailbox.

"Seeing you drive off in that 44," Dad would say later, "it about broke my heart."

That summer, the Lakers beat the Celtics.

Heidi and I spent more time playing Monopoly and watching the Lakers-Celtics rivalry in the eighties than almost anything else. As Dad cycled up and down, the Lakers-Celtics rivalry remained. I was all Lakers and Heidi was all Celtics. The contrast was stark. The Celtics were primarily white guys: the Hick from French Lick, Larry Bird, with his bad blond hair and mustache; the gangly-armed galoot Kevin McHale from Minnesota's own Iron Range; the weaselly-looking Danny Ainge from Eugene, Oregon; the freckled Dennis Johnson, like no Black person I could make sense of; and Robert Parish with his slow, clumsy style that I would have characterized in my infinite Midwest wisdom as more white than Black.

Even the dingy light of Boston Garden compared to the warm, sunshiny feel of the Forum spoke to the difference: white working class versus West Coast playground.

While the Lakers and Celtics battled it out on TV, Dad lay on the couch and snored. After Mom vetoed Dad's California dream, and Dad pulled out of the afternoon snoring pattern that would last for weeks, he was on the lookout for anything else. Dad was going to become a feed salesman or Dad was studying to get his real estate license or Dad was going to sell Herbalife, a line of holistic vitamins and health products, like Carmen's father-in-law. These new, outsized hopes would give Dad energy for a few days until the next time Mom would whisper, "Dad's down again," and we would tiptoe around while listening to him snore at odd hours of the day.

But in early summer, Dad got a job trucking for Bayliner boats, driving little snub-nose trucks that pulled blue fretwork trailers stacked with sleek white-and-blue speed boats.

With Dad gone for big chunks of a fortnight, a crisis in fishing arose. What would I do while he was away? I could fish on my own, he insisted. I knew everything he knew. I could have Mom take me to any of the local ponds we fished whenever I wanted.

As the walleye curse endured, pond fishing had risen in importance for Dad and me. The Cashier in the Sky apparently didn't care if we caught bass and northern and sunnies, as long as it wasn't walleyes.

Actually, there was a pretty rich pond-fishing culture in 1987. There was Chandler Pond, like a mountain lake in miniature, created when somebody thought to put a dam between the hills above Chanarambie Creek. Braving the bull, we'd walk through the cow pasture to fish along the weeds in the way back. Two times one June, I pulled a yellow-eyed beetle spinner and caught a three-pound largemouth bass that danced across the dingy water.

And Johnny De Groot's pond, the same pond-in-the-hills concept on the other side of Chanarambie Valley, fenced off from cattle but with cattail sentinels surrounding the pond on all sides. Someone had cut designated fishing spots into these cattails, where Dad and I spent hours catching big sunfish with deep orange suns under their throats. The whole setting at Johnny's was alive. Red-wing blackbirds trilled and chirped at us angrily, ticks stalked our legs by the dozens, and snapping turtles haunted our stringer, stealing bites out of the sunnies like they were soft cookies. At sunset, muskrats and beavers crossed the pond on their evening commutes and deer stopped to watch us from the hillside.

And there was Van Hulzen's irrigation pond, just off a tributary of the Rock River, where Dad's fishing buddy Johnny Hofkamp had supposedly caught an eighteen-pound northern. We drove through a gravelly part of the nameless creek that fed the pond to get to it. That pond was clearer than the other ponds, so you could see the northerns trail or even strike. We always took an eater or two home from Van Hulzen's, two-to-three pounds each.

Now Dad was deputizing me to fish without him in my favorite corners of Buffalo Ridge.

"And what if I catch anything, what about filleting it?"

"Well, you've watched me plenty of times."

MOM AND DAD distrusted the long-distance trucking life. When you weren't there for your kids, they believed, things went bad. Trucking was a potential move down in class, they also believed, not necessarily financially but because of the rootless life the road turned you towards—irregular church attendance plus exposure to greater temptation equals broken-down morality. Dad would make sure to counteract this tendency by calling home faithfully and by the push-pin map he would put up in the kitchen, to show us where he was going, where he had been. In the summer, he'd take us along on trips, to share his life with us and prove that, "See? I'm still me, moral family man."

I went on a few trips with Dad. On one, we went south to Oklahoma. When I got out of the truck in Missouri, I was stunned that we had driven into another accent, smitten with the waitress because of it.

Another time we went to northern Minnesota, Grand Rapids, where a bat flew into our motel room. When Dad turned on the light, it sat on the wall, a small mouse with wings, and Dad grabbed it with some clothes and smashed it on the floor.

Once we went east, to Rochester, New York. On that trip, Dad's fears of the road were made manifest. Dad was talking over CB to guy at a stoplight who looked down into the car next to him and said over the radio, "Wow, she could breastfeed twins." Before he replied, Dad said to me, "See how they talk?"

When Dad was gone during the summer of sixth grade, I pond fished and hung out at the De Jongs's a lot, especially when Heidi babysat them.

That spring, the farm economy continued to plummet and hair bands continued to rise. The Jim Bakker / Jessica Hahn affair had given a black eye to the church, and the Iran-Contra affair was dragging on on afternoon TV.

Mostly, Shane and I drove around the countryside on their new four-wheeler. We went to St. Kilian where Shane bought chew "for my dad; he's in the field." Then, we went from one abandoned farm place to another, moving the forts where we hung out and where the De Jong brothers and my cousin Drew chewed the St. Kilian chew. We sang parts of Mötley Crüe's *Girls, Girls, Girls* and Guns N' Roses *Appetite for Destruction*. We repeated parts of *Eddie Murphy: Delirious* and *Good Morning, Vietnam* and Andrew Dice Clay's nursery rhymes ("Mary, Mary, quite contrary, shave that pussy, it's so damn hairy"). We told and retold stories that we heard about high schoolers. The basketball team that watched *Stand By Me* and then went out and played actual mailbox baseball. The brothers who would leave the house with a pool stick and tell their mom they were "going wrecking," and her response, "Just don't get caught."

My favorite among these characters was my cousin Lance, from Mom's side. Once, I drove to Luverne with Heidi and Lance in the Chevette, and Lance flipped off every car we met. Later, Lance and another kid, bored and looking for adventure, sprayed fire extinguishers around their church, causing damage in the thousands of dollars.

Then there were the non-jocks. The kid who peed in the open window of an unoccupied cop car. The same kid found a sledgehammer in the back of a parked pickup and put it through the front windshield. The boys who were out selling Bibles—*Bibles*—but, when they didn't find a family at home, threw a brick through their large picture window. The public brawls out front of JJ's drive-in, like a real-life Greasers versus Socs, where the owner of JJ's had to knock out the baddest bad boy, Dirk Van Dyke, with a ball-peen hammer.

So when the De Jongs's parents left for an entire week for a reason I don't remember—most likely for their own exploratory trip to California—and employed Heidi as babysitter, we were poised for our own eighties escapades.

We helped ourselves to the liquor cabinet, sipped at rum and Cokes, tried tequila and vodka. We watched *Stripes*, rewinding the parts with nudity. Clark had stolen the *Playboy* 35th anniversary edition from Cover to Cover in the mall, and we passed it around, a catalogue of breasts through the years. On one page, with a particularly unglamorous pose, Drew pointed to the woman's labia and said, "That's where you nail her."

It was Jessica Hahn.

Later, Shane's mom found the *Playboy*, they got in trouble for it, and she promised to tell his dad. After that, she put it between the mattress and spring in their bedroom, which was where we retrieved it from when they weren't home.

I finally tried Copenhagen in the fort by the old Vanden Berg place, the Vanden Bergs having left for California. It made me lightheaded, and I barfed up the microwave pizza I had eaten for lunch.

MOM LIKES Z so much she makes sure to stop at the nurse's station to give her compliments to the chef. We ask Z as he leaves his shift whether he can be assigned to Dad's room again, but apparently that's not how it works. We don't see him again.

The next night, we have a Somali woman who wears a hijab. She's not as good, meaning that she's not what Z was, a male of a certain type. My family's reviews of her are that she's nagging, meddlesome, just not as good as Z, for whom we pine.

I GOT SHANE to go fishing with me. We schemed taking the three-wheeler all the way to Chandler Pond, but in the end Mom dropped us off. We went to our spot in the back but only caught one modest-sized perch, which we kept because that was the point to fishing for me then, to keep stuff.

I filleted it on the white drain board in the basement bathroom, like I had seen Dad do: slicing behind the head down to the spine; slitting the belly all the way to the anal fin, then carving down along the dorsal fin and over the rib cage. It was painstaking. It was like painting. It took me the better part of an hour to fillet one fish.

I would have my first kiss at Chandler Pond the following summer. I told my parents I was going fishing with my friend Chad, the preacher's kid; he told the same lie in reverse. The mom of my eighth grade girlfriend picked us up, and we dug worms at her uncle's squalid farm and camped out on blankets up near the road end of Chandler Pond—the opposite end from where Dad and I usually fished. Eventually, we coupled off and when my girlfriend—we'll call her Heather—looked deep into my eyes, I knew it was time. We kissed for like a minute. I checked my dobber as an excuse to stop. She broke up with me later that summer.

I pond-fished in response. Pond-fishing was a thing you could count on. Up in the hills above the valley road, or in the ponds along simple streams, there were fish, and you could spend hours there as the sun set with only the threats of bulls in the pastures and ticks in the grass, your whole consciousness taken by the scene, a teeming creation, and the hope that bobbed at the end of a monofilament line, even here, on the flat of the prairie.

NAPPANEE, INDIANA, became a place of promise on Dad's push-pin map. Nappanee was the location of another boat plant owned by the Brunswick Corporation, the parent company of Bayliner, where they made Blue Fin, a brand of fishing boats. Almost from the start, Dad's goal in working for Bayliner was to buy a Blue Fin at wholesale, an employee perk.

Dad had told me all about Nappanee, mainly stories about the Amish, how dangerous their buggies were for him as a truck driver and how they often ended up in deadly accidents. When we got to the plant, Dad showed me the different boats they made and his favorite, the 1706. Then we went to check in at a cheap hotel.

The place had a strange smell to it, smoky and thick. A South Asian couple were working behind the desk. When we got to the room, Dad said, "I thought already this place was run by some of them people—that's what they call sand n—. You smell that? They stink."

I was shocked, embarrassed, but I said nothing. The road really was changing Dad, I thought that night as we snuggled down into white sheets that smelled musky if clean, darkness settling around us.

THE TOWN celebration in Edgerton is called the Dutch Festival, and in the 1980s that still meant two midweek nights of parades and a midway where you could ride the Scrambler, Trabant, Tilt-a-Whirl, and a legit Ferris wheel. You could also play carnival games, the most popular of which was throwing ping pong balls into a pyramid of stacked beer glasses: fifty cents got you three tosses; land one in a glass and it was yours.

For the first time that summer, the Dutch Festival also featured a fishing contest at Chuckie's Pond, around which the city had built a park. I was thrilled. I had heard there were northerns in that pond, as well as good-size bass, and I schemed with my friend Chad how I was going to win it.

I would diversify bait, taking both the night crawlers I had scavenged off the lawn after a rain and the minnows I had discovered in a neighbor's minnow trap since our branch of the Champepadan had almost completely dried up that year. I would have a variety of rigs on a sampling of rods: a Lindy Rig to get down to the bottom but also a casting rod to try both twisters and spoons. I knew ponds. In a pond that small, I could fish every possible square inch.

When Chad and I got to the contest, we found it crawling with dads and their five-year-olds catching tiny bluegills a foot from shore. When someone caught a six-inch bullhead and figured they had it won, I grabbed the casting rod and snapped on the five-of-diamonds. On my third cast, I felt an unmistakable strike and saw a white flash out over the middle of the pond. My stomach jumped.

Mom was our chaperone and played her part perfectly. "Got something, How?" she asked when she saw my rod bend, then, "Oh shoot, a snag." I doubted for an instant myself, but felt the rod pulse in a way that I knew meant not only a fish but a big fish. The line moved across the pond, and when the drag sang Mom knew her mistake. We had no dip net along, but someone else offered Chad theirs, and when it came close, a big northern, he reached as far out as he could, but the fish saw the net and ran. On the next pass, Chad just got it over the lip, but the net was small and cheap and not made for a fish this size. The fish threw the lure just as several loops disconnected from the net, and the northern slipped through the gap and into the water. Chad jumped in after it, new Nikes and all, grabbed it around the middle and heaved it onto shore before it could flash away.

We hauled it up to the shelter to register as little kids and their dads looked on agog. Chad and I high-fived. I was all adrenaline, rubbing my hands compulsively. It weighed in at 7 pounds, 7 ounces. Not only had I won the grand prize, a Daiwa rod and reel combo, I was a Chuckie's Pond fishing legend.

Dad was trucking somewhere out East. When he called, I recounted the story for him in every detail and asked him what to do with the fish itself. Though I had filleted the perch, a northern would be a harder challenge. Plus, I wanted him to see it, so he told me to gut it and wrap it in plastic and freeze it; then we could show other people, too.

I gutted it on the white drainboard of the basement bathroom. Pulling out the long intestines, I found a stone the size of a quarter. This was a pond fish, desperate and reactionary. Unable to resist the rock thrown by some kid on the shore, the impulsive pike had inhaled that rock as it trickled tantalizingly down to the bottom. Had I not caught it, the fish would have probably died anyway.

This was the danger of a closed system.

After the fish was gutted, it didn't look quite right. For several weeks I retrieved it from the freezer to show stiffly to my sisters and other guests, and it looked smaller every time. Then we finally thawed it and Dad filleted it and we ate it, flaking the meat off piece by piece so we didn't choke on the y-bones.

10

Prayer Bouquet

ON THE NEUROLOGY wing, the results of the lumbar puncture are back. No Lewy bodies. It's good news of a sort, but it doesn't feel like it.

Dad's going fast. So fast that he can no longer feed himself. It has been painful to watch him try for a while now, his grasping fingers sending a spoon mouthwards as he leans forward and reaches out with his tongue. And when he drinks anything, he's sputtering badly, coughing shallowly to get the liquid out of his air passage, coughing and coughing.

After more than a week at St. Mary's, we're two MRIs and a lumbar puncture to the good, we're large motor skills, fine motor skills, chewing and swallowing to the bad.

All that's left is a diagnosis *via negativa*: Hashimoto's encephalopathy. The message comes down that they will start the steroids.

I voice my concerns to Carmen, that this feels like a problem with no solution, an inevitability, the abyss. She says, "Well, we've got to pray. Do you have anyone praying?"

"Yes," I half lie.

ONE AFTERNOON when I was ten, I came home from school to find a John Deere tractor and scraper pan working in the bottom below our farm, cutting a smooth ditch straight back from the bridge over Champepadan Creek.

It was the Wierengas, Uncle Klaas's boys, of course.

What were they doing? I asked Dad.

"Moving that crick over," came the reply.

The Wierenga boys had added earth-moving equipment to their arsenal. That way they could cut the land into flat, straight shapes to farm more easily with their other big equipment. It was just Monopoly—owning more and more of the means of production—and my cousins were ahead of the game.

"Why?"

"Well, to improve that land," he said. "Then I can farm it."

Without the finances to buy or rent more land, Dad was landlocked. Making the crooked straight was one of his last attempts to stay in the game a few more rounds. Straightening the Champepadan had been his idea.

I felt betrayed, Dad trading the sharp, quick cut of the creek where Heidi and I got leeches between our toes for maybe three acres of land.

Had I looked up from the bridge, I could have seen evidence of other shortcuts Dad had taken.

The open door of the freestall barn out of which Dad shoved manure, where it inevitably drained into both Champepadan Creek and our well. From the bridge, that door looked like a maw drooling chew spit.

Or perhaps a trail of smoke from the burn pile and that age-old practice of burning garbage, including plastic herbicide and pesticide containers that poured a chemical cocktail into the air that your lungs would tell you was straight up evil.

But changing the creek got my attention. The digging stopped after maybe a day and a half, just yards short of the creek, a perfectly benign, round-shouldered ditch.

"Why didn't they finish it?" I asked Dad.

"The water will find its way into that new ditch over time."

"But won't the old crick be too rough to farm?"

"We'll smooth it out."

It's not much land, I thought.

He never got to farm it.

Not long after, we broke with Uncle Klaas, and Uncle Hein, too.

What happened was this. Uncle Hein, the Chicago Board of Trade player, knew an opportunity when he saw one. With land prices in the shitter, Uncle Hein and Uncle Klaas could step in and save Hank Schaap's farm—especially since Milt had run it into the ground. They had all the money together, even approached the bank without Dad's knowing. Uncle Hein would buy the land, and Uncle Klaas would farm it, and they would free Milt of the farm that had been such a burden to him.

Only after the bank turned them down did they approach Dad about it. And they used Lida, Dad's favorite sister, who had so often rocked him to sleep as a baby, to do it. To him, it was the great betrayal, the kiss of Judas.

At least, that's how Dad told the story ever after, that his siblings "had tried to buy the farm out from under him." It may have been paranoia on his part, or it may have just been eighties economics—hostile takeovers, Midwest style.

Then again, we'd played enough Monopoly to understand Dad's anger. When someone buys St. Charles Place out from under you, the one corner of the Monopoly board you were trying to develop, you don't thank them. And if they tell you it's for your own good, well, hell. . . . We sided with Dad against our Schaap relatives.

And the walls of our isolation pulled in just a bit closer.

AT THE SUPPER table one night when I was about twelve, Dad turned to me and told me that he would no longer be praying before our family meals. Considering the fact that, breakfast aside, he had prayed at virtually every family meal of my life up to that point, this was a significant announcement. Prayer could become just a rote exercise, went his explanation, and he didn't want to fall into the trap of the Pharisee in the parable, praying empty words. "It's not that I've stopped praying," he insisted. "You guys don't know how hard I pray." He intimated that praying was what he was doing before he fell asleep in front of his blaring clock radio at 9:30 in the evening, snoring profoundly, and when he woke up at 11:00 and couldn't sleep for much of the night.

I remember nodding silently, fervently. His logic satisfied me entirely then. In fact I saw it as somewhat noble. And so his deep bass went silent at the table. Silence had become an official position. It may have felt like his only option. Dad had seen the writing on the wall in regard to farming for years: the mountain of farm debt he had taken on; the affliction of disease in his dairy herd; the drop in commodity prices due to international politics. These developments might have not left a mark on Dad's spiritual life, however, if they hadn't correlated to his theology. If a man in the church sat in judgment upon him, Dad could cling to the Gospels, which championed the humble over the hypocrite. But when Republican President Ronald Reagan declared via policies and public statements that Milton Schaap as a marginal operator should be sacrificed to agricultural efficiency, well, that was some Romans 13 shit—submit to the ruling authorities and all that. There was no end around on that.

Protest? Protest was incommensurate with his faith.

A strange position to take for a Protestant from the *Afscheiding* ("secession") tradition. Just a few generations earlier, our landless ancestors had railed against the unholy alliance of church and state. But strong new alliances had been drawn between Leota and the land of the free, home of the brave, alliances forged by the right to run their own schools, and cast in blood by the sons who fought two world wars to secure that right. After the wars, the people of Leota threw in firmly with the Republicans, not the DFL—Democratic-Farmer-Labor Party—because the Republicans kept the appropriate distance from their schools and their land. The new country had been all the Dutch settlers had hoped, and by the eighties, Leota patriotism ran strong, evidenced by the annual Fourth of July parades morning and evening, down Main Street, with fireworks after dark.

Mom and Dad talked in low tones about what some farmers were doing, showing up in large numbers at foreclosure auctions and intimidating would-be buyers into not bidding, leaving the banks holding the bag: a movement called Groundswell.

That was sinister, Mom and Dad made clear—shady, not right. Look what had already happened only twenty miles north of us, in Ruthton, where a father and son had lured two bankers out to their farm at sunset and shot them both. In a town of 467 like Ruthton, these were not faceless stuffed shirts but church members and neighbors.

The perpetrators fled to Texas where the father shot himself later that week; the son turned himself in to authorities.

No, when the sovereign God of heaven and earth has your failure written in the cards via a Republican president, even if that president was a ridiculous movie actor, what were the options? Not protest. And lament was not in our vocabulary then either. Only silence.

The loss of Dad's prayer voice was an absence, like losing one of your senses. Or like a three-legged table; you suddenly became aware of imbalance, that Dad's bass had buoyed up so much of your world.

Meanwhile, between trips to the bank and overheard claims from the relatives that Dad had "run away with the deed," a deal was struck. Dad worked out some calculus to secure the farm, "secure" being the exact wrong word. No doubt he mortgaged it out to his ninetieth year of life. We got to keep the land, but we would never actively farm again. Dad enrolled as much as he could in a government program called the Conservation Reserve Program or CRP (somewhere in greater Chicago, Uncle Hein sniffed at the handouts all these farmers got while he got nothing), rented out the rest to a neighbor, and hit the road trucking for Bayliner Boats.

I love the story of the CRP for how eighties-nonsensical it is, for how it involved us in the Cold War, and for how it transformed our farm.

A decade earlier, Secretary of Agriculture Earl Butz's decree to farmers to "get big or get out" and to plant "fencerow to fencerow" meant that corn and soybeans and bigger John Deere equipment had won the day. Increasingly large green tanks drove through fields to fill "silos" and "bunkers" with only two crops, corn and soybeans. Never again would the Schaap farm see something as exotic as flax if Butz had his way; it would be all corn and soybeans all the time.

When farmers balked at the idea of maximal production, citing the horrors of the Dust Bowl that were still precise and luminous in their parents' memories, Butz promised to find an overseas market to keep prices high, and found it in the least likely of partners: the Soviets. Not very *Red Dawn* of him. By the late seventies, the Russkies were a significant new trade partner propping up the commodities market. Then they went and got involved in Afghanistan, and President James

Earl Carter kept the Olympic team home and declared a grain embargo, famously "weaponizing" grain against the Red Threat. Prices dropped. Not to worry, went the party line, borrow now so that when prices come back. . . . Meanwhile, news reports showed sweeping shots of mountains of grain piled up at ports, rotting.

And there went Carter.

Enter Ronald Reagan, allowing the "invisible hand" to trim those producers the government had been "unable to protect from themselves," and with the other hand, writing off debt for farmers deemed too big to fail.

Then, the eighties reversal: when the left-behind started to protest, and when farmers started to shoot themselves and especially when farmers started to shoot bankers, and when Willie Nelson took Farm Aid on the road, and when it started to look bad for the next election cycle, then the Reagan Administration itself resorted to some serious subsidy-handout-welfare action. The CRP program came out of the 1985 farm bill—the "Food Security Act"—and paid farmers to sow marginal land in a mix of grasses and leave it alone for up to seven years, with the government paying the farmer up to fifty percent of what the land would have yielded in crop value.

So, after the straight lines and big equipment had carried the day, after the fields went all narrow-ruled and even the original linefences that had choked the prairie were removed, then did Dad give up on straight lines altogether. He sowed as much of our farm in CRP grasses as he could, all the sandy knolls above both branches of Champepadan Creek. He rented out the rest to a neighbor, spurning our cousins because of the plot Uncle Klaas had supposedly been involved in.

Now I know things weren't that simple. Then we were totally and completely in Dad's corner against his "enemies." His sanity seemed to depend on it.

Even now, I have the instinct to side with Dad. Whatever the real case regarding politics and write-offs and double-crosses, there *was* a hand on the scale tipping toward big operators and, more importantly, there was no solidarity between farmers when we could have used it most. That was partly because of Dad's paranoia, partly because of blind loyalty to Monopoly itself—maximize what you can get, other players be damned—and partly because the solidarity—and protest—of that *Afscheiding* community, the tiny towns of Leens and Ulrum, had been lost.

But history was also repeating itself in Reagan's rhetoric, echoing that of Governor Pillsbury after the 1870 grasshopper plagues. Poor farmers were problems. Not self-reliant. Indolent.

The 1980s labels divided farmers against themselves. Bad operators and good. Protesters and obey-ers. Foreclosed upon and forgiven.

At least enough hell was raised in the 1980s to give us CRP, a windfall for me. The year we mortgaged our humble Monopoly property, scrambling to just stay in the game a few more turns, that year a tangle of sweet clover grew up along the Champepadan, in white and yellow flowers in summer that turned to a dark, clotted tangle in fall and winter.

It was beautiful and chaotic.

Then the pheasant population also sprouted.

ONE AFTERNOON that fall, Dad pushed himself up from rip-snoring sleep, and, bloodshot-eyed and gravel-voiced, said I should follow him. He dug a fat tin can out of a bag in the basement, pulled his .410 from the closet, and grabbed a box of shells. I carried the gun as we walked back behind what was to have been the new freestall barn for his modern dairy, and along the tangled grove of the original homestead to the grove of row trees that Dad had planted to be the new boundary of the farm. A wind bullied us from the northwest, the bare branches wagging their fingers at us. The landscape opened up here, offering us a clear view of Champepadan Creek below and the fields surrounding it.

The creek drew the eye naturally north where it angled around a flat, roughly square field of twenty-five acres or so. In my lifetime, this field had been alfalfa, had been corn, had been oats. Going far enough back to Grampa's shrewd move, it had been flax.

Now this field, a flat sandy knoll just above the creek, as well as the slopes of hills on either side, were a tangle of brown sweet clover.

Dad instructed me on loading the .410. The lip where the shell was supposed to hook was worn from a lifetime of use, and he showed me how the shell could slip past that lip and create a potentially dangerous situation. I fitted the metal edge of the shell carefully and clicked the gun shut. Then he showed me how to pull the hammer back and how to ease the hammer off again. The hammer, too, was worn. That was another dangerous part he said, because if the hammer slipped, the gun would go off when you weren't expecting.

"OK, pull your hammer back and aim," he said. "I'll throw the can and you follow it and shoot it."

"What? You want me to—do I aim right at it?"

"Yep, just look down your barrel and the can should set right on top of your bead."

"On top?"

"Yep, your BB pattern will spread a little bit when you shoot. Ready?"

I wasn't but nodded. When you're given a gun by your father and told to shoot it, that's what you do. The can spun skyward and then quickly back down, gravity's law and the wind's urging forcing it in a very specific arc with a list to the right. I didn't shoot.

"That's—that's quick."

"Yep, you got be ready."

Dad walked after the can and tossed it up again. I shot quickly this time and missed.

On the third throw I saw the flipping can at the end of my bead, pulled the trigger without thinking. The can shot forward wildly from its regular arc.

"Nice shot!" Dad said, as if he hadn't actually expected me to hit it, as if I was a lot closer to something than he had reckoned on. I set the gun down and ran to retrieve the can. It was flattened, oblong holes torn in its side where BBs had ripped it open.

Below us, a pheasant flushed from the tangle of sweet clover in the CRP and rode the wind down to the long grasses along the creek bank, its cackle trailing behind it.

I WINGED MY first pheasant while hunting with friends in the CRP on the Vis quarter. That quarter had been sowed in mainly brome, for some reason, not sweet clover, which made it much easier to walk, and when the bird burst cackling out of that light grass and banked left, I tracked it down the length of my single-shot twenty gauge and squeezed the trigger. The bird's left wing buckled but it held it in place defiantly, drafting enough air to waver down to the plowed ground below but without any real control. It bounced twice, hard, but kept its wits enough to run pell-mell across the plowed rows of shiny-backed dirt in the plowed field below. I chased it for a quarter mile on pure adrenaline, heart beating in my neck and armpits, stopping once to reload my gun and fire at it as it ran but only peppering the soil behind it. The bird headed for the creek where it entered the deep cover of canary reed grass and cattails. I laid my gun down in a place I thought I'd be able to find it again and then started turning over armfuls of grass. I wasn't a seasoned enough hunter to realize the odds against finding this bird. The God-awful gaudy apparel of a rooster pheasant, the court jester of birds, should be impossible to hide in the tans and browns of fall grasses.

It's not. This is the miracle. Pheasants that are winged just hunker and run. Or, if you've undered the bird, merely split one of its sinewy dinosaur legs, it will just hunker. The odds are perhaps better of finding a hunkering bird over a running bird but they're still not good. Not without a dog.

I worked back and forth on this side of the Champepadan, first randomly, then, once the adrenaline settled out of my system, systematically, working toward the creek, where, pushing aside an armful of canary reed that grew right down at the water's edge, I saw it, sitting in the actual water of the creek. It was a dry year that year, so dry that the creek had stagnated, and my pheasant sat with its auburn shoulders and neck above the surface of the water. It watched me with its unblinking yellow eye, counting on its stillness. I extended my hand slowly, like in cartoons, then snatched it around the neck and swung, spinning the flapping bird and breaking its neck, holding it until the last paroxysms of wing flaps subsided, its eyes squeezed shut and beak opened.

It *had* been fated, and, once I located my gun, I was a happy conqueror, high on adrenaline, already shaping in my mind the story I would tell about the bird that took refuge in the creek.

It was the fall of 1988 and I had just turned thirteen. I'm not sure if Dad was there or not.

I wasn't surprised when Mom asked me one night to put the guns upstairs. I knew it was part of the story. The trend was in the news. Farmers were killing themselves left and right; hotlines had been set up. We had been to see the farm crisis movie, *Country*, where I kept expecting to find the farmer swinging in the barn. It was that central to what was happening. It's what you did on the prairie, I knew then intuitively.

"Say, How, come here a minute once," Mom started. "Dad's really down. I'm sure he wouldn't do anything but—do you know where the guns are?"

Of course I did.

"OK, well, like I say, I don't think he would do anything, but I know he wouldn't if the guns were upstairs, by you. He loves you too much, OK? Is there somewhere you can put them?"

I nodded, moved quickly, padded downstairs on bare feet over the cool cement steps. The first trip I brought up the grooved Winchester .22 pump and Grampa's 12-gauge: the .22 for crows and flickertails and plunking pheasants out of the air when Uncle Hein missed; the 12-gauge that Dad had smuggled out of the house one Sunday afternoon when he was twelve by sticking it down his pant leg to shoot in the pasture with Don DeBoer—kicked so hard it set him on his ass. On the next trip it was the .410, which he was still a good shot with, and my 20-gauge from Christmas last year. I set them upright on the candy-striped carpet in the corner of my closet, crept back down to the crack of light in the bathroom. I told Mom the thing was done, and she gave me a hug. I went back up to my room where the guns stood with their stories in the closet.

I laid down in bed, a human shield, and said a prayer that wasn't a prayer but a curse. The tears were hot in my eyes.

I, too, could retreat into silence.

It's easy for Carmen to say, "We've got to pray." She's good at it, confident and eloquent, respecting that mysterious boundary that is God's will, yet still somehow believing she can move him to act.

Because he is loving and she is sincere. In leaving Leota, this is one of the things she left behind: the uber-predestinarianism that leaves you wondering what—if God is infinitely more moves ahead of you in the game—the goal of praying is.

Sure, I've been praying for Dad, though I'm not sure what I'm supposed to pray. I default to "be with him," try for better, "work through the doctors to heal him," try to get specific, "may they balance his meds to calm his mind." These are tossed up as I think of them, in passing, and mostly melt into a kind of "please, please, please, Lord, please."

For other pray-ers, I have told exactly one person, a guy who catches me off guard after church, asks me how it's going. Maybe because he's not a local but married into the area, I outline the details of Dad's situation for him. It's more than he bargained for, though he's sympathetic.

Of course, I haven't brought Dad as a prayer request to my minister that the church might pray. Too embarrassing. This, too, is a symptom of mental illness. Then again, manic depressive is not a label you want attached to yourself or your family, a boundary you don't want to lay down.

No, the people I have praying are my prayer mercenaries, my children.

When I get back home with the diagnosis, Hashimoto's encephalopathy, I kneel down at my daughter Sommer's bed.

"How's Grandpa Milt doing?" she asks.

I've forgotten by now, twenty-five years later, Dad's tendencies as he prayed, his speech patterns, the familiar ruts his language fell into. I think he typically announced "Shall we pray" beforehand, and already in that introduction his voice shifted into a lower register with a timbre that I will always associate with the sacred. I've also forgotten what he prayed about most, whether people in hospitals or missionaries, whether he "theed and thoud" or used "grant us what we stand in need of" or "keep us in thy tender care." I think he was a formal pray-er, the formality appropriate for the dependency of sinners upon the grace of God.

It's not that he hasn't prayed publicly since then, but it's not the same as it once was. His prayers are more self-conscious and wavering.

He got out of practice, out of the rut, and never got back in. But the timbre is still there; I feel it like an ache when he does pray.

"The same. He couldn't walk and could barely swallow because of inflammation in his brain. Now they're going to give him medicine that could make him agitated and aggressive."

"Oh. So what do we pray for?"

"Just . . . pray that the doctors will be able to balance his medicines."

"Dear Lord, thank you for this day," she begins. She thanks God for the recent rains to bless the crops, though it's been predominantly rainy and we could really use sun. She thanks God that her dance recital is coming up and for all the talents he's blessed her with.

Well, at least she's not self-deprecating. Yet.

"Please forgive me when I pout and don't listen to my parents."

Oh man.

"Please be with Grandpa. Help the doctors to balance his meds so that he's not so aggressive. Lord, please just give him peace."

Yes, Lord, please just give him peace. Peace above all.

I know it's a mistake to think that prayer can be new and authentic every time; I know it's a mistake to think that beautiful words shaped into lyrical praise or effective arguments move God more than other kinds of prayer; I know from experience that often it's the practice of prayer itself, the timbre you get used to hearing in another's voice, that matters; I confess that my own personal prayer life is almost nil, that I've been putting needs and words into the mouths of my own children and having them pray for me, but as Sommer prays for Dad's peace on this night, she also grants me mercy.

This, too, is the grace of God.

ONE NIGHT that first fall of the CRP, a few of us got together to hunt the Vis quarter: my neighbors Shane and Clark and me and Chad, maybe others I've forgotten. We drove out there on Clark's farm permit, like anyone would be checking licenses on the backroads of Moulton Township. We made plenty of racket shutting doors and the end gate, loading 12-gauge pumps and 20-gauge single shots. We went in at twilight, split up to take in the two waterways that wrapped their arms around the three-acre plot where Dad used to grow sweet corn. Those two waterways met in a bounty of dense, raspy canary reed grass that should have been wet underneath except the weather had been bone dry since August. Beyond that was a stand of giant reed with strong, hollow stalks whose plumes eight feet up had gone all silky in the fall air, and then where the grasses weren't seeded right stood a crop of brown thistles that shaded gradually into the tan brome that dominated that stand of the CRP.

It was dusk and calm, evening coming on in measurable moments, ticking off perceptibly as the sun slid down the horizon. It was at the brown thistle patch that the first bird got up, a hen, then, across the way, a rooster and another rooster far up ahead, hens and roosters shooting off pell-mell like fireworks.

Not like fireworks. A group of pheasants as they fly is called a bouquet—it was a bouquet of pheasants, separate blooms crossed amongst each other, the roses of roosters mixed with the plain browns of hens, all woven together and ascending above the dozens of shades of tans and yellows and browns of the CRP, a fall bouquet of the prairie.

We shot some birds that night, dressed them out later in the basement. I don't remember how many. What I remember is that bouquet of pheasants, ascending like prayers from the CRP, prayers that Dad had sowed in silence.

II

The Dead Sea

THE MOMENT COMES late one sunny morning when again it's Carmen and Mom and I in the room with Dad.

He starts coughing, a loud wheezing that builds. He's trying to push something out but his breathing is shallow, his lung capacity diminished. He's trying to get to the full breath stop where his lungs will gather themselves, balanced and full, before he gives a final cough to drive out what's blocking his air, but he can't get there. He doesn't have it.

Carmen and I look at each other and for a moment we know that this is it. He's drowning.

"Can we call a nurse?" I ask.

Carmen shakes her head. "I wonder what Dad's DNR status is."

"Is that where we're at?"

"Listen to him. He can't cough it out. If he goes—"

Just then a nurse comes in to check on something else. He's still coughing, but it's winding down, not because he's winning but because he has no more strength.

"Mom," Carmen asks, "does Dad have an advance directive?"

Mom looks at us, recalibrating or uncomprehending.

Carmen tries again. "Do you know his DNR status?"

Mom searches Carmen's face, trying to orient herself. Mom has not thought of this, will not let herself think of this.

Carmen tries a different tack.

"I'm just trying to think. . . . He's getting worse, and if he can't swallow. . . ."

Carmen's way ahead of Mom, ahead of me. This has always been Carmen's job in the family as the oldest: find the borders and cross them. She was the first one of us who truly left Leota. She was the best and brightest of us siblings, and for that reason, none of us could exactly follow her, though we would always let her lead. Now, she leads us into this other country.

WE NEEDED a boat to cross. That was what Dad believed.

And so one midweek afternoon in May of 1989, a Blue Fin Spectrum 1706 showed up in our yard. Several times since, Dad has asked me if I remember the unloading, the triumphal lifting down by tractor and loader from the fretwork truck and onto our gravel yard in Moulton Township, but it came while I was at school. By the time I got home it was already in the machine shed, safely hidden from the neighbors.

The target launch was Memorial Day, the following Monday. Instead of renting a bathtub from Pete's marina on Valhalla, we'd have our own fishing *machine* to run on Lake Shetek.

We just had to put it together.

Dad had cut every corner he could. He'd gone with the 50-horse motor rather than the 85; had bought boat and motor separately at wholesale through Bayliner, saving the cost of a dealership putting it together; had left off almost all amenities—no trolling motor or tilt and trim, just a live well and an in-dash depth finder, so he wouldn't have to haul along the boxy Fish Lo-K-Tor.

We set to work—Dad set to work. He poured over the instruction manual, hooked up lines and finagled, asked me to read and reread passages. We drilled through aluminum hull and Styrofoam filler and mounted the motor. He asked me to hold stuff and reach my hand in tight corners to fasten nuts. We worked on it Friday night till late, Dad finally getting frustrated and leaving it for the next day. He said, "If we don't have it running by tomorrow night, we just won't take it out Monday, that's all."

"But we have tomorrow," I insisted. "And Sunday—if it just means some final little tweaks."

Carmen and Thor had come down for the holiday, and Thor joined in encouraging Dad. No doubt he looked forward to a boat ride on an otherwise deadly dull holiday on the prairie.

Our nagging worked. By mid-afternoon Saturday, Dad turned the key and it rolled over.

"We've got power," he smiled. I rubbed my hands.

Later that afternoon he filled a 55-gallon drum with water and we put the propeller into it. It took a while, turning and turning, catching and stopping, but the motor finally started and smoked and Dad even put it in gear and churned up the water. We did all of this safely in the machine shed, where no one could see. Dad's demeanor was subdued, like when you get a Christmas present and your parents tell you it was really too expensive and all you can feel is guilt.

But on Memorial Day 1989, we went to State Park as usual, except this time we were pulling our very own boat.

Dad had picked State Park because it had two lanes for unloading and nice docks. More importantly, it was protected from the wind back in there, so that way if it didn't start we wouldn't blow away from shore like at some of the other landings. He was anticipating trouble.

We didn't count on the crowds, the pressure. We had not launched a boat before, and we were unsure how it would go. Dad's unease showed on his face as we pulled up to a busy scene at the docks.

"That's what I was afraid of," he mumbled.

"What?" I asked. "It's fine, Dad."

He would have preferred to do it on an off day, when we had all the time to consider what we were doing, to check all the boxes—take the trailer straps off, unhook the winch cable and chain, tilt the motor up, hook a rope to the front. Then and only then would we back it in, watch it slide off, enjoy it.

That was not this day. A pickup and boat pulled in behind us. Then a truck with a pair of jet skis. Everything was set in motion.

When you're not in a given crowd, be it surfing or chess or boating, breaking into that crowd can be nerve-wracking. And if you're bipolar on top of it, well. . . . For Dad, bipolar meant that crowds and calm could not go together. Every situation with at least two witnesses became potentially pressurized. This one, with new equipment, was especially laden with danger.

Then there were the miscalculations. The State Park launch was deceptively shallow. By the time the back wheels of our S-10 pickup reached the water, the boat was not deep enough to float off the trailer. So we buried the tailpipe and then Dad waded in up to his knees and heaved. A foot, two, and finally, like a scared child, the Blue Fin slid off and into the water.

And it was really busy. When we were all aboard—Dad and I and Thor and Heidi, beyond that I don't remember—we tried to start it, but the motor wouldn't catch. It just spun and spun, the pressure mounting in the line behind us.

"Howard, did we open that air valve on the gas tank?"

We hadn't, so I dove under the vinyl cover that hung across the transom.

"Pump that ball once," he said of the black rubber injection ball on the red gas tank.

I pumped it. Dad pushed the key in as he turned to choke it. It was still only turning over. Dad went back and pumped the ball some more. He got up from his knees slowly, a distant look on his face. This was not how it was supposed to go. I thought, "Please, please, please God, let it start." Finally it caught. He let it run in neutral for a minute. Someone, maybe me, let us drift away from the dock. Dad put it in gear, and it immediately died. We started drifting toward the shoreline. Sheltered as it was, State Park was not immune to the swirling wind.

"Howard, keep us out of the weeds," he said. "We're going to have trouble if we get tangled up!"

Mom and Carmen stood on the dock, hands on hips. Other people were watching, waiting. Another boat had rudely—or maybe this was the way things were done?—pulled into the dock so we could not go back there. This was a test and we were failing.

I grabbed the oar we had shipped for just such an occasion and pushed down to keep us away from trouble. The oar never touched bottom, just feet of mud.

"We flooded it, boys, that's all there is to it," Dad said.

We waited. We were embarrassed. Boats launched and docked around us, and I tried to keep us out of the way with the oar.

Dad tried it again. The Force motor sputtered and finally caught. He revved it high, wide open, and it smoked, a sheen of oil and gas spreading over the murky water.

He was tired. He was sweating. He sat in the passenger seat and said, "Boy, I'm beat. Howard, you take it out."

I was thirteen and had no intention of driving his boat in this Memorial Day busyness.

"Thor? Take it away."

"No, this is your boat, Milt," said Thor. "You should be the one to drive it."

But Dad was not moving. He really was wiped out. "Let's *go*! Get it out of here!"

So golden-haired Thor put down his dark sunglasses with side shields, got in the seat, sniffed, looked around and put it in gear. It sputtered a little and he gave just a touch of gas, and it held. Yes, I thought, Thor would be the one to drive us into peace and freedom, but we had drifted south from the main channel and were not moving.

Without the tilt and trim option, the motor was pointed straight down into the water, which was shallow, just a skim over full feet of muck. We were stuck, churning up the fine silt that flows into Lake Shetek from farm fields in all directions. The first lake water that the new Force motor was sucking up was literally mud.

"Oh damn!" Dad said, moving to the back.

"Should I jump out and push us?" I offered.

"Watch it! You're in the mud," Dad said, "you're gonna wreck it!"

But Thor kept his cool. He alone seemed to remember that people launched boats all the time. He accelerated to get us out of the muck, and black water and mud bubbled behind us, along with the smell of swamp. Then we hit a rock, and the motor visibly jumped.

"Damn, damn, damnit!" Dad said.

But still Thor kept going. In what was probably a few seconds but which felt like a sinkhole of time, we got safely into deeper water.

It seems like overstatement now, but that first launch was pure terror, almost bad enough to load the Bluefin 1706 back up, return home, and lock it up in the shed forever. It was that embarrassing.

The day was wrecked for Dad, and it became another in his long list of shouldn't'ves.

WE FISHED IN the boat that summer without catching. We gathered the paraphernalia for waterskiing. And we planned a vacation.

Up North.

Mom wrote to specific chambers of commerce in Park Rapids, Bemidji, Walker, Brainerd and they sent us resort flyers that we sorted through by cost and look and quality of the lake. That is, by how they compared to *In-Fisherman*, the Up North ideal. We settled on Norway Beach Resort on Cass Lake, with pictures of long sandy beaches, simple cabins, and big, sexy walleyes. Norway Beach Resort, so alluring to poor Dutchmen like us, trying to break into establishment Minnesota-Scandinavia. A week's rental was Saturday to Saturday, but Dad got home from a cross-country trip on Tuesday, and since we needed to take two vehicles anyway in order to pull the boat, we hatched a plan to go up a night early—to scout the lake and get a jump on fishing for the week, maybe catch our first limit, since that was what happened Up North.

Where would we sleep?

In the bottom of the boat, Jesus-like. The Bluefin was wide and flat—we'd pull up the chairs, throw out sleeping bags, and pull a tarp over the top. What more could we want than to sleep on the water? Oh, we'd ask permission to pull it up on shore at the resort, but they wouldn't care.

With hindsight, I can see the flaws in the plan, the mania in it. But back then I was at the mercy of all the myths—of the Miraculous Catch of Fish, of Crossing Over, of Up North.

We left early afternoon. We stopped for dinner at the Red Rooster. We ate fried chicken, fried potatoes, and coleslaw, and drank Dr. Pepper. We got to Cass Lake and launched an hour or two before sunset. It was a huge lake, not one that you can explore in a couple of hours. Straight out from our resort was an island. We tossed out Rapalas, trolled around a sandy point that dropped off sharply into deep blue water, and watched the red lines of the in-dash depth finder, expecting bites that didn't come. Around the back side of the island, it got flatter, weedier, clear for ten or twelve feet, and my Rapala started dragging. I changed to a Mr. Twister. The lake was perfectly calm.

Dad said, "Isn't this the life?" A loon called from somewhere, and I caught a stained-glass aura on the left side of my vision.

"Dad, I've got a migraine," I said.

DURING THE FIRST migraine I ever got, I begged God for my life. First came the visual field cut, which meant a chunk of my vision went all shimmery, like someone was pushing on the back of my eyeballs. Then, numbness, a tingling that became a buzzing on one side of my body, starting from my fingers and spreading to my lips and tongue and cheek and down to my toes. All the while the radiating pain on the other side of my brain built impossibly, till I had to do something, anything, to escape and so I barfed my guts out, at which point it was over.

As I got older, the headaches got worse, repeated barfing without relief. No doubt this was what I was in for as we headed for shore at Cass Lake.

When we got in to shore, Dad pulled the boat up as far as he could onto the sand. He removed the seats from their insets and set them upside down in the front. The mosquitoes descended, singing in our ears. He got the sleeping bags, the bug spray, and finally the tarp that was to be our shelter, then went off into the night to get me some 7-Up or Sprite for later. So then it was just me, lying there on the shore of Cass Lake in the bottom of a Blue Fin boat with a tarp over me, mosquitoes singing a Halle-fricking-lujah Chorus in my ears. The numbness was through my face and tongue and down to my toes. And it was the middle of summer, meaning the tarp and sleeping bag made it oppressively hot.

We had tried all the regular treatments for migraines, over-the-counter and prescription painkillers, even a self-administered injection. Then we tried alternative measures. For six weeks, Mom took me to a biofeedback clinic in Sioux Falls where a short, kindly lady put me in a dark room and made me listen to a cassette tape of a calm baritone voice who instructed me in breathing and muscle-relaxation techniques as electrodes measured my level of tension. She was teaching me to manage my anxiety. When I listened to this tape religiously, morning and night, my migraines went to zero.

When I stopped, they came back. Now, on the banks of Cass Lake, I used the breathing techniques to try to mitigate the pain.

It felt like Dad was gone for hours.

At thirteen, migraines captured the binaries of life. Right brain pain versus left body numbness. Stomach versus head. Body versus soul. Migraines made you consider the terror of pain, which rang through the bones of your skull like pure sound, pain that marooned you in a body and made you yearn for an escape into pure ether. In the midst of a migraine, you could conceive of suffering so severe that life would not be worth living.

Migraines also lent themselves to meditations on Grampa's God v. Dad's God.

The easiest way to understand migraines was as God's punishment of me, long-time looker at the bra section of the JC Penney catalog. Another option was as a "refiner's fire," suffering to purify, to produce perseverance. This was Grampa's God. An omnipotent God had the right to sit in heaven and let you suffer because he's holy. And wholly other. And, since Jesus happened already, he's already done what he could. The rest was on me, to survive if I might.

When Dad finally came back, he let in fresh air and a fresh chorus of mosquitoes, but having your dad there with you on the lake so you're not alone is of course the important thing.

"How are you feeling, Pal? Anything I can do?"

He put his thick hand on the side of my head.

"Boy, I can almost feel that head pound," he said. "Wouldn't you know it? I hate this for you, guy."

I knew that he meant it, that he would take my pain upon himself in a heartbeat if he could. But all he could do was ride it out with me there in the bottom of the boat, with the mosquitoes and the heat. This was Dad's God—embodied, present, locked into the moment with you.

Sometime after midnight, I flipped the tarp back and blew chicken and coleslaw and little bits of fried potato into clear Cass Lake, Dad hanging onto my ankles.

Then, for hours, rinse, repeat.

Somewhere near dawn, I fell asleep. An hour after sunrise, I awoke. The water had washed all evidence of vomiting clean away.

THAT CASS LAKE vacation had so much pressure on it—first vacation with The Boat to the Promised Land of Up North, last vacation before Heidi went to college—that it was destined to fail.

We fished at least ten hours a day. We trolled the sandbar island, marveled at the clear water, at the drop-off to a hundred feet, but caught no fish. We drifted drop-offs, casted shorelines, trolled weed lines, caught nothing.

We tried corners of the lake map marked with W for Walleye or N for Northern Pike. We trolled and drifted, drifted and trolled. We pulled into the weed beds and dropped anchor to bobber fish but could see there was nothing but four-inch sunnies in the clear water.

The sheer size of Cass Lake became oppressive.

We had spent years trying to imagine through the ten feet of dingy water of southwest Minnesota lakes; now we had to imagine through hundreds of feet of the clear water of Cass Lake. We had heard "rock pile" and "weed line," but not how to fish an "inside turn" or find a "thermocline." We fished with fatheads and crappie minnows, but didn't know a shiner by sight, much less a cisco or redtail, all of which made it onto a much more complicated bait menu up at Cass. And we had no sense of the seasonal changes that made you shift from leeches to shiners.

Turns out having the boat to cross didn't automatically mean crossing.

"There's a mayfly hatch," Dad brought back from the bait shop. "You can see 'em in the water. The guides said the fish go right past your bait to take the mayfly. No one is catching a thing. They said it's like the Dead Sea."

We took consolation in that, that we weren't the only ones. God had sent mayflies on the righteous and the unrighteous alike. This was the hopeful piece of despair we lived off.

For Dad, there was always the fact that we were Up North. In the beauty and the calm, he found calm. The deep blue water off a perfect sand point, the bright mottling on sunfish, the stillness at sunset. The fact that we could wake up in a small cabin, go out on the lake as mist rose off the water, listen to the call of loons.

Late in the week, we crossed under a bridge to a lobe of Cass called Pike Bay. We drifted a drop-off in the middle, and on our second pass through, Dad had something take his Lindy Rig. I stood with the net, ready but unbelieving. A walleye! I netted it and, just for a moment, it was how it was supposed to be: light walleye chop, Lindy rig, brown-gold walleye filling out the bottom of a nylon dip net.

Finally. Thank you.

We drifted the same spot all afternoon without another fish.

ONE MORNING while I was on the dock at Norway Beach, looking down at the magic of sunfish in clear water, a high school kid water-skied past, slaloming back and forth in perfect S's, spouting a rooster tail ten feet in the air.

Heidi and I wanted to be that kid, tanned, athletic, water skiing parallel to the water. I had learned to ski earlier that summer and now wanted to learn to slalom. Heidi stated that learning to ski was her official goal for this trip.

This was another pressure of the Cass Lake vacation, another way to cross.

Thursday, long after we were worn out from fishing, we set aside an afternoon for water-skiing. I went first and then we focused on Heidi.

She fought it all afternoon. She fought the skis against friction until she lost balance. She plowed water until it tore out her forearms. Round after round, trying piece of advice after piece of advice.

The motor wasn't strong enough, plain and simple. Dad's boat was big-bodied. It could pull up a thirteen-year-old kid, but not an adult. And not someone who was just learning, not Heidi.

"I should've got the larger motor," Dad said. "The 85-horse. This motor's just not strong enough. Another mistake."

Of course that redoubled her efforts, the importance of fulfilling Dad's dreams to keep him afloat.

She wore herself out, finished in angry tears.

That night we went fishing only for the last hour before sunset, caught nothing.

AT MAYO later that morning, Carmen approaches Dr. Nassar when she rounds.

"Dr. Nassar, can we talk to you privately just a moment?" Carmen asks.

Dr. Nassar is surprised by my sister's tone, and she gives us all her attention.

"So my Dad's clearly getting worse. They're thickening his liquids but it's not working. He's no longer able to cough things out." Carmen is the true believer in the family, the most charismatic of us all about her faith in God, but now she has crossed into clinical-analytical mode. "So, I just wanted to ask about my dad's DNR status, and whether we should have my mom consider adjusting it."

Dad's decline feels inevitable. It's Grampa's God, distant and detached.

"We're wondering if it's time to prepare for the end."

I look at Dad, sleeping, slumped but not restful. His arms are a mess of bruises and masses of hardened blood from old IVs, a hole for his shunt above his heart. All we can do is what Dad himself would do. Be here. Be present. Hold his thick, calloused hand.

That's what Dad's God would do. God *with* you, locked into the moment. God in the boat on the Dead Sea, fishing with you in an authentic wager. God, who loves you *and* he's depressed about the world. At the same time. Manic. Dad's God.

Dr. Nassar is taken aback. "No, no, that's not it at all," she says. "I realize that Milton has been losing ground, but now that the spinal tap results are back, we can be more certain of his diagnosis, and we know how to treat what he has, Hashimoto's encephalopathy."

"OK, because we were just thinking. . . ."

She shakes her head. Clearly, this has not occurred to her in any of the several chess matches in her head. "Hashimoto's is very responsive to steroid treatment. I know he's not been getting better, but we had to eliminate several things first. Your dad is a very complicated case, but he's not in danger. Now that we have a clearer idea of what we're dealing with, I have every confidence he'll respond to the steroids."

And come what may of Dad on steroids, we'll be there, locked into the moment with him.

ONE OF THE last things we did at Cass Lake—did it because Dad asked us to—was to take the boat out on the lake ourselves, just Heidi and me. I drove. Heidi didn't want to.

Dad wanted to stay on shore to witness this thing he had long dreamed of. To be the one marooned on land and boatless, but to be able to say, "I launched my kids. They're out on the lake, free."

I don't remember what we did. What can you do? Drive around fast, hit your own wake. Tip as far to one way as you can so you feel like you'll get thrown out. We did all those things, did them again, then I think we just stopped where Dad couldn't see us and let him imagine.

We knew—what did we know? Heidi was just beginning to understand that we were kidding ourselves, trying to live out Dad's dream; I was still believing the boat might save us. So we just drifted, felt the last minutes of our brother-sister isolation in the sea of Dad's dreams.

Then we went in and went back home to the Moulton Township farm outside of Leota, Minnesota.

We had the boat. But we had been unable to cross.

12

Charon

A NURSE AT MAYO has come to give Dad his pills, to be taken with pudding since he chokes on liquids. He doesn't want to take them, so he keeps his mouth closed, but the nurse, an older lady with short gray hair, is insistent. I see a look come into his eyes. She's not going away so he goes to plan B. He opens hesitantly and takes the pills and pudding. She asks him to swallow, assumes he has, and turns away, but he's just breathed in, and when she turns back, he spits it all over her and himself.

You react, scold him. So does Mom.

It's good news, really—there's a human being with volition in this body that has been shutting down for so long. His will is coming back. His will or . . . something.

It's the look that scares you, from a corner of Dad's personality that, when backed into a corner, will forget himself and turn on the weak, make a dog yelp or disparage the strange, the different; the part of Dad that will come up with "sand n—" for a South Asian couple managing a hotel in a small Indiana town.

And worse.

"THE MISSOURI RIVER," Dad said after the debacle Up North. "That's where we gotta go. The Oahe dam."

Maybe it was the name—Oahe, like the Hawaii of the plains. Whatever the case, it was Lake Oahe, the masterwork of the Army Corps of Engineers, that became our next horizon.

I realize now that most people who were going to "the river" had connections of some sort—a resort that their family went to, a work trip that hired guides who knew the big water. Not us. We'd just figure it out. We would drive around, find a spot like a "point" or a "drop off" or a "flat," whatever that was, and then fish. And then catch them.

It was manic. Or was it? Wanting to take your son on a fishing trip?

"How did you learn them things unless you tried?" That was Dad's exact line.

HERE'S THE context for the "fat squaw" joke, which is to say, there was never any context.

"Yeah, we better make sure to have enough food and ice where we're going—otherwise we might starve!"

We would have stopped for ice in Pipestone to keep the sandwich meat and hotdogs cold, the backup plan should we not catch fish. And Dad had baited the clerk with that line.

"Oh? Where you headed?"

"To find me a fat squaw," Dad said with a smirk. "Warm in the winter, shade in the summer!"

It was Dad's most embarrassing joke, though at the time I didn't really get it. "Squaw" threw me. It was such an old word, gone with the nineteenth century.

I was not looking forward to the drive out there, a great boring plains drive. First Pipestone and then Flandreau, then north to Highway 14. The weather didn't help, windy and hot, approaching high summer. In the heat, the seventeen-and-a-half-foot Blue Fin was all the tan two-tone S-10 could handle.

Up into South Dakota, we saw signs for Lake Thompson, created overnight by a flood and sustained thereafter by mystery. Drove right through De Smet with signs about Laura Ingalls Wilder something. Then the whole lot of nothing I had been warned about, open country where the fields got larger and larger and the towns farther and farther apart.

There was one town that registered on our mental maps, Miller, the high prairie town where Uncle Nick and Aunt Joan, Mom's sister and brother-in-law, had moved their family when Uncle Nick's farm went under in 1985. His was one of the first farms to go in our area. Looking at the place, you might have guessed. The walls of the house they lived in depended on hay bales to keep the winter wind out. The red barn where they tried to milk a few cows was slightly newer than ours but less well equipped. It was the kind of farm they used in the out-of-touch farm crisis movie *Country*, truly marginal, next to which ours seemed a farm of the future.

It was also haunted. By Uncle Nick himself.

Uncle Nick had a truck-driver frame, a big square loping torso with huge hands at the end of long arms that you knew would connect if he swung. And in the early days, he seemed always ready to swing. Mom and Dad whispered about the effects on Aunt Joan, body and mind. When Heidi and I played over there with cousins Lance and Rachel, we'd walk on eggshells when he was around. If he had a kind of half-pout, watch out. On the other hand, if he joked about the ketchup bottle farting, you were OK.

But when the farm finally went under, Uncle Nick suddenly moved the whole family out to Miller in the middle of the school year, disrupting Lance's eighth grade year at Leota Christian. Uncle Nick was going to be a cowboy, to work cattle in the employ of a large ranch, to ride horses and wear cowboy boots, and we hoped it was just the thing the family needed—a new purpose for Uncle Nick that would make him happier, that would soften the chip on his shoulder.

For a while we heard happy stories back from Aunt Joan: about Uncle Nick's adventures on horseback during calving season, about Lance on the basketball team and Rachel in school.

Two years later they moved back. So not that happy. Still, I think of it as the way our family touched the West.

My literary ancestors once again help make sense of Uncle Nick and Aunt Joan's story. *Little House on the Prairie* makes clear the strange position the Ingallses occupy in 1880s America. Pa loads up the family and all their belongings to leave the Big Woods in the middle of the night. Seems like he's fleeing creditors, abandoning one venture when it's underwater for another, a speculative one in Indian Territory, on the Osage Indian Reserve. His plan is to settle there before anyone else gets a chance, to get a leg up on any new settlement. It's adventurous, but you can feel the precariousness of it all through the voice of Laura's child narrator.

The account that Caroline Fraser gives in *Prairie Fires* makes even more clear how brash a move this is on Pa's part. The country has used illegal immigrants to squeeze out native tribes before. But the Osage are wise to this ploy and are not above using violence to defend themselves. Pa goes into the Osage Reserve as a squatter. He's a prospector, an insider-trader, a riverboat gambler, with this difference: he's got a very young family. The Ingallses clearly settle next to a well-used trail, meaning they will definitely come into conflict with the Osage. Their wildcat neighbors are even more racist than the Ingallses are in a place where that doesn't make any sense. Pa's wits seem to be the only real thing between his family and on the one hand, hunger and on the other, violence.

But Pa is still willing to bet on those wits—or something else.

Uncle Nick and Aunt Joan moved West in the middle of February, not the middle of the night. But this is what you do when you're desperate on the prairie: you move, telling yourself another place, another town, will do the trick. And betting on yourself, or something.

After Miller, the S-10 started overheating, the needle pushing into the red. "Roll your window down," Dad said. "I'm going to crank up the heat to draw some of it away from the motor." Though we were miserable—it was ninety-something outside and the heater was blowing full bore on us—the trick worked. We watched the temperature gauge drop steadily until it stabilized just below the red.

THE MISSOURI is amazing because you don't expect it. High country grass and solitude and then, almost without warning, a great river valley and a great river, swollen out of itself, more than the sum of its parts because of the wonder of the Oahe Dam.

We arrived in Gettysburg late afternoon. We pitched our old green tent in the campground of Bob's Resort, a grassy open space in the foothills that commanded a view of the valley, then went down to the river after supper to look at the boat launch: a great cement pad flanked by stones on which the S-10 and Bluefin would look like toys. We had entered a giant's world. The bridge pilings on Oahe, even at this distance, were big enough to have to be circumnavigated, God's own bridge.

We didn't make the same mistake as we did at Cass Lake, didn't launch that night, though I wanted to. The gloaming was on the soft grass hills. A campfire would have been perfect, but we didn't do campfires. We went to bed in the late dusk to get an early start.

It was strange out there on the grassy hills above the Missouri, just me and Dad, lonely. I'd already heard all Dad's tales of woe. It wasn't the same as a fishing buddies trip, ribbing each other and farting each other out of the tent and telling old stories so that if the fish don't bite it don't matter. We were alone above the Big Muddy without really any idea where we were or what we were doing and no one to turn to for help, betting on ourselves.

BEFORE THE eighties changed everything, Dad went on fishing trips with friends: to Fort Thompson, to Lake of the Woods, to Leech Lake, and to Door County, Wisconsin. He went with Don De Boer the car dealer and Johnny Hofkamp the junk dealer, and they hired guides and had adventures and drank beer and farted, and even caught some fish.

Don was the younger of two brothers who owned DeBoer Chevrolet in Leota, the older of whom had been the consistory president for the Acquiescence. Don was younger and less pious. When Dad told a joke, it would take Don a minute, smiling naively, but then when he got it and when he knew it was OK to laugh, he'd squinch up his eyes and giggle. Coming from a family of careful businessmen, Don needed Dad to help loosen him up.

I knew less about Johnny Hofkamp, who seemed to slouch in the shadows of Leota. He was the junk dealer at the back of town to whom we'd bring the aluminum cans we'd been saving. Johnny wore Coke-bottle glasses and always had a cigarette in his mouth. He wore a dark beard with streaks of silver in it and spoke little. I'm not sure where he went to church, but not Leota Ebenezer.

The three of them made a somewhat odd trio: Don, the respected businessman, and Johnny, the not-really-a-businessman, with Dad the respected farmer and dissenting church-goer in between.

THE NEXT morning at Gettysburg, Dad woke me before dawn. We had donuts and juice for breakfast and launched at sunrise. We went north toward a place called Dodge Draw. We trolled points, we drifted, we marked sharp drop-offs on the depth finder and said, "They've got to be here."

We had heard that you just needed to troll fifteen to twenty feet of water on the Missouri, not really realizing the sheer amount of space there was to cover. This wasn't Lake Shetek. But we tied on Lindy Rigs with long snells and green spinners and crawler harnesses with red jewels and silver spinners and two gold hooks and began trolling. We caught tree branches or nothing.

"Do you suppose we're going too fast?" Dad asked.

After several hours, I put on a Rapala, a deep diver, that bent my pole and made the tip shake, and we puttered along in and out of inlets and bays, across rises, up into fifteen feet, then back into fifty.

"Nope, too deep," Dad said.

Late morning, I had a bite. At first Dad didn't react—was I sure it wasn't a snag?

I fought it and gained. It appeared in the water below us, flipping like a snake so I could see its white underbelly, then it flashed and was gone.

OF THE FISHING trips with Don and John, the Lake of the Woods story was Dad's favorite. They stayed on the Minnesota side of the lake, but the good fishing was on the Canadian side. One day their guide took them across the Canadian border to the islands of the Sioux Narrows. The guide warned them about Indian fishing rights. Sure enough, all of a sudden all three men snagged. They pulled and they pulled to get their lures back and Dad, who was at the back of the boat, found they were all tangled in a net. So he started pulling it in. "What are you doing!?" the guide asked. "Well, I'm getting our lures back!" Dad answered innocently. Meanwhile, he grabbed whatever fish he could and when he got to their lures, he took out his pocketknife and cavalierly cut them loose, gouging a big hole in the net.

Back at the resort that night, the guide warned the men not to say anything lest they get in trouble. But when they walked in, says Dad in his stock story, "the whole place cheered and bought us the first round." The guide had already let the story slip about this outsider who had done the white fishermen all a favor.

Dad often counted coup on this blow he struck for the white man in the Indian wars—Dad, betting on himself. Or something.

NEAR THE beginning of *Little House on the Prairie*, as they start out for Indian Territory, Pa promises Laura that if she endures the trip he will show her this one, exotic-sounding thing, a word that Laura has never heard before, but which has a kind of ring to it that makes it stick in her brain. It's the type of promise any father might make to a child at the beginning of a long journey—endure and I promise you'll catch a crappie, a walleye, a northern pike. Except the word Pa settles on is not a thing or fish, it's a "papoose," which he defines as "a little, brown, Indian baby." As kids will do, Laura latches onto the word and asks about seeing one throughout the book. Then, at the book's climax, after the seemingly ominous gathering of the Osage, they suddenly disband. As the Ingallses watch their procession, Laura sees two "Indian babies" in baskets and throws a tantrum, screaming, "Pa, get me that little Indian baby!" It's all weird—beyond weird.

And entirely recognizable.

Once again, Fraser helps. The way white working-class people were encouraged to bet on their whiteness at the nudge-nudge, wink-wink of the powerful—to squat on Indian land, to press their advantage knowing the law would follow—has long created chasms on the prairie between settler and native, between white people and everyone else.

Don't get me wrong. There's an alternate world where poor whites and poor Indigenous drink beer together and tell off-color jokes about each other under the umbrella of solidarity against the Man. But that's not how Dad's jokes worked. Dad's jokes had long been a minder of the gap between whites and Indigenous, whites and non-whites, whether squaw or papoose, Japs or Blacks. Like Pa, it was one of his foundational resources: He may have been poor, but at least he was white. He could always bet on that.

Not that he ever thought of it this way. He saw no harm in it. Just kidding around.

ON DAY TWO at the Missouri, we went across to the far shore, into a long inlet. It was well before sunrise, my hands still thick from sleep. We drifted and casted. I had a hit or two casting towards shore. I even caught a smallmouth bass too small to keep.

"I like this spot," Dad said. "You?"

It was true. There was some magic to it, and more action than all of the previous day. A lone adolescent buffalo came over the hill and down to the water. It looked at us in profile with one mirror eye.

"Isn't that something?" said Dad. We did not interpret it farther. Had we known where we were, the Cheyenne River Reservation, had we known anything at all about Native people or symbolism, maybe we'd have considered more deeply a lone adolescent buffalo's appearance, whether as warning or distraction.

With the sun, we felt the wind rise at our backs. We were protected in the bay for the moment, so we ignored it. By the time the buffalo wandered away, we turned to see whitecaps solid across the river, between us and camp.

"Oh boy, here comes that wind," said Dad. "That's what I was afraid of." We had a dilemma: stay in this cove all day or attempt to cross before it got any worse. We were in for an all-day blow.

I'd been driving, and Dad said, "You want to take it?"

I shrugged.

Dad had me put on a lifejacket.

"As long as you go into the waves, it will be OK."

I turned the boat out of the cove. We had to hit some big rollers sideways to get out of there and Dad grabbed the side for stability. The prow tipped way out of the water and then way down.

"Give 'er the dickens," Dad said when we were out of the bay, and I did. We rose and smashed full on the next wave and then the next. I held onto the steering wheel to keep me attached to the boat and we pounded wave after wave. My stomach was tight. I tried forcing myself to relax, consciously thought of the Apostle Peter walking on the water, of the need for faith. We kept pounding. My stomach tightened again. But aiming straight into the waves, we got across.

THE OTHER FISH story from the Don and Johnny days was about a guide named Frosty, on the Leech Lake trip. On this trip, no one had been catching much, not even the guides. But Dad and his pals lucked out and got Frosty. "Frosty, he'll catch 'em," the other guides said.

And Frosty did: He pulled their boat up into a weed bed where he knew northerns would be spawning, and he instructed his three fishermen, "When you see the weeds come up, drop your bobbers." Then he dropped anchor and put the boat motor in reverse, gouging the weeds, and pissing off the fish that lurked there.

"And I saw, one, two, three bobbers go down just like that," Dad says.

It's a dirty trick, like starting a forest fire to drive out the game, but in Dad's story destruction was indistinguishable from craftiness.

Northern in hand, Frosty beached the boat in lee of the wind, gathered wood and started a fire. From the boat he produced a cast iron fry pan and cooking oil. He brought out potatoes that he cut paper-thin, quickly filleted out the fish and tossed them in breadcrumbs and opened a can of beans and set it among the rocks to heat.

The fire was hot now, the oil ready to fry. Frosty tilted the pan so that he could deep fry the potatoes on one side and fry the fish on the other.

There they are, on the sandy beach of a clear lake set down in the trees of northern Minnesota: Dad, Don, Johnny Hofkamp and the white-haired guide named Frosty.

"He had them potatoes done perfect," Dad said. "And the beans got hot just right in the can. And the fish right outta the water. You couldn't beat it!"

The shore lunch so impressed Dad that one Sunday not too long after he returned from Leech Lake, perhaps in partial payback for leaving Mom with us for the week he was gone, Dad determined to cook us a shore lunch. In the grove.

He gathered rocks and sticks, started a fire, set in the can of beans.

"Dad, the label's burning!" we said. Then the fire fizzled.

So Dad got out the Coleman camp stove.

He fried the potatoes first, then the fish, cod that Mom had bought in town.

It didn't quite measure up to Frosty standards. The beans were lukewarm and had some label ash in them. The potatoes weren't cooked through. "I didn't cut them thin enough," Dad said. "The way that Frosty cut them—paper thin." And the fish itself was soft through the middle and tasted like freezer.

And yet, as we sat in the green grass of the grove, everything on fire in the hot noon sun of July, we could glimpse the vision, taste the goodness.

Shore lunch was the ideal that we strove for as we fished, it became clear to me then, catching walleyes and northern so that we might eat their perfectly white meat that tasted best fresh in the wonder of an Up North setting.

But if shore lunch went to the root of Dad's imagination, it struck a dissonant chord with his jokes. Shore lunches originated with Native Americans, I know now, going at least as far back as Anishinaabe guides making them for French fur traders.

The ideal Dad thirsted after was an Indigenous ideal.

LATE AFTERNOON at Bob's Resort on the final day of our Missouri River trip, we were picking up our last bait. The kid appears in my memory talking. He's got longish, greasy, dirty blond hair. His words have both a lisp and an unnecessary roundness to them, to the point where you have to listen closely to what he's saying. One look at his face and it's clear why. The kid has not just buck teeth but too many teeth in his mouth, two clear rows, one behind the other. At first glance, I can't tell whether he's mentally impaired.

"I's gort this new rord I neerd to try." The kid is addressing Dad in what appears to be a Midwestern Chaucerian dialect. "I seen ye were burring bairt and Ir'm orff now or I carn be'r off. I'll go with ye and take ye out if I can try'r out this new reelr."

Before I know it, he's shipped with us. Dad makes eyes at me like, "Isn't this interesting?" It's not at all interesting to me, and I look earnestly at him to say so.

It's pushing five when we set off.

"If weer go'r up sout to"—some kind of unintelligible or mythical sounding place name—or Welsh perhaps—"the walleyes'll be'r . . . lairing on the sharel."

"OK, South? To that far shore?" Dad says, having apparently turned bilingual.

"Yes, sout, to the sharel. . . ,"

He points, and Dad points the boat across the river.

On the other side, where the shoreline features big slags of rock, he holds up his hand to stop us. This is also the Cheyenne River side. We get situated. He tells us we need a type of Lindy rig—a long snell and plain hook.

"What about one like this?" Dad shows him the kind we have, with a chartreuse float and spinner.

"Ner' . . . walleres lerk . . . plain best. Seer, Er've gert jurst larng snellr that I tierd myserlf."

He shows us his line. It's homemade, just a plain line tied to the weight, no spinner, no floater—and at least a couple of feet longer than the eighteen- or twenty-four-inch Lindy rigs we're using.

We change our lines, and then Dad starts the motor and we begin trolling.

"Carn't you trolls urs arny slerwer?"

"This is as slow as this motor goes. I suppose I need to buy a trolling motor."

"Yems. Them troll mo'ors pull slow. Sharel 'eyes sun theirselves; won't brudge from therms holes until it pulls by reeeeeal sler. Thern ther'll takes it."

Now, I'm sensing Gollum in his dialect.

"Yerm's gert ern oar?"

"An oar? Yep. I wouldn't be out here without an oar."

"I'll rowus. Thaert's the speeds therse walleyers resting ern the sharel wants."

Shale. He's been saying shale. On the shore you could see it in long flat plates. Now, in the late afternoon, fish were laying along the shale on the backside of whatever current there was. He wanted to slow down our approach so that we would creep along these fish.

He moves up to the front, sits on the very prow, feet dangling off, his rod and reel between his knees, and rows us. We crawl the shoreline, imperceptibly. Dad and I watch our rod tips bound and pull as our weights drag along the rocks. The kid looks at mine.

"Art's a bite," he says.

"Me?"

But after playing it a moment, I set the hook into nothing.

"Rorks. Marbe yer poles are loorse gern bouncy." They are loose and bouncy, I'm suddenly aware, and the shale bottom makes it impossible to distinguish between bites and bottom.

"Ers one."

Dad looks at me. The kid gives line, stops, feels again.

"Cormon, terk it." I look down as he sets the hook. When I look up, there's an elegant bend in his rod, the drag sings. I double check the rod to make sure, see it pulse. This is a fish.

"Howard, get the net."

All doubt and distrust disappears at the possibility of boating a fish, even just seeing one. And when he pulls it up, it is indeed a beauty, with dark green saddles across its back.

"That's a gorgeous fish," says Dad worshipfully.

"Thart's arll of twarnty-warn, twarnty twa irnches," he says.

Fish in the live well, we tried to get set again, but whatever magic young Charon had found for us had gone. Dark was coming and he had to get back in. He filleted the fish with an electric fillet knife, zipping off the meat and putting it in a plastic bag for us, like a guide would.

Then he disappeared.

We talked to the resort owner about him. Dad asked, "Where are his parents, that they don't fix them teeth?" And then, the pronouncement I found myself resisting: "He's a good kid."

TRUTH WAS, our trip to Lake Oahe touched a whole lot of the West. We had fished along the Cheyenne River Reservation, home to the Oglala Lakota, with Standing Rock Reservation just to the north, where Sitting Bull is buried. In Gettysburg, settled by Civil War veterans, we could have seen the original Medicine Rock, dated at 350 million years old, a rock marked with footprints and handprints—and bear prints—a rock embedded with story. Lake Oahe itself, marvel of the Army Corps of Engineers, was said to break the heart of the Lakota elders, destroying that most sacred interworld boundary: shoreline.

On the trip home, we descended through the mixed-grass prairie of the Missouri Coteau, the huge fields making a mockery of the Jeffersonian Grid. Then we climbed back up the Coteau Des Prairies, and right through De Smet, the wheat Promised Land that almost killed the Ingallses, then across to Flandreau, burial site of Little Crow, of Dakota War fame, and past Flandreau Indian School, noted instrument of the Indian Wars and one of four Native boarding schools still in operation, and finally back through Pipestone, home to a seam of rock that's said to be the blood of the ancestors by Native people, then home to the Buffalo Ridge and the Moulton Township farm, just above Champepadan Creek, "thorny wood river" in the Dakota language, and just northeast of Leota, Minnesota, named after an Indian woman in a romantic story known by an early settler.

We didn't really know where we were. We were just desperate to catch fish. So we just bet on ourselves, or something about ourselves.

AT MAYO, a new nurse comes in to help change Dad's linen. She's small, maybe 5'4", dark haired. They're about to pull a nursing magic trick, changing the linen in a bed with a confused, 225-pound man on steroids still in it. They've got him on his side and he's not happy about it. The small nurse, younger than me, is talking to him to get him to play along.

Dad's got his right hand on the bar to pull himself over but now his body has shifted and the look comes into his eye. His jaw sets. In an instant his hand flashes out, even makes a fist. With these fists he once concussed his friend Lloyd Bremer in Golden Gloves in Slayton.

The nurse sees it too late and the blow glances her jaw before she can draw back.

"Milton!"

"Dad!"

He knows he's connected. It satisfies something in him. The mean look pulls back into whatever shell it lives in.

No, all it says is that the steroids are working, I tell myself, that Dad has pushed off the far shore.

"Are you alright?" another nurse asks.

"Did he get you?" I ask, but the nurse has returned to the task to finish the job.

Later, I will apologize to her again. "That's not my dad," I say. The pudding-spitting, nurse-hitting man in the room is not my dad. Nor is the racist joke teller, the net-cutter, the wife threatener. Nor is it any part of it me, who is not his father's son, who isn't really even Midwestern because he's left the shark-teethed white trash kids far behind and is now progressive in his attitudes about Native Americans and everything else, who understands the trappings of whiteness and above all is not subject to the forces of history.

"Of course not," she says.

Of course it's not him. Nor is it anyone, ever. And it's especially not me.

Of course not.

13

Pal

"PAL, IT'S TIME to go—can you help me?" he half-whispered in the dark from the hall outside my room. Dad always made work like this, pre-dawn work, something you wanted to help him with by making it optional. Always you had the option of leaving him with all the work, which he'd bear without a word. If you didn't want that, you scared awake to make sure he didn't leave you to your sleep and ease while he bore the brunt of necessity.

"Pal" was always his term of address for me. One Saturday afternoon as I lay under a blanket having whiled away the morning watching cartoons and suffered through the shoddy programming of early afternoon to get to *Mutual of Omaha's Wild Kingdom*, Dad stepped over me in his speed-laced leather work boots and turned off the TV. I thought he was going to make me work, got angry.

"Oh, I'm sorry, Pal," he said that time. "I thought maybe you'd want to go fishing with me to Talcot Dam!"

Of course I did, and, all smiles, I jumped up and ran to change. Dad drove us east to the backside of Talcot Lake, where there was a low dam, a mysterious place of rushing water on the flattest flat of the prairie. You could watch the carp and buffalo swim up into the water flow, like Midwest salmon. That afternoon, our bobbers moved too swiftly in the current, so Dad took them off, pinched on extra weights eighteen inches above the hook, and we fished the bottom with night crawlers. He schooled me in bottom fishing, feeling the tap-tap of the bite without seeing a bobber go down, and we caught bullheads all afternoon, but it was OK because the feel of the unseen bite was a new thrill.

But this morning "Pal" meant work, the kind you didn't want to leave him with. Downstairs, I grabbed a roll for breakfast, a Bismarck fried at Brummel's Bakery in Edgerton, and poured some orange juice while he dressed in the basement. Dad either didn't eat or he'd eaten already, while he waited to see if I would get up. When he came upstairs, we went out to the pickup. The yard was silent, the doors on the outbuildings shut up tight for fear of what may have taken up residence in them. Last year's weeds still filled the cattle yards to the height of corn. It was April, just becoming light.

We rode in silence, our usual mode of communication by then. The countryside itself was silent; no wind buffeted the pickup in a landscape known for wind. County Highway One led straight west, up the hump of the Buffalo Ridge above Champepadan Creek, where the road went dead flat for several miles before dropping down into Edgerton and the Rock River valley. Edgerton was the center of our lives after we transplanted from Leota. A thousand people, Edgerton had five churches of various Reformed gradations, and four schools for those gradations. Its Main Street carried two grocery stores, two hardware stores, and two restaurants, the Leader Café and the Pizza Ranch, a local chain. West was the direction of life and civilization, but we would be stopping on the dead flat stretch just across the Pipestone County line.

On this side of the line, we'd pass the quaint farmhouse with the sign "McVenes Century Farm" posted near the road. The McVenes farm only had a few outbuildings left, and no barn, but it presided over a lush slough of yellow-gold canary reed grass that Chad and I coveted for hunting every fall though it was clearly marked POSTED.

Just over the line into Pipestone County sat QPI, Quality Pork, Inc., where we were headed: three long concrete-and-steel buildings fronted by a boxy office, with a cement manure pit surrounded by chain-link fence out back.

QPI was the first modern hog confinement I remember. Four far-sighted, well-situated Edgerton farmers got together and built the future: three industrially efficient buildings connected by enclosed walkways to breed, birth, and raise feeder pigs with machine-like efficiency, wholly confined to minimize diseases. QPI housed 500 sows and would produce over 10,000 feeder pigs a year, all in a minimum of space, all on concrete floors and steel grates with gutters beneath for the manure to drain to the pit out back, where it would be sucked up as liquid into large tankers and spread on the surrounding fields.

It was the way of the future, anyone could see.

It was also an inferno of stench and control, where you lost track of daylight in the fluorescent lights.

After Bayliner laid Dad off and after a stint at a road construction company where he got tired of being cursed at, Dad got hired on at QPI as a herdsman. One man was supposed to be running all of QPI, even built a house on site, in the midst of all that stink, but eight years into the venture, he was burning out and the place was losing efficiency, so they hired another man: Dad.

On the weekends, Dad and the other guy, the manager, took turns doing the chores. This week was Dad's turn, and I would help him. If things went well, we'd make church; if they did not, we'd return home for a late-morning nap. I had little incentive to make things go well, but there was a special twist to this morning's service: an adult baptism.

AFTER THE NURSE-punching incident, they're using restraints. Mayo Clinic, which was supposed to save him, is going medieval on Dad, tying down his arms with white cloth straps anchored to the bed and looped with Velcro around his wrists. Of course I prefer restraint to punching nurses, but it also means we've come to one of the most advanced hospitals in the world for Dad to be fully institutionalized.

But it's no longer my concern—my weekend on watch at Mayo is over. Once again, leaving will be like prayer to a magician-god: while I'm not present I hope that someone will wave a magic wand and I will return to Dad in his right mind.

The long drive home might itself be like prayer, all that open sky and solitude, therapeutic except that Dad marked this landscape for me. How many thousand farms gone? How many classic barns, old farmhouses, entire farm places? Replaced by bigger, more efficient, but fewer farms, fewer families. In this landscape the confinement, the low tin-and-concrete building, carries the day. CAFO—concentrated animal feeding operation—is a distant, academic term. Confinement gets it right. It means you get to stay.

THE SMELL, the smell hit you first. Not smell—stench, a smell that drenched you. The air was thick with it, made you work to breathe. We were all asthmatics in QPI. It was the ammonia of it, said Dad. It cut your breath when you got out of the pickup and then again past the showers. There were masks you could wear but they didn't lighten the weight of the air, just made you sweaty.

Dad showered first, so he could get the breeding going. I dozed, head in hands, waiting my own turn in the shower, holding a pair of underwear I'd brought from home.

Since hogs are so susceptible to disease, and since high animal numbers increase the risk for pandemics, the way to maximize efficiency is to control the diseases coming in. In open-air farming, pandemics spread from farm to farm without check, sweeping through the countryside. Confinements, which otherwise would maximize the conditions for pandemics, can work only if precautions are taken to minimize exposure to outside influences. Thus, QPI was designed with an office and a shower up front. Employees and visitors would have to shower to get *in* to the building. Likewise, incoming sows would be washed and sanitized before they were introduced to the herd.

The confinement system is not completely foolproof, of course. Little is more threatening to rural communities than deaths at confinements. When bloated corpses pile up outside of a confinement, and when virus turns to pandemic and spreads, against the odds, from building to building throughout the countryside, it's the formula not just for economic loss but revolution. In many confinements today, the air itself gets filtered.

As Dad dried off, his humpty-dumpty body embarrassing to me by then, in my mid-teens, I jumped in.

Breeding was done morning and night, though morning sex among pigs is apparently more popular, as it took more time in the morning. Breeding meant running groups of sows into one of the pens in front of the boar crates, selecting a boar that had not had any action in a while as tallied on a clipboard checklist, and letting it into the pen with the sows, its mouth already frothing at the possibility of getting laid before it stabbed upward with its hard head and snout at the sows' bellies. In response to this clear act of courtship, the sows not in heat would run away squealing, but the ones in heat took these advances silently, standing. The boar would find one of these, sniff it, mount up, and strike its corkscrew penis in the general direction it knew to strike for. Dad would then enter the pen, don rubber gloves, and make sure of the love connection. Then, after, when the boars were "ahnery," cocksure, and would take a shot at you with that big head, even swipe at you with the teeth that had grown in at the sides of their mouths, Dad would tap it out of the pen with a long white rod.

That morning, I spent too long in the hot shower as usual, remembering midway through that I might actually like to catch church. I crossed through the gestation barn to the farrowing building, the labor and delivery rooms of QPI, eighty crates in four rooms, two on each side of a common middle room, complete with a small storage room for supplies. I first checked the rooms with the most expectant mothers, removed afterbirth and any stillborns. Counted and recorded numbers on a clipboard. Checked if there were any sows currently farrowing that were having trouble.

There were two, one having problems for sure, a large piglet already dry and downy under the heat lamps but walking around grunting, hungry, while its mother lay on her teats and panted. I donned a long plastic sleeve from the supply room, jellied it, opened the crate behind the sow, and reached up into the birth canal. The sow rolled on her side, opening the canal to my arm and exposing her udder to the lone pig. Sure enough, I felt a skull, a big skull like the first pig's, too big for the pelvis. I hooked two fingers behind its ears, carefully pulled, the sow tense with the effort. It was jammed there, but after several minutes of cajoling and repositioning, the pressure of the sow's body tight on my bicep, the pig's skull slipped through the bone door and out, dead and bluish in color. I reached back in and found a second, smaller. It came out dead, too, though not blue. I wiped away mucus, blew in the nostrils, pumped the belly. It snuffled, gasped, finally sneezed. It would live.

Confinements get a bad rap in some circles. Sure, hog confinements are their own reality, a controlled environment with their own air spaces and orientation and weather. They're machines created to funnel animal life toward death. But comparatively little death happens in hog confinements. Much more life happens there. Life is tended there, a teeming, short, monochromatic life, some would say, if your livelihood doesn't depend on it, but life nonetheless.

But even the confinement is a state of nature. The machine can't keep nature out: young boars kept in the same pen try desperately to screw each other; sows in heat stand before the boar then suddenly bolt, spooked by some unseen impulse; sows in the madness of labor eat their own young. I once found a piglet half eaten, the back half of its body shredded to ribbons. Another time I saw a sow unwittingly step on her piglet, tearing the skin off its belly, exposing intestines, killing it instantly.

Confinements are a machine built to prevent death, to harness life; even so, like any machine, slip past the guard rails and the cogs of the life-machine itself will kill you. So you try to improve the machine, remembering that without the machine, death still happens and is often even more gruesome.

After checking the other newborns, it was feeding time. As soon as I moved the feed cart one inch, the sows would all rise in their pens and scream, knocking their heads against the steel bars of the crates-- the din of the mess hall or the cries of the damned. Each sow got one scoop or two, depending on the stage of pregnancy and nursing.

Then I processed the two newborn batches from overnight, clipping out eight teeth with a side cutters—two each on top and bottom, both sides of their mouths—cutting the dried umbilical cord and fleshy tail to an inch or two long, spraying both cord and tail with iodine, the tail dripping blood. All of these things done to prevent the state of nature in the third building, I was told, where runts would get shoved to the side and picked on, where, if tails were long and teeth were sharp, other pigs would chew and chew on a given pig's tail until that pig was dead.

All in all, it was a good morning, a busy morning.

IN ANY CLOSED system, converts are notable, bringing a justification to that system that only outsiders can. To Dad, one of the problems of Leota, of small town church and school that was the rural Dutch Reformed culture that we lived in, was that it was a closed system. Outsiders found it hard to break into; insiders found it hard to break out of. Couple that with the pious greed of Grampa Hank and we seemed to be living in some crazy Nathaniel Hawthorne world. At the end of the twentieth century.

Now, this particular morning, our church would be celebrating the legitimation of this system in baptism, not of a baby, a "covenant child," someone born an insider to an insider, but of the most outside outsider I could imagine: a Laotian refugee.

In the early 1980s, before the bad times, a group of families from the Edgerton church we attended got together and sponsored two refugee families from Laos: a man and his wife and their two toddlers, and that man's adult sister, her three children, and their grandmother. To say this family stuck out, the children a chaos of brown arms and legs and black hair biking around white-white Edgerton, is an understatement. They were exotic. The kids went to the Christian school in Edgerton, on the church's dime. The father worked for the town. Our family had been invited over to the tight-knit group of families that sponsored them a couple of times, joining them all for coffee after service in the close little blue house across the street from church: the grocer and his wife; the newspaper man and his wife; the piano salesman and his wife, the kindergarten teacher; and a city employee and his wife; each with two-to-five kids apiece. The small house was packed and smelled of garlic and burnt oil, and we passed around a wicker basket and pulled out clumps of hot rice that stuck to our fingers, then dipped that sticky rice in bowls of dark, salty liquid—soy sauce.

That morning, the oldest girl of that family was making profession of faith at seventeen, which meant she would also be baptized.

This was how it was supposed to work. It was like Dad's work with exchange students, bringing in outsiders to illuminate their lives to us and ours to them.

Dad and I pulled out of QPI at 9:15. Ten minutes home and fifteen minutes back west to church meant we would be late, meant we were not going. I didn't love our minister at the time, Reverend

Blankespoor. He was authoritative from the pulpit and almost too nice face-to-face, patronizing. He toed the Reformed line of conservatism, preaching often on the catechism and twice-a-Sunday church attendance. Likewise, in the sacraments he was a minimalist: one dip in the baptismal font set three times on the head of infants; a one-inch square of white bread and the smallest of sips of grape juice for communion, all eaten or drunk at the exact same moment when he gave the word. Actually, this was denominational practice, emphasizing that the smallest bit of grace was sufficient, a democratic, one-size-fits-all taste of bread and sip of wine, and as such didn't originate with Reverend Blankespoor, but to me all things seemed to proceed from the man behind the pulpit.

Still, adult baptism was strange enough that I found myself wondering how it would go. Would she kneel? What would she do once the water was on her hair? Did you just leave it to dry or what?

It was special enough that there might be an outburst of applause in a congregation who had been specifically instructed by the consistory not to clap for anything. Spontaneous rebellion. Then, afterward, that strange ritual across the street, where sponsors and refugees alike would partake in sticky rice and soy sauce, a second sacrament.

Dad and I drove east, under the belly of the sun, to a silent house.

DAD LIKED THE work at QPI at first. Things were not good when he started. So Dad tasked himself with "turning the place around." He carefully tended the sows, husbanded them. He theorized that piglets, used to feeding together when they nursed, also needed space to eat together when they were weaned. He made feeders out of PVC pipe to recreate the effect, feeders which annoyed the manager. Nonetheless, at least partly due to twice the care after Dad was employed, things did in fact start to "turn around" at QPI according to the numbers, and Dad's narrative about his work there began to take shape.

After the manager of QPI did in fact quit, that position was Dad's for the taking. But Dad declined, his confidence broken. He distrusted himself in any position of authority, it's clear to me now, everything from leading prayer at the dinner table to QPI manager, so no doubt through family grapevine, Uncle Nick, fresh off his ranch rehabilitation out West, swept in to take that manager position, moving a new modular home into the stench of QPI. Dad remained a herdsman in charge of the farrowing unit under Uncle Nick's supervision.

Things started out fine between the in-laws. Then the relationship soured. Or maybe it was the confinement itself.

For example.

One time a sow that was due to farrow had a rectal prolapse, a big deep maroon mass hanging from her rectum, becoming dark and discolored on its way to becoming septic. Prolapses meant ruin; sows with prolapses couldn't farrow and so always went off to market. However, this sow was ready to give birth any day. The pigs in her were more valuable than she was, but since calling a vet to do a C-section on a sow was never done, Uncle Nick took matters into his own hands. He prepped a .410 with a slug, slipped a scalpel in his chest pocket, and dropped some feed on the concrete in the alley between buildings. Dad and I stood ready at the door of the gestation barn with a bushel basket. When the sow bent down to eat, Uncle Nick came up behind her and put the .410 in the space behind her jaw and pulled the trigger, putting the slug in her brain. We heard the bang and the sow must have dropped because by the time Dad and I reached her, she was lying on her side sprinting, as if the part of her brain that had sensed something was up and had told her to run was just now kicking in. Uncle Nick waited for her to wind down, but when she didn't he took the scalpel and sliced open her belly just above where it swelled with pregnancy and reached in trying to find baby pigs. Blood ran down the cement of the alley under our boots. I held the bushel basket and waited for live pigs, but one after another they came out drowned. Dad was on his knees, trying to revive each of them as they came out, but in the end, we saved only two.

When it was over, and we had dragged the sow's carcass out the side door, Uncle Nick shrugged. "Well, better than nothing."

Dad was silent. Though it's a much more common practice in confinements now—I'm told the best way is actually a .22 shell through the front of the skull—I don't think it's something Dad would have done.

CONFINEMENT mentality finally became dangerous for Dad.

I'd entered the silent phase of dealing with Dad's despair. When he wondered aloud about whether the universe was stacked against him or not, I said nothing. When he speculated about the system favoring big operators, I said nothing. When he located the cause in himself, nada.

What he resorted to was of course a cry for help, but I think of it as precipitated by QPI, by confinement. We were headed east, the sun setting behind us. I was driving. We were passing the long low buildings of QPI, industrial hog operation, bomb shelter. He began, "You know, Pal, if I would ever kill myself—not that I ever would, but if I did"—tracking shot of the long, low hog buildings, before the finish of the line—"I would do it so you and Ma never had to find me."

He paused. This was where I was supposed to inquire as to what he meant or to chastise him.

He certainly didn't think of what he said as what it will sound like when I write it down; he saw it as a conversation within his own mind, a conversation between two parts of himself—that's how closely, it seems to me now, he identified with me.

I resisted all impulses, remained quiet, glowered, focused on the road ahead.

"I would strip down in one of those sow pens in the gestation barn at QPI," he continued, "and I'd take Grampa's old twelve-gauge and. . . ." He didn't describe the moment, the actual shot.

". . . the sows in there would clean me up. You and Ma wouldn't find a thing."

I could feel him looking at me. I glowered deeper. We dipped across the county line and past the McVenes farm.

"That's OK, Pal. Just thinking, OK? Don't mean nothing."

I didn't report this to Mom, didn't cross check with her whether or not Dad was in a particularly bad state, didn't cry about it at night. I didn't feel anything. I didn't let it touch me.

Of course, it wasn't the confinement's fault. It was mania, specifically hypomania, a down cycle complete with delusion, irrelevant of setting, of conditions.

And the proper response would have been telling Mom and Mom demanding that he go to a doctor, maybe getting others involved like

Reverend Blankespoor. But when you're an insider to a system with only other insiders, how do you know what to do?

WHEN I FINALLY reached 38, the same age that Dad was when I was born, that fact was not lost on me. At 38 I had a twelve-year-old, my daughter Sommer. I married the Laotian girl, Keodouangsy, Sy for short. I still regret missing her baptism, though she's told me about it. She faced the people, and Reverend Blankespoor dipped once and dabbed three times, and the water ran down her face and neck and, since it was symbolic and she couldn't stop it, into her bra.

My understanding of the world now, in my late forties, the age Dad was before I hit ten, has gotten a little more complicated. I've begun to hear my own tangle of voices, for instance, to understand how easy it is to think myself a teenager when a mirror is not present.

I even know the impulse of confessing to my kids, of inflicting adult pains on them.

It happened during one of the great fights between Sy and me, perhaps over Dad himself, who has never warmed to Sy nor she to him. It was when the distance between us, between that isolated farm in the East and the warmth of sticky rice and soy sauce in the West, had suddenly sprung up again. How can the distance between two people become so unbridgeable?

"Kids," I said—we were seated around the table but Sy stood at the kitchen sink. "Mom and Dad are going to split up. Dad's going to move to Sioux Center by my work and you can stay with Mom. She doesn't love him anymore."

It was instantaneous, as if I had hit them—all three started sobbing.

My God.

I couldn't stand it for more than a minute, so I retracted, knew I had gone too far. "No, that's fine. Dad will stay." Bastard. Arrogant enough to talk about myself in the third person.

"That's OK, Pal. Just thinking, OK?"

Sommer was ten then.

Now, on the drive home through a countryside of confinements, as I think of this sin against her, I have the impulse to ask her if she remembers that day, how she felt, if she'll forgive me.

I will go into her room, so that I can ask her privately—I have to know if she remembers.

No. I won't do it, won't dredge up my sin against her as a way of reminding us both of my place in her life. Plus, I already know her answer and why she would give it: because she has to, because it's the only option.

"Do you remember when I said Mom and I were splitting up?" I would begin.

And she would respond with silence.

14

Reprieve

IT'S LIKE WE'RE the bobber stuck under a rock and something's jarred us loose and—pop—there we are on the surface of Lake Sarah and the sun is shining and the wind light and variable. It's late afternoon and at least late June because we're using night crawlers, and I'm casting an orange-and-yellow jighead with an orange twister tail.

Dad's been talking shit about himself, but it doesn't affect me now.

"You suppose God didn't want me to be successful?" he asks.

"I don't know, Dad."

"Should've worked harder, I guess. Been like Mert Buys. He was successful.

"I tried to raise you guys right, have fun once in a while.

"Take you guys fishing.

"I guess I was wrong.

"Should've done like everybody else. Shorty Smit and those guys—look at their farm. They didn't go fishing."

"You don't want to be like Shorty Smit."

"Huh?"

Shorty Smit was another of Dad's cousins, once a dairy farmer like Dad whose sons were going all-in for the crop-farming game. Eventually, Dad would rent our land to them and they would rip out my favorite waterway—the one we had hunted that fall at dusk when we had witnessed the pheasant bouquet, the waterway we had always hunted—so they could farm straight through it.

"You don't want to be like Shorty Smit."

I don't explain or argue.

It's as if the universe has been waiting for this kind of detachment. Mom and Dad will leave the farm this year, my senior year of high school. Carmen will find a janitor job for Dad and an apartment manager job for Mom in the Twin Cities and they will move in April just like that. No one knows this.

Except the lake.

I'm tipping the jig with a whole crawler, and I'm paying the price in crawlers. Maybe ten casts and the worm flesh begins to tear on the hard barb, the hole widening enough so the worm flies off on the cast, or slips off as the jig moves from thin air to thicker water.

I'm five crawlers into two dozen, and just as I begin the retrieve something hammers my jig, and my reaction jerk sets the hook. It's big; it doesn't give or wiggle like a spastic bullhead bite. It stays down, pulls perpendicular to the path of the boat; you can see the line move.

"Got one."

"Bullhead?"

"I don't think so."

I gain line as it crosses back against the path it had been running. The water is clear for late June, and as it comes to the surface broadside but still swimming—walleye! It's golden, shimmery, and my stomach does a backflip. This is my fantasy, the TV-fisherman dream, and I know the story is that I lose it. I can see the orange and yellow jig head sticking out of its mouth before it dives.

I tire it, bring it up to the surface. Dad has the net and he reaches out with it too quickly, not dipping down under the fish so it won't see the net like he taught me, and the fish runs again, and I'm pissed, and this is how I lose it and it's the cruelest of all. But I work the fish back up and this time, though still not dipping down, Dad lips it in. The fish lies wide and heavy in the net.

Dad is thinking like me. "Wow! Look at that! It hangs in the net just like they do on TV!"

I am a conduit of adrenaline, heart pounding. I put the plastic tube in the live well and turn on the water. I rub my hands. I cannot stop rubbing my hands or calm my breathing. I'm manic.

I twist the lure out of its mouth, pick it up behind the head, hold it and feel its weight, look at it for a moment, a golden fish, a gorgeous golden 'eye. I put it in the live well, it tilts to the side for a second, before righting itself. I can't tear my eyes away.

This may be why we never catch more than one walleye here and there. While I'm obsessing over the walleye, I can't pay attention to where we are, whether we're drifting, what the exact details of the bite are that we must replicate.

"What are you using?" Dad asks.

I tell him but he's bottom bouncing and it would take time to change over. He's given up to fate, no longer convinced that individual effort will produce fish. He drops his setup back down to the bottom and waits.

Maybe twenty casts and I have another take, a smaller one, also golden, still beautiful. Dad nets it and says, "Another dandy!"

I can't help but think the curse is over, cannot help but feel this is a reprieve. I start to hope, look through the Styrofoam crawler boxes to consider. What if.

"Looks like I better switch to what you got," Dad says, but the window is already closed.

That's enough, the lake seems to say. That's your blessing. Now go.

I RETURN TO Rochester on the Saturday before Easter. I check in with Dad, who's stable but still nonsensical and restrained. Week three and we're still waiting for real progress. Carmen's son Thor IV and his wife Kelsey live in Rochester, and my plan is to spend the night at their apartment, join them for church Easter Sunday.

In the morning, I drive in to see Dad early, before service. "Good morning, Dad," I say as I come into the room, almost before I can realize he's sitting up, eyes opened. "He is risen," I say, though the phrase does not come easily to me, even on Easter morning.

"He is risen indeed," Dad responds and it's right there at the forefront of his mind, he doesn't have to look for it at all.

Something has shifted in the night. Someone has moved the stone.

REPRIEVE

THE LAST YEAR on the farm, a lot of things were ending.

Like the USSR. Mom saw an advertisement to host exchange students from former Soviet Bloc countries and she thought I could use the company. We were slated to get Alex from Moscow who loved the NBA. Instead, late in the summer we got Samir from Azerbaijan, who liked boxing. And was Muslim.

Azer-by-what-now? There were Muslims in Russia?

Samir at seventeen has a five o'clock shadow by 11:00 a.m., slightly pocked cheeks, and a dimpled chin. His black eyes sparkle when he smiles, his black hair is thick and close-cropped. He really is a boxer, city champ of a place called Baku. When he runs, his stride is wound a little too tight, but when he settles back into a boxing stance, he is spring-loaded. He has calluses that look like large warts on his middle knuckles from doing closed-fist push-ups. He carries himself nobly but is quick with a smile. On his first night in our house he teaches us a Russian card game, "Stupid."

Also ending was the tenure of my friend Chad's dad as pastor at a local church. So, just before school started, Chad moved in with us, too. Chad at seventeen has dark hair, dark eyes, and freckles over the bridge of his nose. He is the one all the girls dream about, the preacher's kid who, when he isn't scouring town for trouble in his black Ford Probe, sits with a dip in his lip as we play cards.

We became fast friends, the three of us, playing Stupid. We finally got Samir to be "stupid" after something like 100 hands.

One night, after a jog to prepare for the upcoming soccer season, Samir and I walked along the pasture fence toward the CRP where we saw a fox prancing, probably hunting mice. I mused about shooting it with the .22 to preserve the pheasant population. Samir said, "I think if you're a Christian, you should not hunt."

Oh? "Because in your commandments it says, 'Thou shalt not kill.'"

In response, I laid out the story of Adam and Eve.

"I have heard this legend," he said.

So began long conversations in high school apologetics. Turns out Samir was perhaps more Soviet atheist than Azeri Muslim, but more philosopher than anything. The three of us would play Stupid and later three-hand pinochle while eating sheet pans of Mom's cookie bars, dipping them in whole milk and arguing about creation vs. evolution (Samir said he'd seen video footage of a baby born with a tail, which Chad and I dismissed with laughter as Soviet propaganda—we'd seen *Rocky IV*, after all), human nature, and the divinity of Christ. One memorable fight, Samir gestured to the Black Hills gold cross around my neck. I took it off, good Protestant boy that I was, slammed it on the white drainboard in the kitchen, and said, "Fuck this cross. *This* cross doesn't mean a thing." About that time, Dad came out in his tighty-whities and sent us to bed.

The next morning, we apologized to each other, and our friendship deepened.

AFTER MY emotions clear this Easter morning, I give Dad a hug through his tubes and the straps that tie him to the bed, straps he is no longer fighting.

"Wow, Dad—how're you feeling?"

"Oh, preddy good." He's still slurring, but he holds his head up, makes eye contact. He is here, present. It's a reprieve, a small resurrection.

Almost immediately, he goes down a different path. "I'm sure happy the way that guy treated me."

"What guy is that?"

"That guy with that fence."

It takes me a moment. It's a non sequitur, but not to the way Dad's mind works. He is recalling a conflict over pastureland on our farm. A couple years back, Dad had given permission for the man who owned our old farmstead to fence the grass around the creek for grazing, destroying my primary hunting ground. Last fall, Dad had sent "that guy" a letter, asking him to pull out the fence. He went under worrying about it.

"He treated me like a perfect gentleman!" he says now. It's true. The farmer thanked Dad in a return letter and had the fences out by spring. It was taken care of and in the past. But it's at the front of Dad's mind.

He is risen indeed, but risen to the old fixations.

It's a resurrection I'll take.

LATE THAT LAST fall on the farm, on a weekend Samir and Chad were both gone somewhere, Dad and I fished Lake Shetek together one last time. It was a beautiful, subtle day, with mists rising off the water and creating a still, golden light. The leaves were turning and falling, the reds and golds of maples, the profound browns of burr oak.

We stopped to cast the rock points along Keeley Island, then drifted its long sand point, me pulling a Rapala, Dad bottom bouncing, and he had a take, a two-pound walleye, a fish I don't really remember, as if the film of my memory got exposed at that point. We stuck along that sandbar for another hour without any more bites, then fished all the places with the names that were so evocative to us as we sat on the rocks of the second dike: Loon Island, Bloody, Lone Tree.

As the sun set, it turned chill, our hands thick with cold from baiting hooks with minnows in fall air.

"Let's troll that rocky shoreline by the second dike one time," Dad said.

That seemed like a good plan, at dusk, so I headed us in that direction.

"Remember when we fished this when you were a kid?" he asked. Of course I did, but I'd learned to distrust Dad's reconstructions of the past, so I just nodded, whether he saw it in the near dark or not. "And that lady came out because she thought we were going to drown? And I dove for the ones you couldn't get? Remember that? We had a lotta good times, didn't we?"

He wanted a response. "You remember that?"

"Yep, I do," I said.

I was pulling a Mr. Twister, and he was still dragging a Lindy Rig, which snagged several times, so we had to go back to free it. Night was falling fast, oh fast.

"Ho it's rocky," Dad said. "Do you remember it being this rocky?"

That was the whole point of why we swam this shoreline, but I said nothing.

Almost down at Uncle Albert's Rock, where now they'd put in a fishing dock, Dad said, "Whoa."

"You got one?"

"No, I think it's a snag."

He was reeling hard, but gaining.

"That's not a snag—is it?"

His rod pulsed. "That's a fish." I had to say it, to declare it so.

He cranked slow, rod tip down toward the water, not using it as leverage at all against the fighting fish. This was his MO now—leave everything till the last surprise, leave everything to fate, as long as you possibly can. It was so dark that I couldn't see anything in the water. I readied the dip net, and when I heard splashes up by the boat, I dipped for whatever it was—too quick, and it dove again.

"What is it?"

"I don't know—carp." He was sandbagging. If he'd have lifted his rod tip, even in this light, we'd have known.

When it came up again, it rolled and I saw white and the tinfoil layer in the eyes and I dipped for it and got it in the boat.

"That's a walleye!" I announced. It was big, thick through the middle, slightly faded in color. It was all we could do to get it out of the net and get it into the livewell and keep the boat out of the rocks in the dark. Late fall was colder than we were prepared for, and, rather than stay and fish now that they'd started biting and would probably continue into the dark, we sped for home, two lovely fish in the live well, both Dad's.

It was entirely satisfying.

It was also goodbye.

THAT CHRISTMAS, Dad had a manic episode at one of my basketball games.

We were playing Luverne in the holiday tournament, and the kid who was guarding me was short and buff, a football player. Luverne had a big kid down low and a lanky, quick guard who could both shoot and dunk. We had me shooting over the beefy kid and a give-and-go with Chad and me that worked well enough down the stretch for us to win in overtime.

It was after the game that I came to understand that something had gotten under Dad's skin. He had been sure they'd been picking on me—that the game plan was to be physical with me, dirty, and that the idea came from the coach and the player guarding me. And so Dad had been heckling both the kid and the opposing coach all night, to the point that the coach had turned around and said to him, "Sir, you are an A-number one asshole!"

It made zero sense. Dad was not this type of fan, ever. That was Uncle Nick's terrain.

Mom was mortified. It was her idea to apologize. I approached Dad about it, but he only said something like, "Well, they were pushing you around, and that coach. . . ."

That left me to make the phone call, which I did, to the beefy kid. "He's not usually that way," I assured the kid. "I'm not sure what got into him."

There was nothing more embarrassing than having lost control, of having no explanation. We all felt it, but more and more, Mom and I were left to cover for it. So we did.

AT SCHOOL, Samir was so far beyond our Pre-Calc class that he took an independent study in math, occasionally getting up to commandeer the board and creating a problem only he and the teacher could talk about.

That January, Chad, Sam, and I all had Bible class with Mr. Vanderaa, a tall Dutchman, son of a minister and brother to a missionary among the Fulani people in Mali. He introduced us to the concept of the kingdom of God. That it was not all about some exit out of this world but about Christ breaking ever more into this one. He said we can take Christ into every area of life, said that we can farm and do social work and manufacture in the way that Christ would want. I thought of Dad's pride in contour farming, of his care for every cow, of the water filtration systems he built out of five-gallon pails for a missionary in Central America, of raising free sweet corn for the schools, of all the foreign exchange students. The kingdom of God was freeing and demanding at the same time—freeing from the game of "spirituality," demanding in that there is no off switch. Christ wanted it all, pointed us toward the world rather than away from it.

It was just the thing we needed as we graduated. This shit—all of it—mattered.

It stressed Samir out, that senior Bible class did. He sought out Nietzsche in the library but couldn't make sense of it in English. He exchanged it for *Mere Christianity*, which sent him downstairs one snow day in January to tell me he wanted to become a Christian. We prayed together in the living room, then danced around. It's both not our Reformed style, a "prayer of salvation" and all that, and exactly what Dad has been angling for with exchange students, changed lives, lives given to Christ. To me it felt like someone behind the scenes had connected friends from across the world.

That afternoon, I went to school to play basketball. When I saw Mr. Vanderaa in the hall, I told him that he better call my house, that Samir had something to tell him. He started walking toward the phone, then broke into a run to get to it faster to call Samir to hear the good news.

Everything came to a head in April. Samir got baptized by Chad's dad in our high school gym. Dad was down again, and Mom's calls to Carmen had sprouted, taken root. Carmen had found Dad a janitorial job at Eden Prairie public schools, Mom could manage an apartment complex where they could live rent-free, and a neighbor to the south would buy the acreage, making the rest of the farm debt manageable. But it had to happen immediately, so it did: Mom and Dad were moving to the Cities; we boys would live out a couple of weeks of May alone in the farmhouse and then move in with Lisa and her family in Woodstock before Samir returned to Azerbaijan in late June.

It was entirely manic.

BUT SAMIR.

One night we were in Edgerton together. I found a way home to Woodstock, left him with the S-10 to play pickup soccer, even though driving was explicitly against the terms of his exchange student program. "It'll be fine," I told him and myself.

He called me just before sunset. "Can you come get me?"
"What's wrong?" I asked, but he wouldn't tell me.

On the way to town, I met a cop car driving with purpose. When I found Samir at the high school, the S-10 had a transverse dent across the grill, and he started filling in the details. When we had parted at the Dutchmen's Den on Main Street, Samir had driven a roundabout route to the high school soccer field. By that time in the S-10's career—200,000 miles in—you had to really slam the driver's side door or it wouldn't latch. Samir hadn't, and rounding a corner, the door had swung open. As he reached for it, Samir stopped his turn, sending him into the opposite lane. When he looked up and saw an oncoming car, he wrenched the wheel, throwing himself out the open door.

"So there I am, skidding on my ass across the pavement," he told me. "And of course here comes one of our classmates—Sara—who stops when she sees me laying on the ground and says, 'Sam, are you OK?' And I feel around—yep, nothing hurt but my pride. And the car is still running. So I jump back in and go to school. When I get there Mr. Hoekstra is outside with the girls basketball team and he says, 'Yeah, Sam, the electricity went out,' and I think, 'Uh-oh, Sam, you dumbass.'

"Welp, nothing I can do! So I go to play soccer with Vanderaa in the back. 'Hey Vanderaa,' I say, 'I think I put the electricity out in the whole town.' 'Nah, don't worry about it,' he says. OK, so we play soccer. I come out after soccer, and I see a cop car standing there. Oh . . . shit."

After he was thrown out, the S-10 had continued up the curb and struck the guy wire on an electric pole, causing the wires up above to cross or spark and putting out electricity in the entire town. It took the electric company more than an hour to figure out the exact location of the problem so they could fix it.

The cop I had met was on his way to find me. He wanted to charge Samir for driving without a license, for not wearing a seatbelt, for leaving the scene of an accident, and he wanted to charge me for letting Samir drive. He talked to Lisa's husband Brad when he didn't find me. Brad wouldn't give us up so easily. He vouched for us, said we had made one poor decision, mentioned the repercussions for Samir should this go on his record. We met the cop just as he was leaving. Brad stuck it to us, told us we'd done a real number. We were in agony. Then he told us that he thought he had convinced the cop to drop the charges and broke a smile.

In the end, that's exactly what happened. We never even had to talk to anyone in law enforcement. The damage plus the cost of lost electricity was in the thousands of dollars, but Mom and Dad talked to their insurance agent and insurance covered most of it.

Say the Midwest is boring. Say people judge you too much, know all your business and your family line to the third and fourth generations. Say living here is like bipolar II, the one with fewer ups and more downs—long, flat, featureless stretches you just have to get through.

But the reprieves, the small resurrections, when they come, are so unexpected, so good.

This was the place we were leaving.

And would keep coming back to.

15

Lake Independence

ANOTHER DECADE, another living room scene. Even another hip-roofed house, this one in a suburb of Chicago, where Aunt Lida lived, site of a small Dutch enclave. No, come to think of it, it was my cousin's because his house was larger and neutral ground. Since the falling out with Hein and Lida, the relationship between Dad and his favorite sister was still chilly. But my cousin could always put Dad at ease with old stories, get him laughing. Plus, he had this funny Polish-American wife who could defuse any situation.

We've stopped in Oak Park on the way to Samir's wedding in Grand Rapids, Michigan, and Sy is with us. After Samir's stay at our house, near the Dutch enclave of Leota, he went to college in Sioux Center, Iowa, site of another Dutch enclave, where he met a Dutch-Canadian girl from an enclave in Hamilton, Ontario, and they're getting married in Grand Rapids, Michigan, the bullseye of Dutch-Calvinist enclaves and middle ground between Hamilton and Sioux Center, since Samir's visa doesn't extend to Canada.

Sy and I, despite six years together, are not engaged.

But we've stopped on the way to see Aunt Lida. In spite of everything. Things start out a little tense. Dad is quiet in a setting where he is normally the star, all the ribbing and heroic exploits revolving around Uncle Milt. My cousin's son takes me to his room to watch him feed his piranhas. He's out of mice but he throws in minnows and they spin around in terror, the piranhas working up their charge like defibrillators until one nips the tail off the first minnow, and when they all smell blood they buzzsaw until the minnows are gone.

We go back to the living room and comment on the phenomenon. Shock. Awe.

My uncle and his boys are businessmen in their Chicago suburb, the latest one to undergo white flight, though none of us know the term, and the conversation turns to the current influx of workers, Mexicans, and how my cousins don't understand them when they speak Spanish. And the question gets asked, Why can't they speak English? And my cousin is saying, *No habla inglés*, and Mom says, starting it in the middle of the room and turning it toward Sy, "Yeah, why can't they learn English? Your Mom had to learn English, right Sy?" but it's a rhetorical question.

Sy finds a reason to leave. I follow her. "I was getting shaky," she says to me. "I had to get out of there or I was going to do something."

My cousin has moved on to doing jive, "—and I axed him, I axed him, I axed—'Hey, main, what's happenin' my main?'—" and Uncle Hein throws out the n-word, and Dad says loudly, "If they can't learn English, ship 'em back! And if the Blacks can't learn—then ship them back, too!" and he has momentarily forgotten Lida's betrayal, and everyone is suddenly and strangely united.

Almost everyone.

In the kitchen, Sy and I stand against an off-white wall in the midafternoon light. She says, "You don't understand—my Grandma never learned English."

We find a reason to leave quietly for Grand Rapids, fight all the way, Sy wondering how in the world she can be contemplating joining this family, me trying to convince her that that's not me, that that's not the Dad I grew up with, that it's just. . . .

THE EASTER miracle at Mayo subsides into bipolar II normalcy. After three weeks of sorting through Dad's problems—lithium toxicity, adverse reaction to Ativan, UTI, Hashimoto's—he's out of the woods but still disoriented, fidgety, fixated, now with three psychotropics on board instead of the simple salt, lithium.

All us siblings meet with the medical team: Dr. Nassar, an older neurologist, an intern, and a scribe, in a room somewhere between mauve pink and warm tan. We cross-examine Nassar, the Von Schaap family amateur psychiatrists. What exactly has just happened? Why is Dad still so mixed up? Has it really been bipolar that we've been dealing with or was it some other form of depression? Now that he's burned the lithium bridge, what's the next long-term solution?

We get answers that aren't answers. We get a shoulder shrug. They need to get Dad out of the acute wing into something less intensive, so they will move Dad to the general neurology floor and wean him from his aide, which makes us all nervous. The problem now may be hospital delirium, the nondescript nowhereness of the hospital rooms he's been trapped in for going on three weeks. There's no solution now but to get him out of here.

This place makes him sick, it turns out—the placelessness of it.

He needs his own living room, the power station across the road, Pelican Lake down the street. He needs landmarks.

DAD ALWAYS painted college as the great escape, as the way to leave Leota. College would free you from the trap of the farm, of small towns, of the cult. It would launch you into fulfilling, remunerative careers. It would do this naturally, just by you being there. Once you were there, college made you someone.

So upon graduation, I followed Carmen and Heidi to the school that had launched them, Bethel College, in suburban St. Paul. With Mom and Dad's move to the suburban Twin Cities, I also followed them.

The Schaap family time in the Twin Cities was unremarkable. Mom and Dad first lived in a gray apartment with gray walls that looked and smelled like smoke, and then, after a mentally ill tenant set that place on fire three times in one night, they moved to a brown apartment with tan walls, with older, slightly richer tenants and only a few hoarders. Dad cleaned toilets for Eden Prairie public schools and then for the Home Depot. I went to a suburban college that was comfortably white and Protestant, and Sy went to the University of

Minnesota that was not, and we cycled through break-ups and make-ups while Mom and Dad remained cool to our relationship.

We fished when we were in the Cities, but almost no fish have clung to my memory.

I know we went to Lake Minnetonka once, the premier Twin Cities lake, which was big and murky with large houses along many shores. Dad preferred Lake Independence for some reason, maybe because it was a little farther out of the city, a little smaller, a little less busy.

I remember Lake Independence as dingy—not actually as brown-dirty as Shetek, but dingy, like dishwater. I know we caught fish on Independence, sunnies, a bass, a small northern, maybe one rogue crappie. But there was nothing coherent about it. It felt random. I didn't know where I was. Not at Lake Sarah, at the very head of the Des Moines River, fresh and clear and self-sustaining; not the just-downstream Shetek, silted and expansive and islanded; not Lake Benton in the hill country of the Buffalo Ridge, beautiful but stagnant, greening impossibly toxic in midsummer; not the high spring-fed bowl of Summit Lake at Hadley; not the shallow mud of Lake Wilson; not the long beach and two rock points of Currant. I cannot place in time any of the fishing trips to Lake Independence, except to say that they were probably holiday trips. Lake Independence on Independence Day, that kind of thing. It was not the kind of relationship you could structure a life around.

Summers, I caddied at Interlachen Country Club with my Colombian-born college friend Jason, who had caddied there since junior high. On one loop, on ladies' day, a member asked how I'd come to work at Interlachen. "Do you know the caddy Jason?" I asked. She nodded. "Well, he invited me out."

We walked a few more steps before she asked, "Jason. . . . You mean, the Black?" It was like something out of F. Scott Fitzgerald.

Senior year, I went on my college's England Term, a semester of studying at locations across the British Isles. My relationship with Sy was reaching a breaking point. Dad was frustrated with his second job, scrubbing toilets at Home Depot, and was cycling again, while Mom kept everything afloat as manager of the apartment where they lived. As an English major, I wasn't magically being remade into something else and I sure as hell wasn't headed for a remunerative career. I hadn't been able to leave anything. So I went to England in one last desperate attempt.

A week into the trip, on a bus from Edinburgh south into England proper, we stopped at the scenic overlook that Sir Walter Scott was said to have favored, stopping there regularly with his horse, the story went, to look over the countryside, to the point that when his horse carried Scott's bier to rest, it stopped by habit at the place. It was a rural vista I recognized, with fields of golden stubble and old stonewall borders, a landscape plotted and pieced, if in an old-world style. I swallowed hard.

In the Lake District, after climbing a small mountain called Catbells, along the shore of a lake whose name I didn't know, I saw a fisherman standing on a sand point, casting with a reel and lures I did know, Rapalas, spoons. I went and stood near him as you would a fire in the cold. The arc of the cast, the retrieval, the feeling for contact. Finally, I worked up the courage to ask, "Catching anything?"

He politely said no, invited no more conversation, though questions burgeoned in me like swallowed joy, or like Dad's impulse to chat up any fisherman near us. I wanted to ask what he was fishing for, what they bit on at this time of the year, how they tasted when filleted out and fried, what the fish population was, whether he'd had much luck here before, whether he ever used live bait, what his biggest fish was, what his most memorable fish was, what his strangest fish was, whether they ever used dobbers.

In Ireland, in Yeats country, maybe because I'm homesick, the world turns second person. The swans at Coole Park swim at you out of the mist. At Lissadell House, one of many sites of Yeats's passion for Ireland, you're stopping by off-season, and a Brit straight out of the nineteenth century comes out and stops you from getting off the bus and in the Britishest of accents demands you pay him for just being there, but Angus your Irish tour guide refuses and tells him that this man's people have been extorting Angus's people for hundreds of years and he doesn't use the terms "English" or "Irish" but finally he agrees that we'll leave the British accent in peace after a few minutes' stop, but the accent says, "I'd rahtha have your money," and Angus is red-faced pissed off and it's thrilling to touch history.

And then at the strange tower Thoor Ballylee, the river is all in torrent and of course you could be a writer here, anyone could, and then you look up at the hulking Ben Bulben, and in your mind it's like Blue Mound on the Buffalo Ridge by Luverne which you see off in the distance on the drive to Edgerton.

Back in England, in Stratford-upon-Avon, you hear a lecture on Shakespeare, complete with the swarthy picture of the Bard with a gold earring glinting from the darkness around his shoulders, the pub-going Bard, the dashing one, and not the dorky bulbous frontal lobe one. You fancy—fancy?—Shakespeare a person with a libido for the first time. On the walk back to the B&B, you catch your reflection in a plate glass window and imagine yourself with an earring, a little piece of gold hook caught in your ear. The next week, in London, in Camden Town, you get it pierced, and it feels like a big rebellion. Maybe you are finally leaving.

From London you go to Hemingway's Paris with its cafes and butcher shops with full-feather pheasants hanging in the windows and purple water fountains in cobblestone squares and it's freezing cold November and you kiss another girl on the trip.

Near the end of the semester, you have extra time in London. You call John Thwaite, the foreign exchange student who started it all, with whom you share a birthday. You train out to John's, and it's awkward between you, but it's also fine. John is still steely-eyed, steely here connoting color because John can almost not not smile, his eyes are always smiling because he is always smiling and his accent is still so thickly Midlands that you're always asking, "What?"

For lunch, John takes you to eat at the local pub and you have pints with your meal, of course. At night, you watch TV and have a pint can of Boddington's and it's creamy and cold going down and warm in your stomach.

You sleep in his spare bed that is full of dog hair, and the next day John takes you hunting. You walk around farms he knows, not really understanding what it is he wants you to shoot, asking him what the season is, and he's not worried, shoot anything, he says. Then you get that you're really after foxes. You'll never see a fox, you think to yourself, but this is England and there are foxes everywhere: one in the pasture eyeing calves that trots away when you get too interested, one on the farm where John works. Another worker has seen it go in one of the cattle sheds, so John makes a plan to close certain doors to limit its exit opportunities, then he posts you at the last opening and goes in to run it out, yelling to you through the tin that it's coming, and you ready the twelve gauge and pound it against the building when it emerges, slinking along flat-eared like the world has beaten it up one too many times. It dies gasping and John flings it on a pile of manure.

"Sometimes they can be beaut-i-ful crea-tures," he says in that lovely syllabic way, "but this one's just sort of mangy and ugly." He's right, and this has all been sorts of strange and sad and wonderful, and if you weren't so set on leaving you would know you're close to home.

Sy comes to visit, to travel with you at the end of the trip, and she breaks you out of second person, thank God. We can't find each other in Amsterdam, she at Schiphol and me at Central Station, and then finally we do find each other and then find a cheap hotel for the night.

I take her to Paris and we fight when I try to show her around, going down the Rue de Mouffetard, and the little room Hemingway rented with his first wife Hadley before he ruined his life. Then, out of the blue, we call up Jean Luc, exchange student #2 on the Milt Schaap farm, he of the bale hook to the ear. I tell him we'd like to see him the very next day, and he drops everything, tells me to train out to Le Mans and picks us up at the station, grabbing McDonald's drive-thru for his kids on the way home to his farm in the French countryside complete with a stone tower from the twelfth century, and even here I'm living on Dad's merit. After dinner, he and his wife Betty serve us a dozen kinds of cheeses with wine, and he puts Sy and me in the same bed and doesn't ask any questions.

Even so, I try to break up with Sy in Germany, on the banks of the Rhein below the cliffs of the Lorelei, but the ten words of German we both learned under Frau Schoone-Jongen at Southwest Christian in Edgerton, Minnesota, bond us together, and it's the middle of Germany and we have no one else to turn to.

I've had to read Eliot in England, and he's not really my type, but I've come upon something in *Four Quartets* that goes,

> Do not let me hear
> Of the wisdom of old men, but rather of their folly,
> Their fear of fear and frenzy, their fear of possession,
> Of belonging to another, or to others, or to God.

I've had enough of trying to belong to myself, of leaving. I want to belong to others, even if the story is tangled. Especially if the story is tangled.

When Sy leaves to return home, it's not fine, but we have too much story together, our identities melded inextricably. I have not been able to leave. I'm going back.

When I get back to Minnesota, Sy and I have another big fight out of which I say, "Either we break up and never get back together, or we get married. Let's get married. Will you marry me?" It's not a good story. But it's our story.

I tell Dad in the brown apartment, in the four tan walls of the laundry room, and he keeps transferring the laundry and says he doesn't like the way Sy treats me, that it's not her race, just that she controls me. It's not her race at all, he says. He says he thinks I'm making a mistake.

Sy and I go back home to get married, to Edgerton, to the stone church that sponsored Sy's family from Laos when her mom fled communism and her abusive husband—First CRC, Edgerton, the church with parallel pews that is the daughter church of Leota Ebenezer. We get married the same way we dated: with blinders on, looking only straight ahead, crossing borders, walking on water.

Her grandma and mom give her away, and I bawl during the song I try to sing to her.

The reception is in a school gymnasium. I step all over her dress multiple times. Samir is the best man, Chad alongside him, Jason the Colombian-born caddy alongside him. The stars of the wedding are Laotian things: Lao fried rice and egg rolls and sticky rice and meat, and a Laotian singer, Sy's sister-in-law. When she sings, the Lao guests and the tall white guys from my college basketball team come out and do a traditional Lao dance, *fon*, a hand dance where you pull your hands slowly this way and that, taut to the music.

And things are not nearly perfect but they are also fine.

After the wedding and a three-day honeymoon in Colorado, where neither Sy nor I know where we are, I begin teaching high school English. Back in Edgerton, in the place Dad told me to leave, in the landscape that makes him "just tight." Mom and Dad are left to themselves in the Twin Cities.

THERE'S A fish I caught in the Cities that I almost remember. Dad had read about the St. Croix River, and so we drove across the breadth of Minneapolis and St. Paul to fish it, a tight little approachable river, held closely by trees, with a current you could feel, very different from the giant Missouri, from Lake Oahe. We had read about eddies, about "inside turns" where the river bends and creates slack water. Fish there, the article said, so we tried.

Dad threw out a bottom bouncer, the ubiquitous Lindy Rig, his only go-to, and was almost immediately tangled in tree branches. I threw a jig.

Jigging. A jig. To jig. Jigging was the most mysterious term we'd encountered in *In-Fisherman*. Was there really a technique that could produce more fish than others? And was it really called "jigging"? A jig was just a lead-head hook, sometimes tipped with live bait, sometimes with a plastic or feathery body. A Mister Twister, after all these years, was actually a jig. Jigging had to do with feel. Pick up your lead-head jig and let it fall and in between, the walleyes peck at it, sometimes snatch it, but you've got to feel it.

That day, I threw a jig and just flicked it, felt it, let it go with the current and slide slightly downstream. On the dying fall, I found fish snapped it up, that the flick back hooked it in their mouths and left me with that flapping electric pulse of a fish on the end of a line. I brought them to the boat on my spinning reel and lifted them out casually, like I thought the Cross Lake guide would have.

They were sauger, the smaller, more sharply mottled cousin of the walleye, but I can't see any of them clearly in my memory, just feel the feeling, of coming into some insider knowledge, some insight about the unseen world.

Meanwhile, Dad bottom bounced, and snagged over and over.

It was another separation. And a coming home to something I had always known.

Something drove us off the water that day. But we liked the St. Croix, determined to come back, though we never did.

IN THE NEW room at Mayo, off the neurology wing, despite the pictures on the walls of grandkids, of the farm as it was, of Samir, pictures to string together a story with, Dad doesn't know where he is. It feels like the state hospital again, like he's made the move over to Institutional Man.

This is how you leave a story: you set it in four blank walls, make it plotless, pointless, with no tangles. Maybe a hospital room is just a living room with no tension—no passive-aggressive uncles, no family dynamics—that results in its own psychosis: hospital delirium.

After he's as settled as he will be in the new room, I take my leave. I've done all I can do. It's time to return to Sy and the kids, to recross the boundaries of the tangled life we still live. I place my hand on Dad's arm, bruised and marked from wrist to elbow from prickings and IVs, place my cheek next to his cheek, bare across the flat of his cheekbone with stubble only on the jawline, like my own, and I feel the stress go out of him. This is the way he communicated best over the years—bear hugs, knee squeezes, hand pats. Now, as he feels my cheek, we both hold it there and I feel him exhale. I feel us bridge the distances easily, freely. "I love you, Dad," I say. He just breathes, easy for a minute, without urgency.

Then I leave to go home.

16

Shit Buckets

LONG BEFORE THEY actually bought one to live in, while we were still on the farm, I remember looking at them in Sioux Falls. We went inside several models, walked around, and Dad thought they were wonderful. He oohed and ahhed. They smelled new, certainly, a new-car smell. He said something aspirational to Mom, like, "I would love to buy one of these for you some day."

We were standing inside a mobile home—a modular home, they called it, and a doublewide, but a mobile home nonetheless.

I want to give the mobile home its due. They are indeed fine places to live. Uncle Nick and Aunt Joan lived in one next to QPI, and it was . . . sound. It had enough rooms for everyone and a sort of . . . privacy. When the wind blew you generally couldn't feel it. Only sometimes you got the sense there wasn't much depth to the house, no basement, for instance, rooted through the topsoil. Maybe this is tornado paranoia. A tornado like the F-5 that ate half of Chandler and dented the water tower perfectly in the middle of the phrase "In God We Trust"—it was terrifying what a tornado would do to a house like that. Zero chance a house like that could spin all the way to Oz and kill the wicked witch; it would matchstick in an instant, with you inside it.

Then again, maybe a mobile home would just spin and spin. Like a Frisbee.

IN THE END at Mayo, they just stack up the meds on Dad to hold him down: Depakote, Haldol, Olanzapine. Then they send him home. The UTI that had him running the Bobcat on the farm and the Hashimoto's encephalopathy that kept him confined by six-inch bed rails and the steroids that had him punching nurses have resolved finally into hospital delirium. An important part of the cure for Dad now was to orient him to time and place, so they sent him home. One day we just put on his coat and cap for him and put him in the car.

I had great disappointment, tremendous misgivings. Rochester was supposed to fix him. Now, once again we would be leaving Mom to manage a large bipolar man, this time juggling three antipsychotics, alone in the Big Woods. We had been here before.

WHEN WE HEARD Dad had bought a lot Up North, that he was living in a camper while he "got things ready," and that he planned, in time, to move a modular home onto the lot for him and Mom to live in, we didn't much ask about the details. We had long accepted the facts of how Mom and Dad operated. They would do what it took to try to get Dad to his dreams, to live Up North and do some fishing—maybe even become a fishing guide, in the most quixotic version of the dream. If it would keep him busy and his mind occupied, great.

Then, we shaded in a few more details. The lot was not on a lake, since they could never have afforded a lake lot; the camper was from the 1950s and without electric. Dad spent his days cutting down birches and poplars and pines with a chainsaw, clearing a space for the house. Good for him, we said.

Only later did we ask, how far to the nearest bathroom?

A quarter mile. But that was just fine—he could go down to the convenience store when he needed to.

And he always had a five-gallon bucket.

Even then, when it set in that Dad had moved from the Twin Cities up to the Big Woods to live in a camper and, when the need should arise, to shit in a bucket, we didn't ask, "Was this the flashing neon sign of Dad's bipolar? Or was it 'just Dad'?" We had long stopped distinguishing between the two.

Or had never started.

For Dad's part, the willingness to use a bucket was very Charles Ingalls, pioneer resourcefulness and all that. It meant you were ultimately adaptable, could live anywhere, make do—make doo, har-har—with anything. Dad always said that if you hadn't experienced the outhouse when it was -20 in winter or 110 degrees in summer, tearing off a page of the Sears catalog with which to wipe, you had really missed out on something important in life.

He used a similar measure to judge the never-worked-a-day-in-his-life types. "He never wiped his ass and put his finger through the paper," Dad would say about someone too high and mighty for his own good.

To this day, I find it hard to argue with that logic.

From Mom's perspective, stunts like this always worked for Dad, at least for a season. Send him out with his itching foot, and it gives Ma a break, rehabilitates Pa.

Then, to be fair to us kids, Dad had a history. On the farm, Dad would use a bucket when he was in the middle of milking. Made sense. At the gravel pit in California, too, in an unheated, unplumbed trailer, locked behind the chain-link fence at night, a bucket had been called into service, out of necessity. Now this.

Of the three shit buckets, the California one was easily the craziest. It's easy for me to look back and judge Mom for letting Dad go to California at the rock bottom of his depression—instead of going to, say, therapy. You didn't go to therapy in the eighties. Hell, you don't go to therapy *now* in rural Minnesota.

But this idea, that maybe Mom herself needed a break. If I remember the fatigue of trying to carry his self-esteem, she must have been worn out.

Or, darker, maybe she didn't want to live with the results of finding him—or having me find him—swinging in the barn.

But Mom is not the kind of woman to let herself think these thoughts consciously. She's too positive, too hopeful, too nice. Too much a woman of faith—I'm sure that's what she would like me to write. But is refusing to look at the possibilities faithful or foolish? Or both?

In the gravel pit, Dad kept busy during the day working, but at night, alone in a pink trailer for hours, behind the chain-link, he faced the darkness. Dad said he cried himself to sleep often in that trailer.

Mom's faith was faith in Dad. In his love for us. That Dad would look out the window from rock bottom, and re-catch the vision, begin to rebuild their dream.

And faith in God in that American sort of way. That things will work out. That a window would open. That no one would give him a rope.

In both California and Brainerd, Dad *was* able to reset, to see the vision. In California, Dad was part of the California-Promised-Land-endeavor. In Brainerd, he was carving a home out of the wilderness, an Al Lindner dream.

Then again, whether in California or Brainerd, letting Dad live in a trailer and use a bucket in emergencies was also the clearest indication that Mom was profoundly shaped by Dad's bipolar, that we all were.

TREE BY TREE, Dad cleared the yard. Then the house came, a double-wide, complete with indoor plumbing. Then Mom quit her job managing pre-nursing-home hoarders in the Twin Cities and joined him. Then Dad had a large, custom garage built.

It was—nice. There was a kind of—privacy.

Or, put it this way: it fit right in with the Brainerd tourist aesthetic, with faux-log houses and the Paul Bunyan statue, fine unless you looked too close and then a little chintzy.

Mom and Dad's new address was officially in Breezy Point, Minnesota, which took its name from a resort of the same name, a place we could never have afforded ever as a family. Breezy Point seemed like a town financed by the remote rich, staffed by the troubled and wandering, and swelled by weekend warriors. Throw in the retirees like Mom and Dad, and the result was a kind of rootlessness.

Consider the string of murders in the area in light of this instability. Each time we went Up North to visit, Mom seemed to have a new story. Domestic violence: a husband kills his wife and then turns the gun on himself. Family dysfunction: a grandson kills his grandparents; an eighty-year-old man kills his 40-year-old daughter-in-law and then himself; a seventeen-year-old shoots a fifteen-year-old for stealing video games.

Then a *Fargo*-esque crime: a triple homicide in which two men were shot in the head and a woman beaten to death; a week later, the perp stabbed himself to death in a Las Vegas hotel room while authorities pounded on the door.

Finally, abductions: a twenty-one-year-old, found in a shallow grave eighteen months after her murder; and, most disturbing to Mom, a fifty-year-old who was abducted at the end of her shift in a liquor store, her car left running in the February cold, her purse and coat still inside. Her remains were discovered by horseback riders on a side road in Breezy Point when the horses shied at the decaying body, six weeks after her death.

Breezy Point felt like a temporary wager, a Pa Ingalls phase, a patina of wealth covering deeper problems, built on the backs of the desperate.

Here's my problem with Breezy Point in one illustration: Mom and Dad's favorite place to eat was a diner called The Chaparral. *The Chaparral*, like something from TV *Little House*, set in a country of too many hills and trees.

Also, I couldn't catch fish there.

DAD SET HIS doublewide across the road from one of Minnesota's several Pelican Lakes, the biggest, clearest one. I caught one walleye on Pelican in all the years they lived there, trolling Gooseberry Island. It was a fluke. Later, Dad picked up a predictable phrase about the lake from another disgruntled fisherman: "Oh, Pelican? You mean, the Dead Sea?"

So we went over to Lake Edward instead, because it was smaller and Dad liked the boat launch. We could pull enough eater-northerns out of Edward to feel like it wasn't a total waste. One time trolling on Edward, Dad hooked into something large that stayed down impossibly long—as in, he had to pry it off the bottom and mused aloud that it was probably a snapping turtle. I hoped against hope that it was a big pike or musky. When it finally surfaced and we netted it, I had no idea what it was. It was eel-like, with a top fin that extended from mid-back all the way to its tail, not exactly brown like a bullhead but more on the catfish side of the equation. Once in the boat, it shit all over the floor in clumpy, yellow turds.

"I think that's what they call a dogfish," said Dad, pulling the term from I don't know where. I thought he was shitting me at first, but he wasn't. Bowfin is the official name—I looked it up later—an amazing, ancient fish. But because of the shit all over, Dad said he'd never let another one into his boat.

We couldn't catch walleyes, but we could catch dogfish. We looked at this strange creature—like something from a South American river, alive in an obscure corner of a clear Minnesota lake, with a built-in defense mechanism to make us detest it, which we did—but couldn't see it for the gift it was. We got it off the hook and dumped it over the side.

MOM MADE the double-wide her own. She bought loon knickknacks to set around the living room, bird knickknacks for the kitchen. Outside, she set up a congeries of bird feeders and watched them seasonally. She made a little arbor and garden area out back that Heidi added to with a tasteful little waterfall. In the end, that's what Mom didn't want to leave, a little haven that she didn't have in the open of the prairie.

When the squirrels raided the bird feeders, Dad bought a live trap, and the Elmer Fudd games began. When they found acorns stashed in drawers inside the guest bedroom, it was a profound mystery until they caught chipmunks at work, and Dad trapped and poisoned them and tried to find the holes in the crawl space where they were getting in. They fed deer and later a coyote that they told us about for weeks so that we had to come and see for ourselves. Sure enough, at dusk, Wile E. Coyote himself came to pick through the pork chop bones we'd left by a tree out back.

Meanwhile, Dad watered flowers at Home Depot for hours on end. He didn't like corporate. On several occasions when customers couldn't seem to find help because management had left them short-handed and Dad was busy with some other task, he told them to go over to Menards. He cleaned bathrooms and ran the Zamboni and, as always, made friends. Someone with a little drawing skill made a caricature of all the workers, in which Dad is prominent-chinned and dimple-cheeked, with a twinkle in his eye.

As Dad gradually retired, cutting back by percentages as he hit birthdays sixty-six, sixty-eight, seventy, he volunteered, or Mom found ways for him to volunteer. He took disabled kids fishing. He joined Kinship Partners and became a mentor for a kid named Brandon, whose father was not in the picture. Dad taught Brandon how to handle his Winchester .22 pump at a local shooting range, then took him hunting with it. He mentored young men in Teen Challenge, a drug rehabilitation program, got invited to their weddings.

And they made good friends. Through church, Mom and Dad met a retired dentist and his wife, Vernon and Ruth. Dad became fast friends with Vernon, a gentle soul who had his own story of abuse: abandoned by his father, Vernon went to the Navy as replacement, eventually found Christ and Ruth and his way to the gentle demeanor that was palpable when you met him, a kindness that was balm for Dad's own sorrows.

In the time they were up there, Mom and Dad's body of work was formidable. They were finding the pulse of the place, from work and worship to flora and fauna. They were digging in in the sandy, clayey soil of Up North, putting down roots that were well on the way to reaching the water.

And the real behind-the-scenes architect of it all, the fulcrum around which Dad spun, was that girl from the Chandler Hills, Hattie Jean. Sure, Mom was codependent—determined and positive to match Dad's pessimism and despair. During the dark times she nagged Dad out of his chair and out into the world, enlisting his Elmer Fudd know-how against invading chipmunks and squirrels when he was down, providing the soil for Dad's dreams to take root in when he was up. Her resilience came from a combination of Schelhaas calm and Gilman pride, with a healthy dose of faith, with belief in the goodness of the world God created. No matter the place or circumstances, she always had grace enough to share with Chicago nephews and foreign exchange students and the fatherless and broken of Breezy Point.

DESPITE THIS body of work, Up North didn't pan out for Dad as he'd hoped.

"I feel just tight," he'd say from his chair and lock his jaw in that old frightening way.

"Dad's down," Mom would say on phone calls as a way to request a visit.

Once, when Lisa and her son Austin complied with this request, they got blown up at because Dad didn't approve of one of Lisa's decisions, maybe related to her first divorce.

Another time I found Dad hopeful of making a quick fortune by selling something or other, clearly a pyramid scheme.

Then, Dad got old prematurely. He developed the shakes, a side effect of lithium, then balance and coordination issues that left him dependent on others to even go fishing.

One summer when Sy and I visited with our kids, despite Dad's mysterious coolness to the idea, Mom insisted that we take the boat out. I agreed, mainly because the worst thing was to just sit there in the doublewide, a rectangle of six rooms. We invariably barricaded ourselves into the smallest of these, the corner den, where Dad would blare his favorite news channel or we would surf to find something we were interested in and they didn't find offensive.

Hitting the lake was definitely a better option. Dad had gotten permission for us to use a private boat launch, owned by a local man with Alzheimer's whom Mom and Dad sat with from time to time when his wife ran errands. But Dad was not in favor of the whole endeavor, maybe because he was not in control or because we would be on someone else's property.

We blew up the tube, packed snacks, and hooked up the boat to the Blazer. Dad wore a furrow in his brow. We pressed on. I backed the boat in, and he directed me though I didn't need it, and it went smoothly but his furrow deepened. The boat wouldn't start and he knew it, that's what he was afraid of, then it did and we pulled away from the dock. Mom and Dad sat and watched from shore as we tried to tube, but Sommer was terrified alone on a tube that always seemed to be sinking—the boys were too little—and so we headed back to where Mom and Dad sat on the dock. As we pulled in, Dad was convinced I had come in at the wrong angle and a little too fast, and he said, "Watch out, you're gonna wreck it!" I was already coming up to the front of the boat to catch us, but so was he from the dock side, and reaching over he fell to his knees and almost into the water. I yelled at him and Sy did and Mom did, and there he was, on his hands and knees, knees sore and pride sore and too weak and unsteady and awkwardly shaped in early old age to pick himself back up. I got on the dock and tried to help him, but he knew what he had to do, crawl over to the bench and use it to get up, which he did, worn out.

I lectured him but I could have saved my breath. He was physically wiped out but not convinced.

I still had not learned that I couldn't talk him out of his moods.

The kids spent the afternoon in the shallow water and had a ball jumping on and off the tube. They saved us. Then, it was back to their house, to the four walls of the den where Dad retreated to his corner chair and his news channel, relieved to be quit of the world and its anxieties.

Another kind of atmosphere had descended on the doublewide. Mom and Dad avoided many of my grandparents' shibboleths. We could watch TV on Sunday, our kids could get a little loud and wild without worry, nothing was irreplaceable or sacred. But their house in Breezy Point still came to feel like my grandparents' house. Maybe it was their food preferences compared to ours, their habits of viewing, their patterns of conversation. Maybe it was my same old reactions to his same old moods.

Some of the problem was time, the cleaver of the four decades between a fifties couple whom Civil Rights didn't seem to touch and a mixed-race nineties couple. There were major no-fly zones, topics we couldn't find a common vocabulary for. Race seemed unapproachable, unexplainable. They bumbled. Dad, on a visit to our house, in the presence of Sy: "You know what I think we should do with foreigners? Ship 'em back!" Mom, about a Black basketball player on TV: "He's just so ugly—those big lips. . . ." And we took offense.

Some of it was that great Midwestern passive-aggressiveness that won't address what's wrong but just take it out of your hide with smiling meanness when your back is turned. And write a book about it.

And the evil eye of Dad's favorite news channel, just another kind of monoculture, another kind of fencerow-to-fencerow pronouncement from the wizard behind the screen. That there had been too many handouts. Too many people from shithole countries. That he had made it—or not—on his own, so why shouldn't they? Misremembering what had happened, and failing to imagine what might have been.

In this, too, the Ingallses help make sense of things. *Prairie Fires* tracks the Ingallses' slide to the right. Charles Ingalls joins a populist party. Laura's daughter Rose flirts with fascism, praises Mussolini. Laura herself scoffs at people who would take handouts, selectively remembering her own father's story as pure heroic self-reliance. She and Almanzo manage to stay out of the poorhouse through her books, but just barely.

After the fall at the dock, we didn't really try to launch the boat anymore when we visited. By the time Dad started falling around the yard and in the house, it was clear their vision of Up North was drying up.

As Dad is discharged from Mayo, we kids determine to do a better job supporting Mom in her life with Dad Up North. To keep an eye on them. To call and visit more often.

Carmen accompanies Mom and Dad on the trip home. She sends us a picture of Dad on a stop for ice cream, in his maroon-and-gold Gophers sweatshirt and cap. His eyes are lifted and he wears a smile that is trusting. He doesn't quite know where he is.

Yes, he does. It's The Hub, or may as well be The Hub, and he's responded to Mom's request for a smile and to Carmen's purity of voice and to ice cream the way he always responds to those he loves and to the good things in life, somewhere out in the world, on the way Up North.

Despite everything, I carry on the shit bucket tradition. Go fishing with children for any real amount of time to places off the beaten path where you might actually have a chance of catching fish, and a bucket is bound to come in handy. When your kid says, "I've got to go number two—now," and you could either pull up stakes and drive a half mile to the hole-in-the-ground outhouse or set your kid on a bucket twenty feet away, it's an easy choice.

Even when you're ice fishing, it's ten degrees, your kid needs to disrobe from his coat, snow pants, pants, underwear, and then poop. In a bucket.

It makes for a funny story, at least, or a memory. It's just you, your humanity, and a plastic bucket.

And your dad.

What more could a person need?

17

Minnesota Wild

"SO, DAD WENT crazy last night," my sister Lisa said when she called. "Not crazy—there was murder in his eyes."

Sy and I were married and living back in Edgerton, where I was teaching high school English. Mom and Dad were visiting, down from the Big Woods for the weekend, staying at Lisa's house in nearby Pipestone. Lisa's phone call would set in motion the first intervention, the time we had Dad committed. He was sixty-nine years old.

"Oh?"

"It's that look, when his jaw goes hard and he grits his teeth. It's the one he used to get when there was a fresh heifer that wouldn't milk."

The precipitating event was, surprise surprise, about church. He'd come home from my sister's church, Cornerstone Evangelical Free Church of Pipestone, which had voted to plant a church in Edgerton, town of 1100 with five churches already. This was ridiculous to Dad, even offensive, the Protestant game of protesting the protesters. He came home from service agitated, and the argument began, him stating his position—it was ridiculous to start another church in Edgerton—and Mom countering it. "Well, what's it to you? It's none of your business, anyway."

From there, it went and went. Dad couldn't drop it, and Mom couldn't either. "She just keeps picking at him," Lisa said, "almost egging him on, but that doesn't mean he can do what he did."

The argument spun throughout the day, Dad ruminating and reopening the topic, only to get, "Now would you just drop it? If they want to plant a church there, let them do it. It's no skin off your nose."

"And that's when he got that look," Lisa told me the next morning. "That look is *not* my dad—and the voice wasn't his either."

Dad had looked at Mom, clenched his jaw, and growled in an otherworldly voice, "I could slit your throat." Then, as she "scampered" up the stairs, she of two hip replacements, he had swiped ineffectually at Mom's heels. Lisa was frightened enough that she took the butcher knives into her room that night.

"I don't think he'd do anything," Lisa said to me now on the phone, "but at the same time, there was murder in his voice. I can't let them go back up north that way."

I know what's coming.

"I thought if maybe you could talk to them—he listens to you," she said. "I could just never forgive myself if they went home and something happened."

Later, we pieced together that he'd forgotten his meds (no lithium, no sleeping pills), had ballpark eight cups of coffee on Saturday which meant a sleepless Saturday night. Add in all that ruminating—the obsessions of an up cycle—plus his decreased cognitive ability at his age to find the right words or even to get a word in edgewise, and once again he'd become a bomb, culminating in the Satan voice and the heel-swipe Sunday night.

I took a personal day that Monday and called their cell phone in the morning, half hoping Mom wouldn't answer. She did. "I hear yesterday wasn't a good day," I began. "I'm coming to talk to you. Stay put till I get there."

What probably kept them from leaving was the way I leaned into the guilt of it: "I've already taken the day off," I told Mom. Her consternation was palpable.

"Oh, you didn't have to do that. Why did you do that?"

In hindsight, I wish they had gone.

When I got to Pipestone, their dark gray Buick Park Avenue was parked along the curb, a little ways down the street from Lisa's house and probably in gear. Dad was ready to bolt. I could see him in the driver's seat and Mom as far over in the passenger seat as she could be, looking frail and scared.

I rolled the window down and met them with my winningest smile. "I hear we had some problems last night," I said to Dad as if nothing could be that serious, ever, Dad's own approach.

Dad was unsmiling, his eyes bloodshot.

I did have the day off and wasn't going back to teach even if they left, I told them in all honesty, so we may as well talk about what happened. Then, with appeal to authority, "I can't let you treat Mom that way." You had to talk to Dad man to man, I knew, like you were in his head. "That's not acceptable."

"I didn't mean anything by it," he said. "I would never do it."

"Yeah, that's fine, but you don't get to say it either," I said. "There's a park over here. Let's go there and talk for a little bit," and for good measure, "Don't make me take a day off all for nothing."

He was embarrassed, he was ashamed. "Oh God," he said, looking off into the distance, like he knew he was caught, already powerless and under arrest.

I had a place in mind a mile from my sister's house, and I watched closely in the rearview mirror to see what Dad would do, but he followed dutifully. On the way, I called Carmen, who would really know what to do. The plan we hatched was this: hold Dad until she could get down there. She would take off work, could leave almost immediately. Then, with the two of us, we would see if—we would make Dad enter a place that could help him, a treatment facility. It was time.

I couldn't believe we were actually going to do it, the thing we should have done years ago, yet the idea of standing up to Dad still seemed impossible.

I took Mom and Dad to the Three Maidens on the outskirts of Pipestone, looking down toward Pipestone National Monument. I don't know that we had any business going there. It was not our place. The Three Maidens are three large rocks perched a short distance from Pipestone Creek as it wanders its way down from the east and tumbles over a line of short pink cliffs into a shallow bowl of prairie on the north side of Pipestone. Among miles and miles of flat topography frosted in fat black glacier dirt, any kind of escarpment is remarkable, and so the cliff line at Pipestone, perhaps thirty feet at its highest, feels like a sort of up-periscope of the underworld, the bedrock of our lives peeking up into the mess we've made of things. The rock itself is Sioux quartzite, a hard, pink rock that can be hewn into blocks and used to build, as testified by the pink buildings of Pipestone's main street. More importantly, running through this rock is a vein of pipestone: red, soft, soapy stone that can be carved by hand into the sacred pipe central to ceremony in many tribal cultures.

In Native stories, pipestone is the blood of the ancestors. Touching the stone, feeling it give slightly on your fingers and leave its residue, you can believe it. The Three Maidens stand just south of this sacred place, Pipestone National Monument, as guardians. Hulking, strangely isolated, vaguely pink, the three maidens aren't cut from the same stuff as the cliffs but are actually massive granite chunks, set here poignantly by glacier or God or Great Spirit. They are like Abraham's three visitors, in appearance like men but of a different quality: the three maidens were assigned by the ancients, moved from afar to testify to the pipestone.

We sat on a bench looking across the prairie. Mom left me alone with Dad, went off walking somewhere. It was September, and the tallgrass prairie was in all its glory. In the spring, the prairie is muted, even lazy, a notorious bedhead, last year's growth all matted and tangled and grayed by winter's attrition and needing to be pushed through by the new greens and humble flowers. I couldn't have done what I did—had the conversation we were about to have, held Dad for hours—in spring.

But those flowers accrue to a modest tide of color, yellows and blues, by late June, paving the way for the coming of the king, the winey bluestem, by mid to late July. By late September, the bluestem stands at full height, proud three-pronged heads arching above other members of its royal court: the golden spears of Indian grass, the late blooming black-eyed Susans, the receding leadplant, and the newly blooming goldenrod, its yellow fire slowly burning down from its tips. If only we could have just sat there and steeped in that prairie and then gone home, let the medicine of the land work upon us.

But that was not our tradition, either.

When you don't talk to your father, when you've stopped talking to your father, suddenly talking to him for four hours, holding him by talking while your sister comes down from the Twin Cities so that together you can perform an intervention, is like running a marathon at gunpoint: you start because you have to and realize there's a good chance you'll die either way.

I started talking. I talked about the tallgrass prairie, how I was coming to know prairie grasses by name and noticing when big bluestem shoots up in roadside ditches. I talked about the Dakota War, which I was just learning about, how one of the southernmost events of that war happened at Slaughter Slough, on the banks of Bloody, where Dad had returned the twenty-two-pound northern while working for Donnie LeClaire, and where fifteen settlers had been killed. How a little farther up north a white agent turned away starving Dakota saying they could eat grass and how he was found dead, mouth and anus stuffed full of grass. How that war culminated in the largest mass execution in US history at Mankato, thirty-eight Dakota men hurriedly sentenced to death, the final total determined arbitrarily by Abraham Lincoln himself, far away in Washington, DC.

I was rambling.

Maybe it was the Three Maidens that did it. Here we were, immigrants who had benefited directly from that mass execution and exile, just learning the story that had secured the land that we were both, in different ways, fixated on.

At some point we rehearsed what happened between him and Mom. "Sometimes I just get wound tight," he said. He intimated that Mom had a role, that she kept picking and picking. But that doesn't mean you can do what you did. Yes, he knew that. He made ready to leave.

It was like role-playing, like a kid with a principal. And I was the principal.

"No, Dad. We don't want this to happen to you anymore. It's not OK. Carmen's on her way down from the Cities. You can't leave until she gets here."

"Carmen's on the way down?"

"Yes."

"Oh, what the hell . . . ."

"She already left, probably an hour ago. She wants to talk to you too. We want to help you. You don't have to 'get wound tight' anymore. Just wait for her. I'm sorry, but when you say things like that to our mom, this is what happens."

"Carmen doesn't have to come down! I'm not going to hurt anybody—you know me!"

"OK, but then why even say things like that? That's not OK, Dad."

Silence.

I launched into another round of talk. I told him about my job teaching. Of how I got tired of babysitting, trying to manipulate kids into working in study hall. He ate it up. He loved when I talked about work, when I gave him a window into that part of my life.

I worked my way around to my own sins. I drew a straight line for him from the *Playboy* at the De Jongs's to repercussions in my own marriage bed.

He was grateful again. "You know I had the same problem," he said. "They say the sins of the father are visited to the son."

Taking sins upon himself, always.

It wasn't nothing. But it was just so Evangelical Protestant, so Arthur Dimmesdale of us both. So desperate for confession. So sure we were the greatest of sinners. So sure our personal sins blotted out the rest of the world.

As we looked down from the Three Maidens, across a landscape cleared in part by the largest mass execution in US history, gazing down at a quartzite cliff line that contained a seam of stone so malleable it was like human blood, the most sacred of places to native people now somehow under the control of the federal government, we were simply overwhelmed by our individual sinfulness. Our interior landscape determined what we saw and didn't see in the landscape before us, the way we think about land and body being in the end very much the same.

WE HAD Hardee's for lunch. The time was interminable. At any moment I was sure he would defy me, drive off. But he stayed, and the sun's angle lit the full prairie ever more brightly from above.

Finally, Carmen came with her oldest-daughter magic. She took the burden of conversation, and they revisited the details of the previous night. Then we told him our specific plan of action, that we were going to take him to a hospital with a mental health unit. Didn't he want to not have to feel tight anymore? He shrugged. But was that really possible?

Heidi arrived. Carmen had called her on the way. He said, "Heidi—you, too?"

We all wanted this for him, we said.

Dad agreed, maybe to get out of the purgatory of confrontation, maybe because our accumulating presences convinced him. We had decided on Brainerd, the closest mental health unit to their Breezy Point home. We were going to caravan the whole way there, five hours, take him to the ER, see what the options were.

We all got into vehicles. Carmen led. Heidi and Mom followed. I brought up the rear, with Dad. We had taken him out of the driver's seat. A mile out of town, Carmen called me.

"No," she said. "We're doing it again. We're catering to him. Brainerd is way removed from any of us. We're going to take him to Worthington, to the mental health unit there, because that's easier for us—it's closer to you and Lisa."

I broke the news to him. He said, "OK. Let's *go*," and it was a command.

We turned around. I led. We went through Leota.

Lisa met us in Worthington. Intake was with a doc who didn't know whether to be conversational or deadly dull. When asked his name, Dad brought out the old gag, Clem Kadiddlehopper, and he told the story of his F's hanging on the wall in Leota school at parent-teacher conferences as if it had happened yesterday and he almost broke down. He admitted to being depressed, that he didn't know where to turn. It seemed like a capitulation. We signed on the dotted line, committed Dad to an involuntary hold in a 72-hour locked unit to assess his condition.

Finally, Dad went through a big, metal institutional door with diamond wire glass. It locked behind him. His face, hardened and glowering, almost crumbled.

Outside, it was dusk, the last vestiges of the long nights of summer. I was strangely, perversely elated, the burden lifted, of the Place Hypothesis, of Leota the Cult, of the Theological Musings as to the Fate and Failure of Milt Schaap. They had been given to professionals who knew how to dispose of them. I had done the impossible, cornered the bull, talked the Hulk down to Bruce Banner, wrestled with

God until the dawn that was Carmen's arrival. Now they would fix him. The system would fix him. This is what hospitals did. It was bad now—it hurt to see him pained like that behind the clanging door, but Mom was safe and he was safe and they would fix him.

We looked out over Main Street, Worthington. The downtown was buzzing with ethnic businesses, people from three continents walking around in the fall evening. We had no idea what we were doing, what we had just done.

DAD WAS IN the Worthington unit for three days. On day one, he cried on Mom's shoulder in apology. He would never do it again. Another day, during exercise time, he did it mockingly, the life of the party. Now, Dad the comedian, Dad the subversive, could finally be looked at clinically. For the first time, behind diamond wire glass, Dad's humor became primarily a symptom.

At the end of the second day we all met. Carmen had come down early, walked around downtown Worthington.

Worthington sits at the bottom of the Buffalo Ridge. Growing up, Worthington was a destination for us, with its own mall and K-Mart where we went back-to-school shopping, with downtown businesses called Cows Outside and Brown's Shoes. Then the mid-eighties began a long decline—the hollowing out of Main Street, shuttered businesses, empty buildings—that was reversed by an immigrant culture and ethnic stores, central among them an Asian grocery story and a Mexican bakery. Entering Top Asian Foods was like entering another realm. Sy and I loved the Worthington downtown for all its people of color and ethnic foods, though Sy was certainly my passport into that world.

Carmen commented on the change, on how strange it was as a white person to walk around downtown Worthington now. No, this was not the world any of us had grown up in. That doesn't mean it wasn't a better one.

We entered the locked unit, were clicked through to a meeting room. Dad came in. He looked pale, as if all that institutional light were already changing him. All four of us siblings were there, plus a psychiatrist, a social worker, and Mom and Dad. I can't remember the psychiatrist; I remember the social worker because Sy knew him. He had limp, gray hair and thick rimless glasses. He talked to Dad softly, with an almost feminine voice. The question was whether to release Dad or continue treatment, to double down for another fourteen days. Of course it was awkward. Dad was restless—the formality of it, the questions about his behavior, his inner life, and Mom's safety. He'd already told us about being tight, recounted again his pain from adolescence. He got up and left. I don't know if he didn't understand that he was ceding the decision to us or if he did know, trusting that, on the basis of our knowledge of his character—Dad the big-hearted bear-hugger, Dad the life of the family—we would not do this thing.

But we didn't trust him—or we saw our chance.

Lisa recounted the terror of the otherworldly voice, the threat against Mom. I reacted out of the wrestling match at the Three Maidens and the long fear of living with guns. We kids were all tantalized by the idea that we could get a stable Dad out of the ordeal, a Dad who was always level. Mom was taken aback. She'd spent so long managing Dad's moods that we could read her skepticism as codependence, and in the end she was neutralized. The professionals heard that we wanted him committed, and the plan was made to transfer him to Brainerd the following day, to the Grace Unit, a mental health ward with a good reputation at St. Joseph's Hospital.

We never asked what legal steps are involved when you take away a grown man's volition, or how he would be transferred. And I swear they never volunteered that information.

Dad came back in. We told him we wanted him not to have to feel tight, once and for all. We told him we didn't trust him to do it voluntarily. We told him that two weeks more under the care of professionals and he would come out healed. It was not what he thought we would do.

The truth is, we were inattentive. We had asked the best questions we knew how to ask but not every question. We had entered that form of American elder care that trusts institutions with their management. It was *King Lear*, but no one was playing Edgar.

DAD WAS transported the next day by a sheriff's deputy, handcuffed to a pole in his squad car for five and a half hours.

Dad was removed from the squad car, not at the Grace Unit, but at the state hospital in Brainerd. There he and Mom faced an official hearing before a judge, with none of us kids present, no context.

Afterward, Mom called Carmen, crying, telling her, "Never contact us again!"

It took two weeks for Mom to reach out for help. Then, once Carmen realized that we were losing Dad down a hole of rotating psychotropics, her nursing instincts kicked in. She was granted access to Dad's chart and transposed Dad's medical records, interspersed with her own commentary. That's how we pieced together what had transpired at the state hospital.

Intake was October 2. The first week, his lithium was doubled, and he was started on Geodon, an antipsychotic.

That weekend, I went and saw Dad. The state hospital was what you would expect: a stone building, forbidding and unyielding. Dad came in and was pleasant if colorless, clueless, with little idea where he was or what was going on. Stoned. I teased him and his expression didn't change, a kind of almost smile. Mom and I thought it was progress. If this was the Dad we had been after, it looked like we would get what we wanted, a Stay Puft Marshmallow Man permanently whistling between his teeth. I left hopeful.

But in hindsight, it was strange. After everything, did we just want someone we could control?

On October 10, Tuesday of the following week, the official note is three lines: "Milt cries uncontrollably with his wife. 'I just feel terrible inside.' Wife notices he is more restless and increased tremors."

On October 13, Mom talked to a psychiatrist for the first time. Dad was having trouble sleeping, so he was given Ativan.

The next day, the medical note is again perfunctory. Dad has become a zombie: "Milt is lethargic, difficult finding words for conversation, shuffling gait."

Then, Sunday, October 15, he's wired: "agitated, restless, displaying akathisia [restlessness], dystonia [involuntary muscle contractions], thoughts are erratic and difficult to make conversation, signs of aggressive behavior."

On October 16, in the most heartbreaking of medical minimalism, he's given Zyprexa, and then additional Zyprexa "IM . . . for episode." Carmen's commentary fills in that he'd hit an aide and had to be tackled and restrained—and that's when he was given more Zyprexa "IM," by muscular injection.

I imagine it as your generic horror scene in a mental hospital—a patient in a white-walled institution is gang-tackled by men in white uniforms so a doctor with a syringe can stick him with a long needle, which wipes him out instantly.

Except it's my dad.

The first time we kids hear about all of this is when Mom calls Carmen that same day, begging for help.

"In two weeks," Carmen's summary reads, "he had become disoriented and confused. He walked around naked. He was paranoid or made no sense at all." She takes them to task for their care. "Doubling and tripling his medication without increased hydration to match that change. Adding new strong psychotropic drugs. No intake/output on his chart. Small succinct sentences updating medications, but nothing to counsel him."

Maybe most heartbreaking of all is the status quo for the type of person who happened to find their way to this state hospital. Apparently any kind of family presence or support was not normal. The social worker told Carmen as she poked around for answers, "This is new for us. We don't usually have families involved."

On October 20, Dad is transferred to the Grace Unit at St. Joseph's Hospital in Brainerd. On October 27, he has another aggressive and combative episode, perhaps connected to "additional med trials"—at least his fourth different psychotropic drug.

"I found him naked in his shower," Carmen writes, "pawing the walls, groping and mumbling after the second episode of violence when he hit a nurse." Carmen called his psychiatrist and asked for a "medication holiday," saying that drugs were creating worse effects than being bipolar. He agreed.

That weekend I spent a night with Dad at St. Joe's to get him through one more night before his release, convincing him at 2:00 a.m. that it was too early for an early morning fishing trip.

Dad was discharged on the same dosage of lithium as when he entered the mental health unit at Worthington.

But the nightmare continued: "Months of restless wandering the house during the night, opening and closing cabinet doors. Little or no sleep. Two emergency room visits with a prescription of Ativan each time, even after the first prescription created an adverse reaction. Increased anxiety with doors locking, clanging shut."

THAT DECEMBER, more than a month after he'd been discharged, when he was still recovering, when we were all still not on speaking terms, Sy and I broke the ice by inviting Mom and Dad down for the grandkids' Christmas program. They didn't want to come but did for the grandkids' sake. That night Dad confronted me. We had locked him up, he said, had tried to take away everything from him. We were just like Hein and Lida and Klaas and Agnes, when they had gone behind his back to take the farm, and if that's the way we felt about him, then he would stay Up North and that would be it.

I felt the anger rise in me.

Yes, it was terrible what happened to him. No, that's not what we intended. No, had we known what he was going to go through, we wouldn't have done it. I said he could choose to cut himself off Up North if he wanted, but whatever went wrong, we had done it out of love. And when we realized what hell we had banished him to, we hadn't abandoned him but had come to spend nights with him, had done what we could do to get him back out. That we were sorry, but we loved him, and he could choose to make us part of the conspiracy if he wanted, of Red Nose and Write Offs and the World Set Against Milt Schaap, but that we would still love him, that he had a disease and we had tried to get him help and had failed but now it was his choice to let us back in or not and if he didn't believe that then. . . .

I would have fought him over it. He could feel the passion in me. That was all he wanted. I could see that he believed me. It was the least I could do.

Mom told me the next morning, "He slept better than he has in months."

AFTER DAD'S release from Mayo and after their return Up North, I was on duty for Dad's first appointment at a new geriatric psychiatrist. It was about a half-hour to the big box stores in Baxter. There, beyond Costco and the Home Depot where Dad had worked, we found it, a house-like building with a timbered entrance, Northern Psychiatrics Associates. As we turned down the drive, we passed another building which caught my eye: Lindner Media Productions, home of *In-Fisherman* and the source of so many of our dreams. I craned my neck as we passed. Three large pickups were parked out front. Had the boys been out fishing that very morning, now retired to the studios to film commercials and edit?

We felt good about Dr. Andersen and his nurse, an unpretentious blond woman in aqua scrubs who was personable with her small talk and thorough with her questions and who appeared truly interested in Dad's case. It was good to know there was someone right up the road that we could match Dad and Mom up with. Mom could find this place herself, she insisted, it was easy. If we were going to abandon them to the Big Woods again, at least we could assure ourselves that this professional was on watch and a phone call away, day or night. And Dr. Andersen planned to peel back the medicines Dad was on, now that Dad was on the additional medicine of being home.

I looked over to Lindner Media again as we left. I couldn't help but feel resentment, at the false ideals that had drawn Dad Up North only to leave him in a double-wide unable to back his boat in the water.

No, that's not quite fair.

Wendell Berry says a few different forces can bring us to the places we call home: preference or history or accident.

In the end, Charles and Caroline Ingalls just stay in De Smet because Caroline says no more moving, because Charles runs out of energy and money, because he catches on as a man of the town. History and accident.

Dad preferred the Big Woods. History and geography had coincidentally centered Al Lindner in Brainerd, Minnesota, next door to a geriatric psychiatrist.

History has brought me to the place, the shallow mud lakes of Buffalo Ridge, where I prefer to catch walleyes.

Or be skunked.

18

Lake Wilson

AFTER DAD RETURNED from Mayo, Mom gutted it out one more winter Up North. Then she put her foot down. They were moving back: back by their kids, back where they had some support, back to the landscape of melancholy. The next summer they put their doublewide on the market and it sold quickly at a good price, to Dad's pride, and with the cash they bought a house in Edgerton, the town where I live.

Dad was tremendously anxious about the move. How would they ever accomplish it?

We'll help you, we said. We can find trailers to move your stuff.

For everything in the house? he asked.

Yes, we said, this is what people do for each other. People move all the time.

He was not convinced.

Or you can hire it done, we offered.

Yeah, but isn't that expensive, he worried.

Your kids'll pitch in, I said, but it was finally dawning on me that it doesn't matter what I say, that maybe I shouldn't take away his perturbations.

And there were always perturbations. After the move it was the house itself.

They bought a modest two-bedroom house just off Main Street in Edgerton, but both Mom and Dad regret it. Mom wants a second bathroom so they can host guests more easily, and Dad thinks he has figured out that the main structure was originally part of a barn, not a house at all, and is embarrassed. He sits in his corner recliner kicking himself.

"I should never have bought this cracker box," he says, hands on his head.

It's a manic episode, I finally figure out, but not until we've argued and I've stormed out to leave him with his fool thoughts.

Dad has aged quickly after Mayo. His balance is gone. He fills his days by walking with his cane about the house or on the sidewalk for exercise and putzing around the garage, arranging things perfectly. Adjusting a wrench a quarter-inch one day, he smells gas, traces it to the snow blower where he sees a spot on the cement.

That night, he says to Mom, "What will we do when this house explodes from that gas and insurance won't cover it?"

Mom calls me the next day, and I go over to talk him down.

How will we ever get that leak fixed, he asks.

There's a guy in town. All you do is call him and he'll even come pick it up.

I don't know, he says, meaning he won't take my word for it.

I leave, shaking my head. All this time, and I still try to reason him out of it, out of illness. We're both still trapped.

A FEW YEARS pass, and a new fishing season finds the walleyes biting at Lake Wilson, fat little fourteen- and fifteen-inchers, with an occasional seventeen, an entire stocked class that's outgrown the bait in the lake and bite eagerly, desperately. We bring home a stringer-full three, four times before I'm convicted: I have to take Dad.

I'VE ATTEMPTED to pass on fishing as a tradition to my kids, with mixed results. They all got starter fishing poles with updated characters—Dora the Explorer, Spiderman, Bob the Builder. We went to the dikes at Lake Shetek in the spring and I taught them to read bites by their dobbers, to tighten the line and set the hook, and when they reeled in crappies, we celebrated it like the rite of passage it was. After, we stopped for ice cream at The Hub.

But maybe because we started them so young, or because of how often I direct them to cast and recast, to "watch now," to not pull their line in too much, to reel up the slack, or because when the fish start biting around sunset I tend to get a bit demanding of five-year-olds to pay attention, to stop playing around now because the bite window is closing, because, in short, I tend to get a bit manic about it all, none of the three has lasered in on fishing like I did.

But when I tell them one day, "We're going to Lake Wilson with Grandpa," both boys, ages twelve and ten, are game because they know it will mean action.

With his grandsons as bait, I figure, Dad won't be able to turn down my invite. Plus, think of the optics: three Schaap generations catching walleyes back where it all began, with a broomstick pole on the banks of Lake Wilson.

It's a Tuesday in late June but cool and windless with high clouds and I stop by midmorning and tell Dad, it's a nice day, I'm taking you fishing. I know where we can catch walleyes from shore. Lake Wilson.

Lake Wilson! He purses his lips and shakes his head.

Oh? Why not? I'll set you up, have the boys fetch minnows. There's a place to set your folding chair and the boys and I can cast for you.

He can still cast, he insists.

Then it's settled, but he has not yet agreed. He's looking for reasons not to go. There's his nap, for instance.

"Oh, you can skip that one day," Mom butts in.

Yeah, but he didn't sleep hardly at all last night.

Insomnia again, that long and faithful companion.

Well, I'll get you good and tired today and then you can sleep well tonight, I say.

That's right, Mom says.

I think when I leave that I have him convinced, but fifteen minutes later Mom calls to tell me that Dad has decided not to go. Too cold.

It'll be fine out there, I tell her. He can sit in the car if he gets cold.

I know that, but he's got it in his head.

I'll stop by again later, I tell her.

OK, she agrees, but calls back a half hour later to tell me Dad will go after all. I know what's happened: she's willed him into it.

I've told Dad 1:30 and when I show up just a little late, he's waiting, as if for a first date, shoes and cap on and maroon Minnesota Gophers jacket, equipment sitting ready. But also like a first date, he's ill at ease.

We drive over the peak of Buffalo Ridge and then down into Lake Wilson. I turn down a side street to get to the shoreline.

This where you fish? Dad asks.

Yep, I say.

I didn't even know this was here.

There's room right where we've been catching them, in the space between a mid-sized cottonwood tree at the lake's edge and the boat dock belonging to the house up the hill. Actually, someone is sitting down toward that dock. I see that it's Al Top and Steve Visser, from town, so no problem. The ground slopes slightly down between the road and the rocks that protect the shoreline, but we set up Dad's chair safely on the edge of the gravel. I set out the minnows and tackle box and poles and get a minnow on Dad's, his rig an oversized dobber and swivel and half-ounce jig head, all big so he can work with them with his large, shaky hands and bound not to catch small walleyes.

Let me put on a little smaller jig head for you, I say, grabbing one like we've been using. Then I cast it out for him and hope.

ON THIS DAY at Lake Wilson it takes a bit, but Aidan finally catches a walleye on a jig. It's too small and we drop it back in, but then he catches another one and then another, a keeper, and then I do. Micah catches one on a dobber, but it's clear that they really want jigs today—of course, since jigging is a skill Dad never mastered. I consider whether he might not just drag a jig head across the bottom and still have better results.

Dad is just happy to be here, taken with the place. "I never knew this was here," he says. "Has it always been here?" It dawns on me that he thought we were going to the rocky shoreline along highway 30, impossible for him to navigate, and that's why he was hesitant to come.

I take off his oversized leader to see if that might help, set his line deeper.

Finally, he gets a bite and reels without really setting the hook, so after a few seconds the fish gets off.

"Gotta set the hook, Dad," I instruct him. "Did you set the hook?"

Dad goes on marveling at the place. "Lived here all my life and never knew this was here."

It hasn't always been here. Like many things, this spot has come with development, a shoreline cleared for docks for the houses along this shoreline. And yet it captures the tragedy of place, to not know what's right beneath your nose.

We've got several fish on the stringer when Dad gets another bite. I see him pull his pole awkwardly out of the corner of my eye, and this fish stays on. He reels with his rod tip down and it seems to take forever to land and I want it to be a walleye but when it gets to shore it's the yellow belly of a bullhead, the first one we've caught.

"Oh, Mr. Bullhead," Dad says. "Boy, that feeling, of not knowing what you've got on the end of your line—I don't even care if it's a bullhead—I just like to feel it fight like that. And wonder."

AL AND STEVE have been fishing Lake Wilson all morning and they have a nice stringer of fish. They go to the other Christian Reformed Church in town, Bethel. They pack up to leave shortly after we arrive. I'd hoped that Dad could fall in with men just like them when he moved back to Edgerton, men who fish regularly yet casually, following the bite to whatever shoreline on summer afternoons, but Dad keeps his distance from almost everyone, partly from bipolar paranoia, partly from embarrassment at having gotten old. Dad and I are both back at First Christian Reformed, Edgerton, where Mom and Dad monitor if we're in church and we monitor if they are. If they're not, it means one of them is ill and I stop over after service. When he's there, Dad always leaves early to beat the rush, using imbalance as a reason to avoid fellowship, just the latest in a long line of excuses. Mom allows it, shepherds him along as always. They have couples over for coffee at their house that was a barn at her insistence.

Leota mainly doesn't touch Dad now. He drives through Leota on occasion, but the school where he was bullied is closed, and Leota Ebenezer is struggling, which Dad himself says is a shame. Dad hasn't made his peace with Leota exactly, but it's clear that a way of life is ending. Actually, a minister with tattoos up and down his arms holds combined services with Leota Ebenezer and Leota Reformed, a new kind of Reverend Entingh, perhaps, to lead Leota into a new era. But Dad himself wouldn't be able to see past his tattoos, his earring. He would pick and pick at those things until the guy left. And so in the end, Dad may have more in common with the Leota founding fathers than he ever would have thought.

Then, it turns out the minister does leave, that he's bipolar.

As for the church we both attend, First CRC Edgerton, we follow proudly in that Leens and Ulrum tradition of small town churches, skeptical of the outside world and its progressive ways that love to ignore lowly folks like us. We stick to that great leveler, original sin, and that greater leveler, God's grace, which everyone needs equally. But we're still trying to put the brakes on a world that's going to hell fast. We see ourselves as the salt of the earth. We read the law Sunday mornings, recite the creed Sunday nights, and expect everyone to be there both services. We regularly bemoan the worldliness of the world and the slide of the denomination and, as testimony to our biblical faithfulness, resist any kind of change.

But Sy and I stay. Because—because leaving isn't always the answer. Because of inertia. Because we have history. Because some of these same people, community leaders and heads of households and small business owners, have so often sat around a low table eating sticky rice with Sy and her family. Because of relationships and despite structures. Because we've determined to. Because there's nowhere else to go but exile, which I can't help feeling is where Dad went. Because I've come to believe there's no leaving, no escape, no arrival.

Officially at First Church we worship the logical, law-giver God of clarity, the sovereign God and his unchanging, infallible Word.

Who also puts coins in the mouths of fishes. Who will make an ax head float like a dobber. Who will tell you to try the other side of the boat to teeming results. But who will put you through long bouts of silence.

AT LAKE WILSON on this day, Dad still hasn't caught a walleye. "Man, isn't that something? I just can't catch 'em and you guys can," he says. I steel myself for some kind of self-deprecation, "I never was much of a fisherman," or "I always was a failure," and consider my response, whether silence or a deep sigh or taking the bait and propping him up with a compliment, but he doesn't say anything, and it's clear again that he's satisfied to be here, to have us catch fish, as he always was when we went fishing—as long as the kids caught something, he was satisfied.

"I'll let you reel in the next one," I offer.

"Unh-uh," he says. "You guys just catch 'em. I can catch bullheads."

On cue his bobber goes down, slow, like something is walking it down steps.

"There you go, Dad!"

"Oh, I'm sure it's Mr. Bullhead again."

Once again he reels without setting the hook but I stop myself from saying anything and also say nothing about how he reels, so damn slow, with that infernal rod tip down. I stumble down the rocks to see what it is, not hopeful. He's right, it looks like a bullhead bite.

But it's not.

"There's a walleye," I announce as it gets to shore. Just like that, the fish tosses the hook on the small rocks near shore, and though I grab for it, wetting my foot, it flops back in the water and darts away.

Aidan brings me another walleye, maybe the nicest one so far. We have six fish on the stringer, a meal for us and, more importantly, a meal for Mom and Dad, who still love fresh fish.

As I drop the stringer back in the water, Dad sets into his bobber again and reels his painfully slow reel.

"Bullhead?" I ask.

"I imagine," he deadpans.

But it's not. As the fish emerges I see its white belly and look to see where the hook is, but it's so deep in its mouth I'll have to cut the line or keep it.

"Well, what do you know?" He lifts the fish up on the grass near his feet. I want him to love this moment, to revel in it.

"Finally—a walleye, Dad! Here, let me get a picture."

He sets the rod down and holds the fish, the walleye dwarfed by his thick hands. No matter. It is the gift I wanted to give him.

He smiles a soft smile, the depth of it coming from his eyes, the look of satisfaction.

It's the gift he's wanted to give me, or it's the gift I've wanted.

IT'S BEEN a long struggle with Dad, but I know now what point we're at, the one where we're supposed to look forward to "that other shore." Like that other fisherman, Huck Finn, I have no time for visions of robes and harps, for eternal praise and worship.

So I try to imagine a new earth but with local pictures. Like the fish breakfast Jesus made for his disciples after a long night of fishing. Except it's on the shores of Lake Wilson. It's Dad's ideal of men in nature, a shore lunch made special by Jesus himself. And since the original shore lunch originates with Native Americans, the Christ Dad looks up to is an Ojibwe fishing guide. And he's there to serve Dad fresh walleye and paper-thin potatoes. But it's just the necessary sustenance for a long conversation, one in which the Ojibwe savior burns away Dad's impurities, as someday, Lord willing, the Christ I need will burn away mine.

It's a flawed vision, of course. Perhaps I should just stick to the present moment, Dad with the last walleye he will catch, a pretty good taste of glory on this shore, the muddy Lake Wilson, where, after all these years, we have this, another miraculous catch of fish.

THE ROCK RIVER, up near Woodstock, is anything but a signature Minnesota fishing experience. But it's my family's spot, one that Lisa brought us to when she first lived in Woodstock. To get there, we pass the place where her son Austin lives now, Austin who also farms the Moulton Township farm, who is putting the waterways back in that were taken out, sowing cover crops off season, restoring the land. Two miles north of Austin's place, the Rock turns against a soilbank, a line of hills the last of which has been topped by payloaders and dump trucks for its gravel deposit. We park in the gravel pit and walk down the hill to a wide spot, maybe twenty yards across and a hundred long. The river here turns to literal shit by late June, thanks to the cow pastures upstream. It is not a beautiful place. But in spring and fall when the water runs fresh, the northerns get aggressive and their meat is firm and white.

Spring, and our spot has once again been good to us. We're back home, filleting Rock River northerns at sunset in the front yard. This is the kids' favorite part, where, after I have the meat slipped off into a steel pan, I slit the stomachs to see what the fish have been feeding on. What we find in the northerns' stomachs never ceases to amaze: the still-hard shells of crayfish; the leathery skins of frogs, five of them packed together in the stomach of one pregnant female; and once something unrecognizable—but with feathers.

This night, under a lavender evening sky, Micah asks, "Where's the heart?"

With the meat already off, I find the muscley lump for him, up under the gills behind the head. As my fingers stroke the nerves around the heart, it beats between my fingers. Though both fillets of meat have been sheared off the skin and are lying in the steel pan, again and again as I handle the heart, it beats. With the promise of summer glowing around us, it beats, and for a moment it's something prophetic: I'm an ancient haruspex examining entrails, looking down to look up, the universe in the belly of a fish.

This is the greatest gift Dad gave me, the gift of a universe woven with terror but also grace, the knowledge of an OCD God, who tracks every swooping swallow, who remains silent and distant somewhere among the prairie grasses, who broods over the waters of a windswept lake, but a Creator madly in love with every flower in the prairie, who promises to make all things new, and who would send his own Son to do it. A manic decision. All or nothing. All *and* nothing.

With each slight stroke of my thumb, the heart beats.

"Whoa," Micah says.
"Whoa, that's cool," Aidan says.
It is a portent of life.
"Do it again," Micah says.
And I do.
Again and again and again.

Acknowledgments

Traveling through the landscape of memory is not an easy thing to do, whether with your father or alone. There are mirages there, and the light is erratic. In Dad's case, his mental illness cast a definite kind of light on things. These are my memories, shaped by my life with him, and cast in the kind of light I needed to write a story. In cases where the memory may be contested or the quality of light less than ideal, I have changed the names of the people involved.

It's been a ten-year sojourn in this landscape so there have been quite a few important signposts along the way. Thanks first of all to Paula Huston, who with one email made me believe I had a book to write and gave me inspiration that lasted ten years.

A number of books took me to a different level of thinking about the Midwest. *The Witness of Combines* by Kent Meyers first made me think I had lived a life worthy of literature. Janet Timmermans's book *Draining the Great Oasis* and her master's thesis on Joseph LaFramboise both opened up local history for me and made me consider how that history might have been different. Caroline Fraser's book *Prairie Fires: The American Dreams of Laura Ingalls Wilder* helped me make connections between Dad, myself, and the Upper Midwest and explained the forces that continue to shape us. Emily Martin's book *Bipolar Expeditions* helped me think about bipolar disorder culturally and metaphorically. And Sarah Smarsh's *Heartland* modeled what it meant to weave it all together.

So many people shaped the material along the way, knowingly or not. Thanks especially to my writing mentors at Seattle Pacific University, Lauren Winner and Paula Huston, and my creative nonfiction cohort, Callie Feyen, Chrysta Gustwiller, Rachel Woldum, and Laura Turner. Thanks to everyone in the SPU MFA who created such a vibrant writing community, especially Aaron Guest, Matthew Slye, Seth Riley, Jill Reid, Adie Smith Kleckner, Jessica Gigot, Melissa Gardner, Paul Luikart, Bryan Bliss, Chris Hoke, Rachel Hammer, Alissa Wilkinson, Joanna Campell, Kate Schifani, Chris Warner, Bruce Kirby, and Christian Downes.

Thanks to my colleagues at Dordt University for providing a culture of thinking and letters. Thanks especially to Jim Schaap (no relation) for being both mentor and friend and the first person I turned to with a fledgling manuscript, to Dave Schelhaas (some relation) for his insistence that I had written something the world needed to see, and to Luke Hawley (not even Dutch) for sharing countless conversations about writing and creating.

Thanks to those colleagues who listened to me read portions of it year after year and encouraged me in the writing: Bob De Smith, Josh Matthews, Mary Dengler, Bill Elgersma, Sara de Waal, Rose Postma, Shaun Stiemsma, and Leah Zuidema. Early versions of "The Miraculous Catch of Fish," "Ebenezer," and small portions of "Prayer Bouquet" appeared in *Pro Rege* at Mary Dengler's insistence. Thanks to Angela Kroeze Visser and the Kielstra Center for funding various endeavors to both shape and seek an audience for the book.

I made a whole bunch of people read early versions of this book that were pretty rough. Thanks to good friends who doubled as readers: Samir Gassanov, Kevin Caspersen, and Jason Como. Thanks also to Margaret Gassanov, Monica LaRose, Cameron Dezen Hammon and her workshop, Fred Bahnson and his workshop, and Shelbi Gesch.

Thanks to the teachers who first got this punk to write and thereby lifted my eyes to see the world: Mr. Bryce Fopma, Ms. Janie Van Dyke, Dr. Julia Janeway, and Dr. Thomas Becknell.

Thanks to Greg Wolfe for his patient and frank pestering to see the manuscript, for "getting it" once I finally sent it to him, and, along with Emily Kwilinski and the team at Slant, for shaping it for the world.

This work comes out of everyday life of cooking dinner and cleaning toilets and fixing roof leaks. I share that daily grind and wonder with the love of my life, Keodouangsy (Sy) Schaap, who has always kept my eyes on what matters. We're each other's anchors in important, sometimes tug-of-war ways, and I wouldn't have it any other way. Thanks to our children, Sommer, Micah, and Aidan, who allowed me to plunk away for years of our lives on this project and gave full-throated whoops of joy when they heard it was becoming a book. You are the best of us.

I started this book intending to just focus on Dad and me, to keep my sisters out of it so that they would be protected and I wouldn't have to . . . deal. Then I realized that leaving them out was its own sort of arrogance and would leave out so much beauty and grace from the story. So I wrote them in and shared it with them—afflicted them with it. In doing so, I asked them to relive parts of our lives that it was clear they would have told differently or let lie completely. However, with typical grace and strength, they've allowed me to tell the story in this way. In portraying them, I have of course flattened each of them into characters to serve the story, meaning they're not portrayed as completely and vibrantly as they deserve, but I hope they feel that their representations are treated with respect. Carmen, Lisa, and Heidi, thanks for supporting your little brother in this book as you always have. Thanks for being remarkably strong women. When I look at the way we worked together to care for Dad and now Mom, it's clear we share something remarkable.

Thanks to Mom and Dad, who were so faithful to each other and us, and who, despite some hard circumstances, gave us a good, rich life.

This book was set in Plantin, designed by Frank Hinman Pierpont and Fritz Stelzer and published in 1913. It is based on the "Gros Cicero" type created by Robert Granjon in the sixteenth century, which the modern designers found in the Plantin-Moretus Museum—an institution devoted to the history of printing —in Antwerp, Belgium.

This book was designed by Shannon Carter, Ian Creeger, and Gregory Wolfe. It was published in hardcover, paperback, and electronic formats by Slant Books, Seattle, Washington.

Cover photograph: Travis Ridings, via Unsplash.

www.ingramcontent.com/pod-product-compliance
Lightning Source LLC
Chambersburg PA
CBHW031435160426
43195CB00010BB/738